ƒP

ALSO BY RICHARD BROOKHISER

Alexander Hamilton, American
Rules of Civility
Founding Father: Rediscovering George Washington
The Way of the WASP
The Outside Story

FOR
WILLIAM F. BUCKLEY, JR.

THE FREE PRESS

A Division of Simon & Schuster Inc.

1230 Avenue of the Americas

New York, NY 10020

First Free Press trade paperback edition 2003

The Free Press and colophon are trademarks

of Simon & Schuster Inc.

For information about special discounts for bulk purchases,

please contact Simon & Schuster Special Sales:

1-800-456-6798 or business@simonandschuster.com

Designed by Chris Welch

Manufactured in the United States of America

3   5   7   9   10   8   6   4

The Library of Congress has cataloged the Fress Press edition as follows:

Brookhiser, Richard.

America's first dynasty : the Adamses, 1735–1918 / Richard Brookhiser.

p.   cm.

Includes bibliographical references and index.

1. Adams family.   2. Adams, John, 1735–1826.   3. Adams, John, 1735–1826—Family.

4. Adams, John Quincy, 1767–1848.   5. Adams, Charles Francis, 1807–1886.

6. Adams, Henry, 1838–1918.   7. Presidents—United States—Biography.

8. Statesmen—United States—Biography.   9. Historians—United States—Biography.

I. Title.

E322.1 .B76   2002

973.4'4'0922—dc21

[B]   2001051276

ISBN 0-684-86881-4

0-684-86864-4 (Pbk)

America's
First Dynasty

The Adamses
1735-1918

Richard Brookhiser

The Free Press
NEW YORK LONDON TORONTO SYDNEY SINGAPORE

ACKNOWLEDGMENTS

I must thank the Massachusetts Historical Society for their help with unpublished portions of the diary of Charles Francis Adams; John Lukacs, for pointing out Tocqueville's thoughts on democracy and history; and Judith Kaufman, Paul Romaine and Ross Douthat for help and suggestions.

I would also like to thank my editor, Bruce Nichols, and my agent, Michael Carlisle.

Between John Adams's first writing and Henry Adams's last, the rules of spelling and punctuation changed. Ignoring these developments would make for a deceptive uniformity, while following them faithfully would make the earlier Adamses seem even more idiosyncratic than they were. My compromise has been to modernize most of the punctuation and capitalizing, and to keep most of the original spelling.

CONTENTS

CONTENTS

Introduction

CHAPTER 1

---

*T*HE FIRST TIME anyone asked a member of the Adams family about his famous ancestors, she was joking.

In April 1778, John Adams, lately of the Continental Congress, arrived in Bordeaux, France, to represent the new nation as a diplomat. His second day ashore, he was introduced to polite conversation at European dinner tables. "Mr. Adams," a pretty young woman asked him, "by your name I conclude you are descended from the first man and woman." Did he know of any family tradition that might explain how Adam and Eve "found out the art of lying together"? "I believe at first I blushed," wrote Adams in his diary that night, but "I was determined not to be disconcerted." He replied that a "physical quality," like magnetism, caused any pair of Adams and Eves that drew "within a striking distance" to fly together, "like the needle to the pole." "It is a very happy shock," the lady said.[1]

John went on to assignments in Holland and Britain, as well as honors and offices at home, and soon enough Adamses were being questioned about their forebears in earnest. In 1795, John Quincy Adams, John's eldest son, was in London on a diplomatic mission of his own, and met George III, the king against whom his father had rebelled. His Majesty asked if all the Adamses "belong to Massachusetts"? An attendant minister told him they did, whereupon he asked John Quincy if his father was now governor.

"No, Sir, he is Vice President of the United States."

"Ay," said the king, "and he cannot hold both offices at the same time?"[2]

If the new nation was still only dimly understood, its first dynasty was already known.

Twenty years later, John Quincy was back in London, this time as American minister to Great Britain, and had a similar conversation with

3

George III's son, the Prince Regent, who ruled during his father's final illness. After they exchanged greetings, the Prince Regent asked John Quincy if he "was related to Mr. Adams who had formerly been the Minister from the United States here. I said I was his son."[3] One member of the House of Hanover was preparing to succeed his father on the throne of England; a member of the house of Adams was following in his father's footsteps.

John Quincy went on to be secretary of state, president, and, as a congressman, a scourge of slavery and its political representatives. While he was in the White House, he hosted a dinner for Lafayette, the aged hero of the Revolution, who had met him and his father almost forty years earlier. At dinner, Lafayette pointed to nineteen-year-old Charles Francis, the President's youngest son, and the man who would be most famous among the third generation of famous Adamses, and solemnly asked the First Lady to see to it that he never "entertain thoughts of becoming President save by the free choice of the people." Charles Francis never entertained such thoughts, nor did the people ever choose him. But in 1848, he succeeded his father in the affections of antislavery men, when he was nominated to be the vice presidential candidate of the Free Soil party. "Yes, Sir, we want him," said a delegate from Wisconsin. "There he is *with the crape on his hat.*"[4] John Quincy had died six months earlier; Charles Francis, still in mourning, was treated as if he bore his transmigrated spirit.

Not everyone viewed the Adams family history favorably. Henry Adams, Charles Francis's third son, moved to Washington, D.C., after the Civil War, to represent the fourth generation of Adamses there, as a political journalist rather than a politician. One of his targets, Senator Timothy Howe of Wisconsin, declared that Henry belonged "to a family in which statesmanship is preserved by propagation," like "color in the leaf of the Begonia, perpetuating resemblance by perpetual change." "To be abused by a Senator is my highest ambition," Henry wrote a friend. "My only regret is that I cannot afford to hire a Senator to abuse me permanently."[5] Henry wrote with the enthusiasm of youth: He would go on observing senators, with diminishing humor, for another forty-eight years. By the end of Henry's life, the Adamses had been center stage, or in the front row of the orchestra, for almost a century and a half. They had been present at the creation—not, French banter aside, of the world, but of the country—and at many of its pivotal scenes.

The United States is formally an egalitarian nation—the Declaration of Independence (John Adams was on the drafting committee) states that all men are created equal. Yet political families weave through its history. In the 2000 presidential election, Vice President Al Gore, Jr., son of Senator Albert Gore, ran against George W. Bush, son of President George Bush and grandson of Senator Prescott Bush. The wife of the outgoing president, Hillary Clinton, became a senator. One of the signers of the Declaration was Benjamin Harrison (an "indolent, luxurious, heavy gentleman,"[6] John Adams called him), a charter member of the Virginia gentry. His son, William Henry Harrison, became president, as did William Henry's grandson, Benjamin Harrison. Franklin Roosevelt was Theodore Roosevelt's fifth cousin; Eleanor Roosevelt (her maiden name) was TR's niece. One of Henry Adams's friends and intellectual foils was Henry Cabot Lodge, who became a senator from Massachusetts. Lodge's great-grandfather, George Cabot, had been a senator from Massachusetts, and an enemy of John and John Quincy Adams. Lodge's grandson, also named Henry Cabot Lodge, became yet another Massachusetts senator, until he was beaten by John Kennedy, and a fresher dynasty. Political families regularly flare to national prominence, or sink to lower levels (like the Tafts); or they keep percolating along as local fixtures. In 2000 the representative for the eleventh congressional district of New Jersey was Rodney Frelinghuysen. The first political Frelinghuysen, Frederick, represented New Jersey in the Continental Congress in 1778, the year John Adams went to France.

Political families pass on inclination, as well as opportunity: The founding pols give their children prominence and contacts, while the talk around the dinner table, and the family pictures on the wall or in the scrapbooks, provide inspiration and example. John Adams expected these hereditary concentrations of power: They had marked the relatively free institutions of the colonies, and would survive independence. "Go into every village in New England," he wrote in 1787, "and you will find that the office of justice of the peace" has "descended from generation to generation in three or four families at most."[7] No family will ever be as famous as the Adamses, whose role in the founding gives them a leg up even on the Roosevelts, but, as long as there are elections, people will vote for candidates whose names they recognize. It is the tribute democracy pays to aristocracy.

The Adamses also defined themselves as a meritocracy. They inspired their descendants to hold office, but they also required them to work for it. They did not expect fame and power to come to them by virtue of their birth alone. They trained themselves to live up to their birth—and then they expected fame and power to come to them. John Quincy Adams's parents told him that his career should reflect his "advantages"; if it did not, it would be due to his "lasiness, slovenliness, and obstinacy." When Charles Francis Adams suggested that he might drop out of college, his father threatened him with "perdition."[8] The Adamses who could not make the grade often did suffer earthly forms of perdition. In the second and third generations, there were six sons: one president, one diplomat, and four drunkards, one of whom was a suicide, and one of whom may have been driven to drink by the pressures of being gay.

The family employed carrots as well as sticks. Adamses took their sons with them to Europe on diplomatic missions; they also employed them as private secretaries. Young Adamses lived, as a matter of course, in Washington, London, Paris, and St. Petersburg, and hobnobbed with congressmen and kings. Home life was a long tutorial, a graduate-level course begun in infancy, conducted by presidents-in-residence.

Yet Americans have played a trick on this intensely political family. They tell the Adams story as if it were a purely domestic saga, a Yankee *Buddenbrooks*. The first historian to do so was Charles Francis Adams, who began publishing the letters of John and Abigail Adams in 1840. "The great men of the Revolution," he wrote in his introduction, "in the eyes of posterity, are many of them like heroes of a mythological age. They are seen, chiefly, when conscious that they are upon a theatre, where individual sentiment must be sometimes disguised, and often sacrificed, for the public good." But Charles Francis Adams offered, in the private thoughts of a great man and woman, the intimacy of the inside story. "Students of human nature . . . look for the workings of the heart." Only "the solitary meditation, the confidential whisper" provide true "guides to character" and to "the springs of action."[9] Charles Francis's approach struck a chord. The husband and wife letters of the Adamses, detailed and tart, pop up in every history or biography of the period, and keep coming back into print. Phrases from them are sung by John and Abigail in the musical *1776*. Publications about the first Adamses and their nuclear family constitute an industry, while smaller industries have grown up to cover the private lives of later Adamses, chiefly Henry and his wife and friends. *The Adams Family Chronicles* re-created the whole clan for public television, and the scholar Paul Nagel has tirelessly distilled the vast materials of the family archives into manageable narratives.

The Adams family saga satisfies our curiosity about famous figures, which is part gossip—a venerable genre, from Suetonius to *People*—part identification. Few of us are going to be president, and no presidents nowadays get to be revolutionaries. But all of us had families, and most of us form new ones. In the Adamses we find every variety of parent, child, and sibling. Abigail is—mistakenly—thought of as the only political woman of the late eighteenth century, and her letter to her husband asking the Continental Congress to "remember the ladies" is treasured as a proto-feminist appeal. Among her unsung peers was Mercy Otis Warren, an Adams family friend until she published a history of the Revolution that ferociously attacked John. But the Warrens have been deficient in PR.

Presenting the Adamses at home not only serves our needs; it also serves the family, coating its flaws with empathy and pathos. The Adamses need the help, for although they are admirable, and frequently lovable, they are seldom likable. Benjamin Franklin's famous judgment of John Adams, with whom he worked and fought for several years— "Always an honest man, often a wise one, but sometimes, and in some things, absolutely out of his senses"—can serve as a motto for much of his family (Abigail included). The Adamses typically envy the talents and achievements of others, while venomously reckoning their real or imagined failings. When the Adamses are engaged, they are apt to be prickly and temperamental ("I am the drollest little, peppery, irritable, explosive old man of sixty-two that ever was,"[10] Henry told one friend); when they are not on the offensive, it is often because they are deeply depressed (sometimes for good reason, sometimes for reasons that they themselves have created). Charles Francis, who was the most equable, accomplished this only at the cost of being more than a little dull.

All men have flaws and tics; the flaws of the Adamses limited their public effectiveness. Although two of them became president, they were failures in office. If the two Adams administrations were the family's only legacy, we would not be interested in them. For the last fifty years there has been an effort to re-evaluate John's administration upward, by positing him as a moderate midpoint between the extremism of Thomas Jefferson's Republicans and Alexander Hamilton's High Federalists. It would be more accurate to say that John Adams was an extremist throughout his four years in office, who switched sides (from High Federalist to crypto-Republican). There have been fewer efforts to salvage the presidency of John Quincy Adams, because the task is so obviously impossible. Adams presidential revisionism is thankless work; family history is a welcome distraction.

There is another way to look at the Adams family, which is the way that they mostly saw themselves—as figures in the theater of history. Charles Francis might pitch his grandparents' letters as a backstage view, but all the Adamses, even at times Charles Francis, lived for the roles they played, and the effect they had on the audience, which was the country, and the world. In early July 1776 John wrote his wife a prophetic letter describing Congress's vote for independence: "[I]t will be celebrated, by succeeding generations, as the great anniversary festival. . . . It ought to be solemnized with pomp and parade, with shews, games, sports, guns, bells, bonfires and illuminations from one end of this continent to the other, from this time forward forever more." "[Y]our letters," she answered, "never fail to give me pleasure, be the subject what it will." Yet the pleasure she took from his last "was greatly heightened by the prospect of the future happiness and glory of our country; nor am I a little gratified when I reflect that a person so nearly connected with me has had the honor of being a principal actor." John had played a leading role, and the drama would always be in the repertory. More than a century later, the stakes were different but equally high. Henry Adams complained in a 1904 letter about the atmosphere of Theodore Roosevelt's White House—"a boys' school run wild . . . mortifying beyond even drunkenness"—but added that "one wants to listen at the key-hole. I think this place is now the political centre of the world."[11] The Adamses did great things, and when others did them (or failed to do them) they watched closely.

Their family history was History. When they looked at their past, they saw the nation's; when they looked at the nation's past, they saw themselves. Their inherited likes and dislikes (mostly the latter) were political; the crafty acquaintances and treacherous neighbors who did their fathers and grandfathers wrong were generals, senators, and cabinet members; the friends who gave them a helping hand were presidents. In 1818, when John Quincy writes in his diary about calling on the painter John Trumbull to see the progress of "The Declaration of Independence," one of his historical paintings for the Rotunda of the Capitol—"I cannot say I was disappointed with the execution of it," wrote Adams, "because my expectations were very low"[12]—we may need to remind ourselves that John Quincy's father is in the picture, in a brown suit and white stockings, right hand on hip, left leg bent. John Quincy and every other Adams, including John himself, could never forget where they stood.

The constant companion of the Adamses, like an extra member of the family in each generation, is the idea of greatness. *What is a great man? How great am I? Am I as great as my ancestors? As great as my contemporaries? Why doesn't the world recognize my greatness?* These are the family questions, inspirations, and anxieties. They begin with young John Adams, during the French and Indian War ("I talk with Sam Quincy about resolution, and being a great man," he wrote at age twenty-one, "which makes him laugh"),[13] or even earlier, when at age ten he heard his father discussing with friends King George's War; they are still being asked by Henry Adams on the eve of World War I. The idea of greatness crushes and stimulates them; it is reinforced by the great deeds they witness firsthand, or in which they have a hand. The Adams family wished to be judged, and constantly judged themselves, by the standard of greatness. Our interest in their domesticity confuses the picture. Only when we strip them of the spurious advantages conferred by sentiment can we do justice to their achievements and see them as heroes (when they deserve the title), not mascots.

Great men have large and positive effects on their times and on the future, either through their actions or their thoughts. This book will look at the four Adamses—John, John Quincy, Charles Francis, and Henry—who meet this test. John's wife and Henry's brothers are interesting, but only these four touch greatness: John, as a patriot and a diplomat during the Revolution; John Quincy, as a policy maker before his presidency and an enemy of the slave power after it; Charles Francis, as a diplomat during the Civil War; Henry, as an artist. If you had to jot their achievements on a business card, it would be a speech and a treaty (John), a doctrine and a fight (John Quincy), a sentence (Charles Francis), and a book (Henry). This is a heterogeneous list, but everything on it changed the world or, in the case of Henry's book, has the potential to enlarge our minds.

Despite their differences in talents, careers, and circumstances, each of the Adamses goes through three phases of public life: initiation into the family and its public role; comparison with the great non-Adamses who are his peers and rivals; justification of what he, and his ancestors, have done. Certain themes run through all their lives and continue to engage us today, more than eighty years after Henry's death: the importance of writing and the meaning of history; the jostling of empire and republic in American history. One theme that preoccupied all the Adamses, and that concerns Bushes, Gores, and Clintons today, is how to perpetuate a legacy that must also be learned. Great actors often have great exits, and two of the Adamses had deaths as dramatic as those of any American public figure.

The Adamses were a public family. Politics, war, and peace were their vocations; politicians, warriors, and diplomats, past and present, were their soulmates and enemies. When the family lost contact with public affairs at the highest level, they snapped out like a candle in the wind, and became ordinary sons of Adam, like the rest of us.

John Adams

*J*OHN ADAMS was born in Braintree, Massachusetts, in 1735, to a family that was neither powerful nor famous. Even so he felt the weight of ambition and past achievement. The "first" of the Adamses did not feel himself to be first.

One great predecessor was collective: the community of Puritans who came from England to New England in the 1630s. French ladies of the Enlightenment could be amusing about Genesis, but the Puritans of the great migration believed they lived in the Bible. England under the Stuart kings was Egypt; they were Israel fleeing to Canaan, to establish a refuge for godliness, a city upon a hill. The hills they picked overlooked Boston Bay, a large shallow bay ringed with inlets and flecked with islands. Boston, the Puritans' capital, was then virtually an island, a peninsula connected to the mainland by the narrowest of necks.

Other Englishmen with competing visions who appeared in their midst were driven off. In 1637, some newcomers named a hill ten miles southeast of Boston Mare Mount, because it had a view of the ocean, or Merry Mount, because that is how they intended to live. They set up a maypole, wrote a shocked neighbor, "inviting the Indian women for their consorts, dancing and frisking together . . . and worse practices." A punitive expedition of the godly broke up the alien community, without bloodshed, except for one man who was "so drunk that he ran his own nose upon the point of a sword."[1] One of the Puritans who resettled the liberated area was a Somerset farmer and brewer, Henry Adams.

By the mid–eighteenth century many aspects of Puritan dogma and society had fallen away, but the people of Massachusetts continued to honor their ancestors. John Adams considered them bearers of freedom, a cause that still had a holy urgency. When he was thirty years old, he wrote that "our fathers" had bought liberty "for us at the expense of their ease, their estates, their pleasure and their blood." They had flown "to the wilderness for refuge from the temporal and spiritual principalities and powers and plagues and scourges of their native country." In New England they had established governments with popular branches to check the power of priests and kings, lest New England become "the man of sin, the whore of Babylon, the mystery of iniquity."[2] It does not matter that the Puritans limited freedom to themselves, or that later historians have argued that their motives were also economic; this is what John Adams felt emanating from them like light from a not-yet-distant star.

The spirit of freedom and ardor still marked their descendants when Adams was a boy. In 1745, the colony of Massachusetts besieged the French fortress of Louisburg on Cape Breton Island, off the north coast of Nova Scotia. France and England had been engaged in a series of wars since the late seventeenth century that were both ideological and imperial. Catholic France was an absolute monarchy, spinning around the sun of Versailles, while Protestant England after the Stuarts was ruled by Lords, Commons, and a law-abiding king. The rival nations and their systems competed for territory on a world scale, from Europe to India.

In 1745, in the phase of the struggle known as King George's War, the immediate danger to New England was the fortified harbor of Louisburg. The great French military engineer, the marquis de Vauban, had designed its forty-foot walls, at a cost of one million pounds (perhaps fifty million modern dollars). French privateers sailing from Louisburg could raid New England merchant ships and harass fishing fleets on the Grand Banks off Newfoundland. In wartime, the French navy might descend on the New England coast. William Pepperell, a wealthy merchant and a colonel in the Massachusetts militia, was asked to lead the expedition. He consulted with George Whitefield, the celebrated English evangelist, for spiritual guidance. A Yankee army, half strike force, half crusade, landed before Louisburg, hauling its cannon, a hundred men hitched to each gun, over marshy ground to the fortress's base. After a seven-week siege they prevailed; Pepperell was made a baronet, the only native-born American ever to be so honored. The men of New England were still capable of great deeds. John Adams remembered when he was ten years old hearing his father talk about the Louisburg expedition. He also remembered the discussions three years later when Britain, ending this round of warfare by the treaty of Aix-la-Chapelle, agreed to give Louisburg back to France, in return for the Indian town of Madras. Old England had set New England's victory at naught, and for reasons of imperial housekeeping had put its Massachusetts subjects back in danger. John was learning that his spiritual parents, in New England, were purer and more principled than their political parents, in England.

John Adams had a personal goad and inspiration, in the form of his father. Henry, the redeemer of Merry Mount, begat Joseph, who begat Joseph, who begat John Adams (1691–1761). John Adams the elder was a farmer and a cordwainer, or shoemaker. He was a solid citizen of the town of Braintree, with a farm of about fifty acres; a deacon of the Congregational church; a lieutenant in the militia; and a selectman, or town councilman, who helped oversee schools and roads.

In diaries, letters, and autobiographical jottings, John Adams recorded a few details about his father: that he discussed politics; that there was on occasion "passion,"[3] or high temper, in his home. The most interesting vignette, however, concerns education. Deacon Adams had not been sent to college, which, in Massachusetts, meant that he had not gone to Harvard. Only his eldest brother had enjoyed that privilege. John, who had been deprived of it, was determined to confer it upon John, his oldest son.

But young John remembered that he preferred swimming, skating, shooting, and kite flying to attending the local public school, where the knowledge required for entering Harvard, such as Latin, was to be learned. One day when he was about ten, he told his father that he did not want to go to college. "What would you do, child?" the Deacon asked. "Be a farmer," the boy said. "Well, I will show you what it is to be a farmer," the Deacon replied, and woke him early the next morning to harvest thatch.

The Adamses worked together all day—it was "very hard and very muddy," John remembered—then at night, Deacon Adams asked his son if he "was satisfied being a farmer." "I like it very well, sir," John answered. "Ay, but I don't like it so well," the Deacon told him. "So you shall go to school."[4]

This story had no doubt improved in decades of mental retelling. But it shows two traits that characterized Adams as a man, and may well have come from his father. Obviously, there is willful stubbornness, in matters of pride and right—the son sticking by his opinion, the father sticking by his plan. Less obviously, there is stern self-judgment: the son, who became one of the most bookish of the founding fathers, remembering himself as a truant; the father, in his hope for his son's future, breaking out in bitter words about his own station in life. The Adamses could be hard on those around them; they were always hard on themselves.

The Deacon's expectations for all his children were fulfilled. John, the eldest, went to Harvard and advanced in the world. John's younger brothers, Peter and Elihu, who did not go to Harvard, spent their lives, in or near Braintree, farming, like their father.

John graduated from Harvard in 1755, fourteenth in a class of twenty-four (class rank was determined by social standing, not academic achievement), then moved to the town of Worcester to teach school. He was not happy there. "I must be within smell of the sea," he once wrote, and Worcester was fifty miles inland. The imperial struggle resumed as the French and Indian War, and Adams was conscious that he took no active part in it—years later, he would write that he was the first of his family to "degenerate" from the status of a soldier—though he did manage on one occasion to take a military dispatch from Worcester to Newport, Rhode Island. He also worried about his career: schoolteaching was a stopgap, fit only for "base weed[s] and ignoble shrub[s]."[5]

Deacon Adams had wanted his eldest son to be a minister. The thought patterns of a fading religious establishment would survive, transmuted, in the minds of even secular New Englanders for generations. Like many a Puritan, Adams kept a copious and anxious diary, although for him it was a record of his pilgrimage through life, not toward Heaven. Terms of art in such remote fields as politics carried (as the critic Peter Shaw noted) a religious afterglow: "election" meant being chosen by God for salvation, as well as chosen by the people for office. Ministers, meanwhile, addressed politics directly: When Adams was twenty, he heard the Reverend Jonathan Mayhew, a Boston cleric, deliver a famous attack on the doctrine of the divine right of kings, which Mayhew called "altogether as fabulous and chimerical as transubstantiation."[6] But Adams had no calling to the cloth, and the time had passed when a young New Englander would choose the pulpit as the only avenue of ambition.

The avenue he picked was the law. While not teaching school, he studied with a Worcester lawyer and was admitted to the bar in 1758. Over the next twenty years—even after he had become a famous man—he would argue cases, in Boston, where he intermittently lived, or following judges as they made the circuit of Massachusetts county courthouses, which then covered Maine. He started small, taking what work he could get, and arguing against cheap amateur lawyers called pettifoggers (in other words, the competition). Legal lore and treatises provided grist for a curious mind, and a side-door to political theory. Adams also found he could argue effectively on his feet. He once improvised in a courtroom for five hours, while his client went home and back to retrieve a necessary document.

All the time he was studying and establishing a practice, he pondered about greatness in the pages of his diary. "[D]illigence and attention" could make him "a man of sence." But he would only be "a great man" if nature had given him "a great and surprizing genius." What then was genius? On another occasion, he jotted down a page of analysis, concluding "I have not patience to pursue every particular attentively. But," he added, perhaps patience is "one of the greatest marks of genius."[7] Mere diligence wasn't enough for greatness, but maybe the great were always diligent. So he chased himself in mental circles.

When his career was well-launched, he married Miss Abigail Smith of Weymouth, the next town down the Plymouth road from Braintree. She was the daughter of a prosperous clergyman, and though, as a female, she had had no opportunity to go to Harvard, she had been well-tutored at home in Milton and Shakespeare. A pair of primitive portraits taken at this time shows John with a high forehead, a double chin, and a surprisingly bland expression. The artist had better luck with Abigail, who looks attractive without being friendly. Theirs was a marriage of true minds—smart, clever, censorious, and passionate.

Most important, as a lawyer Adams met his first great contemporaries, whose example drew him into politics.

Half a century later, John Quincy Adams would tell an English lord that only three Americans had desired independence before the Revolution: his father, James Otis, and Samuel Adams. This was a curious opinion, squinting at history through the lens of Boston Bay. But it accurately reflected John Adams's view of the men who set him on the course his life would take. James Otis, Jr., was a natural orator and a flamboyant courtroom performer—"a flame of fire!," Adams described him admiringly.[8] Though Otis was a born insider from a rich Cape Cod family, he had fallen out with the establishment when his own father was passed over for a plum of a legal appointment. He defended his clients in Boston's merchant class when they were harassed in the early 1760s as smugglers—which indeed they were (New Englanders traded with French colonies during every imperial war). Otis cast the contest as a matter of principle, arguing that Parliament's efforts to control the black market infringed on the colony's long-established prerogative of policing itself. John remembered Otis's performance in the case all his life— when he was an old man, he would ask John Trumbull to paint it. Deacon Adams, coincidentally, had died in 1761—just at the time John had found a new inspiration.

Otis helped Adams see that the parent country, which had sacrificed New England's interests in King George's War, continued to do so in peacetime. At the end of the French and Indian War in 1763, Britain had captured not only Louisburg, but all of French North America, and many other possessions as well. The expense had been staggering, however, and Britain sought to pay down its debt by raising revenue from its American colonies—either from stamps on legal documents, or from duties on sugar, paper, glass, lead, and tea. Britain contemplated other innovations in its empire as well. There was fearful talk in the colonies of establishing an Anglican bishop for North America (a scheme that inspired John Adams's 1765 paean to his liberty-loving "fathers"). There was talk in Britain of paying colonial civil servants from London, thus making them independent of the colonial legislatures. Thomas Hutchinson, who had beaten James Otis's father out of the job he coveted, and who had since been promoted to be lieutenant governor of Massachusetts, wrote the politicians in London a secret letter warning that "there must be an abridgment of what are called English liberties" if unrest in Massachusetts was to be controlled.[9]

Otis, ten years John Adams's senior, was a colleague and role model. But in the mid-1760s, he began to lose his mind (a blow on the head in a fistfight with a customs collector in 1769 sped his decline). Leadership in Massachusetts politics, and in Adams's political education, passed to his second cousin, Samuel Adams.

The two cousins had certain superficial similarities: Samuel was named after a deacon father, who sent him to Harvard intending him for the pulpit. But Samuel's family was enmeshed in Boston politics, which lured him from the ministry. The elder Samuel Adams was a brewer, an officeholder, and editor of a contentious newspaper, the *Independent Advertiser*. To win his master's degree at Harvard, young Samuel defended the proposition that it was "lawful to resist the Supreme Magistrate, if the Commonwealth cannot otherwise be preserved."[10] He ran through his inheritance and lived in the rundown family property in Boston's South End, with a collapsing brewhouse in the yard. He wore, and wore out, one coat. He kept himself going by holding a series of small-time government jobs, including tax collector, though his collections (thanks to a long economic depression, and his own incompetence) came to be so deeply in arrears that he nearly missed prosecution for embezzlement. His hands shook with palsy in his forties, but he had a bright eye and a direct, engaging manner.

The ne'er-do-well was learned and principled. Samuel Adams knew his John Locke, and he quoted him to good effect, in clear, sarcastic prose. He was also versed in the culture of the city's taverns. His father had formed the Caucus Club, an early political clubhouse, taking its name from an Algonquin word meaning "advisor" (later in the century, Tammany Hall would continue the tradition of urban Indian political lingo). Samuel was friendly with the Loyal Nine, a group of artisans who met on the second floor of a South End distillery. He knew how to impress talented young men, like his cousin John, by inviting them to smoky confabulations. Finally, he studied Boston's mobs. Traditionally there were two collections of neighborhood bruisers, from the North and the South End. On November 5, or Pope Day, they would parade mocking effigies of the pope and other unpopular figures, and each gang would try to destroy the other's images, brawling with cudgels, sometimes fatally. In 1765, a mob, inflamed by Samuel's polemics, razed the mansion of Thomas Hutchinson. Samuel Adams called the action a "high-handed enormity," and held a "Union Feast" to make peace between the two gangs. The result was that he had an orderly, amalgamated mob under his influence. Englishmen observed that Boston rioters, unlike those in London, now acted "from principle."[11]

The principles Samuel imparted to his brawlers and to John embodied what historians call the Whig Myth: the belief that the ancient liberties of Englishmen were threatened by wicked, power-hungry men, sometimes bad ministers, sometimes bad kings. This myth had propelled the Puritans and continued to run like a creek in a storm drain under the surface of eighteenth-century English politics. In the colonies, the Whig Myth could be used to dignify every local squabble with colonial governors; it also seemed perfectly to explain Britain's postwar imperial policies. Myths sometimes tell the truth.

More important to Samuel Adams was his emotional connection to a lost New England past. Like many radicals, he had a deeply conservative core. Thirteen years older than John, he seemed older yet. Accused by his enemies of being a revolutionary, he worried that the revolution had already occurred: the undermining of New England's virtue and purity by "Luxury." As a young man he had been stirred by the Great Awakening, the 1730s religious revival led by George Whitefield. He was a regular churchgoer and sang hymns with a "charming" voice. Enemies and friends recognized his austerity. "He eats little, drinks little, sleeps little, thinks much, and is most decisive and indefatigable in pursuit of his objects," wrote one critic. John Adams wrote in his diary that his cousin had "stedfast integrity . . . real as well as professed piety, and a universal good character, unless it should be admitted that he is too attentive to the public and not enough so to himself and his family."[12] Even that flaw was to his credit: Samuel Adams ignored his own affairs for the same reason that he ignored his clothes and bungled his tax collecting. His mind and soul were devoted to other matters. He was the first Adams, even before John, to be inspired by a glorious past and disheartened by a lax and puny present.

John Adams was drawn but slowly into his cousin's orbit. He was liable to be distracted from politics by concern over his career, and by his and Abigail's growing family: Their first child, also named Abigail, was born in 1765; their second, John Quincy, was born in 1767. He also deeply disliked mobs and violence—a consequence of his argumentative personality, for mobs end argument with coercion—and condemned the

disturbances that coincided with the burning of Hutchinson's house as a "very atrocious violation of the peace."[13]

Tensions rose to a new level in 1768 when London sent three regiments under General Thomas Gage to keep the peace in Boston. The deployment had the opposite effect. The mere presence of soldiers on the city's streets was a continual provocation—Samuel Adams trumpeting their real and imagined misdeeds—and Bostonians responded by provoking them, calling them "lobsterbacks," after their red uniforms, and worse. The only surprise is that it took a year and a half before anyone was killed. In March 1770 a mob of four hundred surrounded a party of eight soldiers and a captain in King Street, threatening them with curses, snowballs, and clubs. Without orders, the soldiers fired, killing five. John Adams, who was attending a discussion group that night, rushed out as the city's bells rang, expecting to fight a fire. Paul Revere, a silversmith and ally of Samuel Adams, produced a print of the "Horrid Massacre," showing twelve corpses. After the dead were given appropriately spectacular funerals, the soldiers and their commanding officer were tried for murder.

John Adams agreed to head the team of defense lawyers, very likely at Samuel's urging. Defending the soldiers made excellent long-run political sense, from their point of view. The colonial administration had an interest in scapegoating the redcoats; Hutchinson himself had appeared at the scene of the killings and assured an angry crowd that the soldiers would be tried. An acquittal would shift blame for the military's presence back to Hutchinson and his superiors, instead of their instruments. After successfully moving to have the captain and his men tried separately, Adams argued that the captain was not guilty, because he had given no orders to fire, and that the men were not guilty, because their lives had been in danger. Two privates were convicted of manslaughter; the rest were set free.

But Adams was also attracted to the defense by its very unpopularity in the short run. A friend of his ruefully remarked that he was "perhaps rather implacable to those whom he thinks his enemies." He could be equally so to his friends. Adams's lifelong suspicion of parties was already well-developed: He was willing, as he put it, to "quarrel with both parties and with every individual of each before I would subjugate my under-

standing, or prostitute my tongue or pen to either." Singularity was the
outward and visible sign of virtue. He knew the purity of his own motives, but he could only demonstrate it if he was braving the scorn of the
world, especially that of his "own" side. Adams cherished, as an image of
embattled righteousness, the opening lines of a sonnet by Milton.

> *I did but prompt the age to quit their clogs*
> *By the known rules of ancient liberty,*
> *When straight a barbarous noise environs me*
> *Of owls and cuckoos, asses, apes, and dogs.*[14]

Adams's temperament took comfort from the baying and braying of
others. In this case, his own side chose not to quarrel with him: When a
Boston seat in the Massachusetts House of Representatives became va-
cant, Adams—backed by Samuel—was elected to fill it.

Adams's next election raised him from a colonial stage, bound by
Boston and Braintree, to a continental one. In a slack period after the
Boston Massacre, Samuel Adams and another of his protégés, the
Boston doctor Joseph Warren, formed Committees of Correspondence
to link like-minded souls throughout the colonies. Soon they had much
to write about. In late 1773, Americans up and down the coast refused to
buy tea, rather than pay the taxes Parliament had levied on it. In
Charleston the tea sat in a warehouse; in New York and Philadelphia it
stayed on ships. Boston dumped it in the harbor. London responded by
closing the port and suspending Massachusetts's charter, making General Gage the governor. A Continental Congress was called to meet in
Philadelphia in early September 1774, "to consult upon the present state
of the colonies and the miseries to which they are reduced." Half the
four-man Massachusetts delegation were Adamses.

A few of the delegates had been trained as lawyers in London, and
Colonel George Washington of Virginia had cosmopolitan experience
of a different kind, having fought French and Indians west of the Alleghenies. But many of them, like John Adams, were leaving their re-
gions for the first time. Not all of them shared Massachusetts's view of
the crisis. Joseph Galloway, a lawyer and a leader in the Pennsylvania Assembly, would offer a plan to reform the empire by establishing an "infe-

rior" American branch of Parliament, giving the colonies some say in imperial measures, yet binding them more closely to the system. Warned on their arrival by friendly Philadelphians of the Congress's divided temper, the Massachusetts delegation resolved to be subdued, and let the case for being left alone be made by radicals from other states, such as Richard Henry Lee of Virginia.

John Adams attended daily sessions and nightly formal dinners. One meal, he wrote in his diary, ended with "Curds and creams, jellies, sweet-meats, twenty sorts of tarts, fools, trifles, floating island, whipped sill-abubs." "Parmesan cheese, punch, wine, porter, beer" were also served. He spent his free time gawking at Philadelphia, which, as one of the largest cities in the English-speaking world, and the most tolerant, was full of sights unknown in Boston, including a Roman Catholic church. He was both impressed and disturbed. "Here is every thing which can lay hold of the eye, ear, and imagination. Every thing which can charm and bewitch the simple and ignorant. I wonder how Luther ever broke the spell." [15]

The delegates gawked at each other. Thomas Lynch, of South Carolina, reported (inaccurately) that Colonel Washington had offered to outfit one thousand men and march them to Boston. Silas Deane of Connecticut thought that Roger Sherman, also of Connecticut, had the graces and personality of a "chestnut-burr"; he was also disappointed to learn that the firebrand Patrick Henry looked like "a Presbyterian clergyman." Caesar Rodney of Delaware struck Adams as "the oddest looking man in the world . . . his face is not bigger than a large apple." James Duane of New York he thought "sly" and "squint-eyed." What whetted their attention to each other was a common consciousness that they were engaged, for good or ill, in something momentous. They might defend their liberties, transform the empire, or involve themselves and their societies in ruin. "We have not men fit for the times," Adams had worried in his diary before setting off. "Great things are wanted to be done," he had written Abigail from the judicial circuit during the summer, "and little things only I fear can be done." But a week after he had arrived in Philadelphia and met his peers, he felt inspired by their presence together. "There is in the Congress," he wrote home, "a collection of the greatest men upon this continent." [16]

As soon as the brotherhood of greatness settled down to work, there followed a sizing up and a sorting out. After a month's experience in the Congress, Adams could be sarcastic at its expense. Because "[e]very man in it is a great man," he explained to his wife, ". . . therefore every man upon every question must shew his oratory, his criticism and his political abilities."[17] As in every masculine arena, the great men in Philadelphia were showing off, and some of them were falling short.

A torrent of events, beyond their power to orchestrate, now seemed to sweep them along. Galloway's plan was tabled by a margin of one vote (the colonies voted as units) and stricken from the record. The Congress adjourned in late October, calling for an embargo on trade with Britain and for a second session in May 1775. In London the American expatriate Benjamin Franklin met with pro-American politicians such as General Sir William Howe, to try to arrange some compromise. But sympathetic Englishmen were too small a minority in Parliament to effect policy. Americans meanwhile formed parallel institutions— Committees of Public Safety and provincial Congresses—to replace the colonial ones, and seized weapons and powder from storehouses. Colonel Washington, elected commander of his county militia, ordered muskets, drill books, and silk sashes for officers' uniforms from Philadelphia. Back in Boston, John Adams wrote a series of political essays under the pseudonym "Novanglus" (New England) that struck a radical pitch. "How, then, do we New Englandmen derive our laws? I say, not from parliament, not from common law, but from the law of nature."[18] In mid-April 1775, General Gage sent eight hundred men to Concord, twelve miles northwest of Boston, to secure a cache of munitions, and to arrest Samuel Adams, fomenter of so much trouble, who had fled town. The British easily routed hostile militiamen at Lexington, in the middle of their route, and at Concord. But neither Samuel Adams nor the munitions were to be found. Their return trip was one long rolling ambush as enraged farmers picked off officers and men. By day's end, more than three hundred British had been killed, and nearly one hundred Americans. Once news of the fighting was known, thousands of New Englanders streamed to the Boston area to besiege the town.

Before returning to Congress at the end of April, John Adams went to Lexington and Concord to talk to eyewitnesses and see what had already become sacred ground. These were great events marked in blood. But Congress had its own duties to attend to. "No Assembly," he wrote, "ever had a greater number of great objects before them." Many of the personnel were different. Galloway, seeing the drift of things, had refused to be re-elected. Benjamin Franklin had returned to America and joined the Pennsylvania delegation as a radical sixty-nine-year-old. Virginia sent a radical thirty-two-year-old, Thomas Jefferson, a shy, rich planter. Congress's first order of business was to pick a commander-in-chief for the spontaneously generating but disorganized American army. Their choice, as Adams wrote his wife, was "the modest and virtuous, the amiable, generous and brave George Washington Esqr." He had reason to be pleased with the selection, since he had nominated Washington himself, seeing an alliance of Massachusetts and Virginia as a foundation of energetic policy. Congress also voted to dispatch ten companies of light infantry from the Appalachian back country. "They use," Adams wrote, "a peculiar kind of [musket] call'd a rifle—it has circular . . . grooves within the barrell, and carries a ball, with great exactness to great distances."[19]

Adams's family was closer to rifle balls at this time than he was. The neighborhood swarmed with patriot troops and refugees from Boston; British ships plied the bay, and occasionally anchored at nearby offshore islands. John Quincy, age seven, was taught the order of drill by a militiaman, and when he broke a finger, Joseph Warren, the patriot doctor who was president of the Massachusetts Provincial Congress, set it. "In case of real danger," John warned Abigail, "fly to the woods with our children" (two more sons, Charles and Thomas, had been born in 1770 and 1772). It did not come to that, but it came close. General Howe, who, whatever his political opinions, was obliged to suppress rebellion, had arrived in Boston to serve under Gage. In mid-June, Howe ordered a frontal assault on the militia (neither Washington nor the riflemen having yet arrived) who occupied Bunker Hill, which guarded the heights north of Boston. Twice the British attacked and were repelled. "To be forced to give up Boston," Howe remarked to his officers after the second repulse, would "be very disagreeable to us all."[20] On the third charge, they took the position, at a cost of over one-thousand men. More than three hundred of the defenders had been killed.

"My bursting heart must find vent at my pen," Abigail wrote her husband. "I have just heard that our dear friend Dr. Warren is no more, but fell gloriously fighting for his country.... Those favorites lines [of] Collin[s] continually sound in my ear.

> How sleep the brave who sink to rest
> By all their country's wishes blest? . . .

[T]he God of Israel is he that giveth strength and power unto his people. Trust in him at all times, ye people, pour out your hearts before him.... The constant roar of the cannon is so distressing that we can not eat, drink or sleep . . . ten thousand reports are passing vague and uncertain as the wind."[21]

Greatness in its most appalling forms—rumor, chaos, death—had come within sight (for the smoke of battle was visible from Braintree) and earshot. But so had its inspirations, and—for whatever they were worth—its consolations. Noble words, and words meant to be noble, from the Bible to the sentimental patriotic verse of William Collins, became as timely as the newspaper, and as personal as one's own name. "You are really brave, my dear," John wrote back, "you are an heroine."[22]

American affairs now followed an obvious division of labor. On the military side, while the British burned coastal towns and encouraged slave revolts and Indian attacks, the Americans mounted an almost-successful invasion of Canada. As these sideshows played out, Washington settled into a traditional siege of Boston, waiting for British cannon captured in northern New York to make the hundred-mile trip across Massachusetts.

On the political side, the Continental Congress had to try to supply and fund the fighting and carry on badly frayed negotiations with London. Since there was no executive, all the detailed work had to be done by committees. Over the next two years, Adams would serve on ninety, and chair twenty-five. His efforts were prodigious, and the drudgery gave him rashes, insomnia, headaches, and fears for the state of his eyes. Sometimes the work was enjoyable. On a trip to Massachusetts, Washington introduced Adams to a party of French Indians as "one of the grand Council Fire in Philadelphia." They "made me low bows, and scrapes &c. In short I was much pleased with this days entertainment."[23]

But beyond war-making and administration stood the great as-yet-unanswered question: What were the war, and the Congress, for? Redress of grievances, or something more drastic? To many, the bloodshed in Massachusetts, and Britain's resolve to persist, made the situation plain. Philadelphia journalist Thomas Paine, a recent immigrant from Britain, saw the issue with the clarity that outsiders and sharp writers tend to find in things. "[U]ntil an independence is declared, the Continent will feel itself like a man who continues putting off some unpleasant business from day to day, yet knows it must be done . . ."[24] His pamphlet making this case, *Common Sense*, had record-breaking sales (150,000, out of a population of less than 3 million—the equivalent today of 14 million). Adams read it with appreciation, and sent a copy to Abigail.

Congressional resistance to such a step was led by John Dickinson, a wealthy Pennsylvania lawyer from a lapsed Quaker family. He too had a clear and forceful style; his 1768 pamphlet, *Letters from a Pennsylvania Farmer*, had been the previous American political bestseller. Then, he had argued that Britain's new imperial taxes infringed on established rights. Now, he feared that independence would be the rash innovation. His mild manner, and his great reputation, won him the respect of even his most impetuous colleagues. In deference to him, he was allowed to draft a conciliatory petition to the king, three weeks after Bunker Hill, assuring "your Majesty" that his "faithful subjects" would be faithful still, if only their grievances were addressed. When the motion passed, Dickinson declared that there was "but one word" in it "which I disapprove, and that is the word *Congress*," since it suggested a politically independent body. Benjamin Harrison of Virginia, unable to contain himself, retorted, "There was but one word . . . of which I approve, and that is the word *Congress*."[25]

Adams recorded his reactions in two letters home. To Abigail, he complained of the "fidgets," "whims," and "caprices" of "some of us." To a friend, he wrote that a "piddling genius, whose fame has been trumpeted so loudly, has given a silly cast to our whole doings."[26] Adams's letters were captured on their way to Massachusetts by the British and published in hostile newspapers by the end of the summer. His sentiments were too harsh to be ignored and not witty enough to raise a laugh. Dickinson cut him in the street.

In March 1776 the military situation changed dramatically. After the cannon arrived from New York and Washington mounted them on the heights overlooking Boston, the British, knowing it was futile to remain, withdrew to their naval base in Halifax, Nova Scotia. Harvard awarded General Washington, whose formal schooling had stopped at age fifteen, an honorary doctorate; Massachusetts still celebrates Evacuation Day today. Liberation brought no relief, however. Every important town in the colonies was vulnerable to attack by sea: Where would the British strike next?

At the beginning of June, Adams went to a stationery shop on Front Street, a few blocks from the State House in which Congress sat, and bought a folio book in which to make copies of his letters. Duplicating his correspondence "will be an advantage to me in several respects," he wrote his wife. "In the first place, I shall write more deliberately. In the second place, I shall be able at all times to review what I have written." [27] In the third place, he sensed that he would soon be writing letters worth saving. On June 7, Richard Henry Lee of Virginia moved that "these United colonies are, and of right ought to be, free and independent states." Adams was appointed to a committee to draft a revolutionary statement of purpose.

Congress debated for the next three and a half weeks. The representatives of the middle colonies and South Carolina offered the contradictory arguments of a weakening position: Independence should not be declared, or it should not be declared just yet. The motion's supporters maintained that independence was already an "existing fact."

As events had called forth stronger and stronger measures, the Massachusetts delegation had abandoned the strategy of lying low. Adams took the lead in arguing for action, firmness, and now independence. From descriptions of his speaking style, it seems that he did not employ the flowers of rhetoric or theatrical effect (when Patrick Henry had cried, "Give me liberty, or give me death!" he had underlined the last word by striking his chest). Adams moved his listeners, when he was at his best, with directness and power. According to one congressman, when he spoke it seemed as if "an angel was let down from heaven to illumine" his audience. [28] Angels do not give stemwinders; they make a plain demonstration of what they wish to be done.

As June ended, seven states in New England and the south favored independence. The New York delegation's instructions, which had been drawn up almost a year and a political era ago, did not allow them to vote for it; at most, they might abstain. New Jersey was sending new delegates who would be instructed to vote in favor. Delaware's two delegates in Philadelphia were split; the third, who was pro-independence, would have to be called from home, where he was nursing a cancer of the face. Pennsylvania, Maryland, and South Carolina would have to be won over by horse-trading. On Monday, July 1, Lee's motion was brought to a vote.

The last speech against was given by Dickinson. He said as he began that he knew his words would destroy his "once great and . . . now diminished" popularity, but he imprudently made the case for prudence one more time. Adams answered him, speaking for several hours. During his talk, the new New Jersey delegation arrived, requiring him to review what he had said. He kept no notes of his speech, could never recall it afterward, and indeed thought that giving it had been a waste of time. "Nothing was said but what had been repeated and hackneyed in that room before, a hundred times, for six months past." He did himself an injustice. If men could comprehend an argument the first time it was made, the history of philosophy and politics would be very short. This particular argument merited effort and repetition, for it would have momentous consequences. Three days earlier a British fleet had attacked Charleston, and another, larger fleet had been spotted off Long Island, heading for New York. Adams "was our Colossus on the floor," a pro-independence delegate wrote. "His reasoning demonstrated not only the justice but the expediency of the measure," wrote Richard Stockton, one of the New Jerseyans who arrived in midspeech. "I call him the Atlas of American independence."[29] Stockton would have to back these judgments up personally. The British captured him later in the war and treated him so harshly that his life was shortened.

At day's end, nine states were for independence (Maryland having also switched). On July 2, the third Delaware man—Caesar Rodney, he of the small face—arrived to tip his state. Dickinson and one other reluctant Pennsylvanian were persuaded to stay home, so that the pro-independence faction of their delegation would prevail; South Carolina went along for unanimity, and independence passed, by a vote of 12–0 (New York abstaining). Despite his loss, Dickinson immediately enlisted to fight, while the British, unmoved by his arguments, had orders to burn his mansion should they ever capture Philadelphia.

It was the second of July, and the passing of Richard Henry Lee's motion, which Adams believed, as he wrote his wife, would be commemorated "from this time forward forevermore." In the near term, the new country and its leaders faced a string of disasters, which would not end until the battles of Trenton and Princeton six months later. By then it was clear that the British evacuation of Boston would not be followed by a next phase, but by a series of phases, trying and unpredictable. That did not make the act of declaring independence a trivial moment, any more than Adams's speech of July 1 was a wasted effort. Time may be a stream, but it is remembered as steps, and the step Congress had taken was a great one. In March 1777 Abigail wrote her husband that "posterity who are to reap the blessings, will scarcly be able to conceive the hardships and sufferings of their ancestors."[30] Adams and his peers no longer had to look back to the Puritans, or to the men who took Louisburg. They themselves were great ancestors.

CHAPTER 3
_____

ONE OF ADAMS'S first important undertakings for the
new nation occurred in September 1776. The British fleet,
which had been spotted offshore in midsummer, had landed
an army on Long Island, which crushed the Americans under George
Washington at the end of August. Lord Howe, who had replaced Gage
as British commander, also carried credentials as a peace commissioner,
and wished to meet with American representatives on Staten Island
after his victory. Congress sent Adams, Benjamin Franklin, and Edward
Rutledge of South Carolina. On their way north from Philadelphia,
Adams and Franklin had to share a room in a crowded inn. Worried
about his health, Adams shut the window for the night. Franklin told
him the air in the room was worse than anything outside. "Come, open
the window and come to bed, and I will convince you. I believe you are
not acquainted with my theory of colds."[1] Adams fell asleep as Franklin
talked (and Franklin got to keep the window open).

The meeting with Howe was fruitless. He had no power to recognize
American independence, or even to acknowledge that Adams, Franklin,
and Rutledge were sent by Congress, and the three Americans would
not negotiate on any other basis. Adams said he did not care what he was
called, so long as he was not called a British subject. When Howe said
that he would regret the fall of America as the fall of a brother, Franklin
told his London acquaintance that they would use their "utmost endeav-
ours to save your lordship that mortification."[2] As the three diplomats
left to be ferried back to American-controlled territory, Franklin offered
to tip the sailors with gold and silver, to show how well-off the new government was. It was a splendid gesture, but there was nothing to back it
up: Days after the meeting, Howe landed on Manhattan and began driving Washington and his men before him.

This episode foreshadowed much of Adams's life for the next twenty-three years: dealing with Benjamin Franklin, and dealing at a distance with George Washington. Adams would serve at the highest levels of American diplomacy and politics, where he continually encountered two men of even greater fame and (in the opinion of most people) greater ability.

Adams met Washington, who was three years older, at the first Continental Congress. Washington was the younger son of an ambitious Virginia planter; but his father had died when he was eleven, and he had had to make his way in the world by the traditional back stair of aristocratic societies—the kindness of in-laws. The Fairfaxes, a noble family whose American holdings were the size of New Jersey, gave him work as a surveyor and got him a commission in the Virginia militia. Washington did well in both jobs, particularly the second: His frontier exploits as a twenty-two-year-old were recorded in London newspapers and noticed by George II. Only a commission in the regular army, which he most desired, eluded him. After the deaths of his elder half-brothers, he inherited the main family estate, Mount Vernon, named after an English admiral.

Despite his aspirations and his connections, he took the radical side in the controversies of empire and rights. "Parliament," he wrote his loyalist step-brother, "hath no more right to put their hands into my pocket, without my consent, than I have to put my hands into yours for money."[3] His first portrait, painted by Charles Willson Peale in 1772, showed a smooth, almost mild face, with brown hair, blue eyes, and round rosy cheeks. But it had a tough line of a mouth. Washington came to the Second Continental Congress in his old French and Indian War uniform, letting the world know that he was ready to fight.

The president of Congress, John Hancock, a rich Massachusetts merchant who was a protégé of Samuel Adams's and a sometime client of John's, entertained the belief that he could lead America's armies, though he had no military experience. When John Adams rose to nominate a commander in June 1775, saying that he would propose a gentleman of "independent fortune, great talents, and excellent. . . . character,"[4] Hancock beamed—until Adams added that the gentleman came from Virginia. After some backstage conciliation of New Englanders who wanted one of their own, Washington was chosen unanimously.

Adams joined the congressmen, militia, and other well-wishers who saw Washington off to Boston, with bands playing, at the end of June. The spectacle left him disgruntled. "Such is the pride and pomp of war," he wrote home, while "I, poor creature, worn out with scribbling for my bread and my liberty . . . must leave others to wear the lawrells which I have sown." War may be politics by other means, but warriors cut a greater figure than politicians, especially when a war has just begun. John and Abigail Adams shared the feeling themselves. "Every man who wears a cockade appears of double the importance he used to," Abigail wrote her husband. "Oh that I was a soldier!" he wrote his wife. "I will be. I am reading military books. Everybody must and will, and shall be a soldier."[5] But Adams, unlike John Dickinson, never became one. Washington had been one twenty years ago and was now the most important one in the new country in its moment of trial. No wonder everyone looked to him, more than to Congress.

Adams also felt simple envy, of the most personal kind. He was a much better orator than Washington—who spoke seldom and briefly— and he could summon far more erudition. But in every other public quality, Washington outshone him. The General was tall, strong, and graceful, and could flirt without being a rake. Adams was short, stout, and sedentary; he cannot "dance, drink" or "talk small talk . . . with the ladies," as one friend put it. Many testified that Washington was the finest horseman they every saw; Adams had taught his cousin Samuel how to ride on one of their trips from Boston to Philadelphia, but by the time they arrived, Samuel had become a better rider than John. "I was struck with General Washington," gushed Abigail in July 1775, when she first met him. "Dignity with ease . . . look agreably blended in him. . . . Those lines of Dryden instantly occurd to me:

Mark his majestick fabrick! He's a temple
Sacred by birth, and built by hands divine.
His soul's the deity that lodges there,
Nor is the pile unworthy of the god.

Years after the General's fabric was in the grave, the contrast still rankled: Washington, John complained, had been chosen to lead because like Saul, the first king of Israel, "he was taller by the head than the other Jews."[6]

One characteristic way that Adams responded when unresolved differences loomed was by throwing himself into whatever work lay at hand. There was much for him to do. Twice a day he met with the Board of War, the congressional committee, on which he sat, in charge of overseeing and supplying the army. What with his other committee assignments, his typical day began at 4:00 A.M. and went until 10:00 P.M. His absence from his family lengthened, and his letters home shortened. In March 1776 Abigail wrote her famous plea to "remember the ladies" in the new political system Congress would establish. "[B]e more generous and favourable to them than your ancestors. Do not put such unlimited power into the hands of the husbands. Remember all men would be tyrants if they could." She began with a plea that he remember one particular lady: "I wish you would ever write me a letter half as long as I write you."[7]

Adams's work was frustrating as well as taxing, because the problems confronting Congress were daunting and its resources slim. The victories of early 1775 had been won by swarms of militiamen against badly deployed regulars. When the British moved in a more considered fashion, as they did against New York in the summer of 1776, the Americans were virtually helpless. There was no tradition of professional military service to build on, and Congress in any case had no dependable sources of revenue with which to pay for long enlistments.

Like most Americans, and almost all congressmen, Adams had little feel for military matters. In early 1777 he wrote General Nathanael Greene, one of the best officers the country had, a lecture comparing Trenton and Princeton with the Battle of Quebec in the French and Indian War, and the Battle of Pharsala in the Roman Civil Wars. (Adams did not finally send the letter, judging it to be "too impolite.") There was much anxious and pointless military erudition in the air; Greene himself had acquired his early training by reading military books in a Boston bookshop. But at least Greene and his comrades were in the field learning, where the incompetents among them were being winnowed out. Adams wanted faster winnowing: He called for the death penalty for officers who were taken by surprise and suggested (without any apparent thought of *Candide*) that it would be good to "shoot a general."[8]

Adams's ignorance and his severity grew out of the prevailing political ideology of the day. Americans believed, from their reading of history, that standing armies and generals were a perennial threat to republics. A free people defended themselves by serving for short periods; their officers should come from civilian life and return to it. Louisburg and Bunker Hill were ideals; Julius Caesar, whose victory at Pharsala destroyed the Roman Republic, was the danger. Even though experience would modify the views of all but the most ideological, the military model of classical republicanism would tug at American minds, like an undertow.

After driving Washington from New York ("it was a fine sight," a British officer wrote, "to see with what alacrity [we] dispatched the rebels"),[9] Howe pursued him across New Jersey, Congress fleeing Philadelphia for Baltimore. The small but timely battles of Trenton and Princeton ended the campaign of 1776 on a victorious note. But in the fall of 1777 Washington lost two major battles outside Philadelphia, and the city itself. Congress fled again, to York, Pennsylvania. Only the defeat and surrender of a British army invading New York from Canada seemed to show any great skill—and Washington had nothing to do with it.

The victor of the battle of Saratoga was Horatio Gates, a British army veteran who had fought in the French and Indian War and settled in America. His tactics justified military republicanism: His army had been swollen by militiamen from neighboring New England, encouraged to turn out by the folly of the British, who had marched into trackless forest at the rate of one mile a day. Although Adams had been alarmed by the jubilation that greeted Trenton and Princeton—"some members" of Congress "idolise an image which their own hands have molten. I speak here of . . . Genl. Washington"—he was grateful for Saratoga. "Now we can allow a certain citizen"—Washington again—"to be wise, virtuous, and good, without thinking him a deity or a savior."[10]

Others went further than Adams. In Congress and the army there was now sentiment—Washington called it a "cabal"—to bring the commander-in-chief down a peg. "In all such juntas," one congressman wrote, "there are prompters and actors, accomodators, candle snuffers, shifters of scenes, and mutes." Historians have not been able to assign all the parts, or to agree how scripted they were. When Thomas Paine accused Adams of belonging to the cabal, Adams called it a "scandalous lye"; nor did he wish to make a counter-idol out of Gates: "the idea that any one man alone can save us," he thought, was "silly." [11] It is easier to know which officers wished to rise at Washington's expense: Gates; Thomas Conway, a Frenchmen of Irish descent, with a high opinion of himself; and Charles Lee, another British veteran of the French and Indian War, who was learned, witty, and odd (when Abigail Adams met him, he insisted that she shake the paw of his pet Pomeranian, Mr. Spada). It was ironic that the champions of military republicanism should ally themselves, even provisionally, with foreign-born professional soldiers. Nothing good came of any of them. Lee was courtmartialed for his performance in the battle of Monmouth in 1778; Conway's manner so offended his comrades that he was challenged to a duel and shot in the jaw; at war's end, Gates fanned the grievances of unpaid officers into a near-mutiny that was quelled only by Washington's charisma and loyalty to civilian power. It was not wrong to fear a man on horseback. But Washington, the native-born hero, turned out to be as good a republican as his congressional critics, and a better one than his military rivals.

By the time that Washington was back in the ascendant, Adams had left Congress for his next important assignment. Most of the talented men in Congress were gravitating back to their states, where the real power lay: Patrick Henry and Thomas Jefferson had already gone; Samuel Adams would stick it out until 1781. At the end of November 1777 Congress asked John to go abroad and join the American diplomatic mission in France. In February, John and his eldest son, John Quincy, set sail.

Except for one brief trip home, Adams spent the next ten years as a diplomat in Europe. Europe's capital cities—he was posted to Paris, Amsterdam and The Hague, and London—struck his American eyes as centers of wealth and ease. These qualities sometimes trickled down to him: In Holland, he wrote of himself in the third person, "he begins to be a courtier, and sups and visits at court among princesses and princes." [12] Travel between these cities and America was tedious, sometimes hairraising. On his first transatlantic crossing, three sailors on his ship were struck by lightning. On his third, the ship sprung a leak, Adams and the other passengers had to man the pumps, and the boat limped into Spain, forcing Adams's party to take a month-long trek on muleback simply to reach the French border. One short jaunt from England to Holland was lengthened by a three-day storm, an emergency landfall, and a four-mile walk through the snow to get to the nearest village; an ice-boat and a peasant's cart helped complete the trip.

As work engaged Adams's attention, Abigail found herself less and less remembered. His letters, slowed by long ocean voyages and his own failure to write, arrived three times in eight months, once in nine months, once in eleven months. Only in 1784 would she herself cross the ocean and join her husband.

The United States' first man in France had been another ex-congressman, Silas Deane. Deane had arranged for French assistance to the cause, funneled through a dummy "private" company since France did not yet recognize the rebellion. Congress soon sent Benjamin Franklin and Arthur Lee, a brother of Richard Henry Lee, to join Deane, then replaced Deane with Adams.

Washington was the rising celebrity of America, but Franklin was the established one, and he loomed over his fellow diplomats. Fifteenth child of a Boston candle maker, Franklin had moved, two decades before John Adams was born, to Philadelphia, where he became a printer and politician. He loaded his adopted city with improvements and activities: a hospital, a college, a fire company, a Masonic lodge. When he decided that the Penn family, the feudal owners of the colony, were a venal and incompetent gang, he placed his hopes for good government in a reformed imperial system. He spent sixteen years in Britain, serving as a lobbyist for the American colonies, and soaking up and dispensing patronage (he made his illegitimate son royal governor of New Jersey). When Parliament proved to be as high-handed as the Penns—and disrespectful to himself—he returned to America.

Politics was the source of only a part of his reputation. His almanacs and their maxims provided a self-help guide to bourgeois life. His experiments with electricity were partly scientific, partly magical: No one understood electricity, but everyone was in awe of it, and of him, for mastering it. On a practical level, he developed stoves, spectacles, and a set of musical water glasses—he called it the "armonica"—for which Mozart would compose a lovely quintet.

Franklin used his accomplishments, and his humor, as a card-dealer at a carnival uses his dexterity and his patter, to keep the world distracted, entertained, and at a distance. When Adams's daughter Abigail first met him, she hit this quality exactly: Franklin, she wrote, is "always silent, unless he has some diverting story to tell, of which he has a great collection."[13] He kept his thoughts to himself and used his multiple personae for diversion.

Adams had first met Franklin in the Second Continental Congress. He found him, he wrote his wife, a "great and good man," though he felt compelled to point out that he was not a prime mover: British "scribblers will attribute the temper, and proceedings of this Congress to him. But there cannot be a greater mistake." Franklin's only role in Philadelphia was "to co-operate and assist."[14]

When Adams arrived in Paris in the spring of 1778, he found Franklin settled into a new role. His goal was to create a good impression of the United States and of Benjamin Franklin; this he did by playing the part of the simple sage. Though he occupied a mansion with nine servants and ran up huge expenses, he appeared in public in a brown coat and undressed hair. Religiously he was an eclectic deist, and politically he had fought the Quaker party in Pennsylvania for decades, but he was content to let the French think of him as a simple Friend. His intellectual stature was real enough, and he milked it for all it was worth. In April Adams attended a meeting of the Academy of Sciences, at which the crowd called for Franklin and the even more elderly Voltaire to stand up together. "The two aged actors upon this great theatre of philosophy and frivolity then embraced each other," Adams noted sourly in his diary. "And the cry immediately spread through the whole kingdom and I suppose all over Europe . . . 'How charming it was! Oh it was enchanting!' " "Women and children come to have the honour to see the great Franklin," he wrote later, "and to have the pleasure of telling stories about his simplicity, his bald head and scattering strait hairs."[15]

It was one thing to be overshadowed in America by a hero; now Adams found himself overshadowed in Paris by a showman. Nor was his self-esteem helped by the fact that the French at first mistook him for

Samuel Adams, *le fameux* Adams. But there were more concrete reasons
for his ill humor. Because Franklin refused to attend to paperwork—he
saw receiving visitors and dining out as more important, and he was
right—the accounts and correspondence of the mission were in chaos.
Several of Franklin's associates, including the mission's secretary, were
British spies. Franklin professed not to be concerned: "I have long observed one rule . . . to do nothing but what spies may see" without dam-
age. Arthur Lee suspected Deane and Franklin of lining their pockets
(his complaints about Deane had led to his recall). Lee himself was can-
tankerous and impossible to work with. Adams responded to difficulty,
as he had in Congress, by plunging himself into day-to-day work—"the
business of the commission would never be done, unless I did it," [16] he
complained boastfully—and by studying French. He eventually came to
speak the language more correctly than Franklin, who made many mistakes, although Franklin was more fluent.

The political problem that dominated Adams's first five years in Europe was, how helpful would France be to the United States? And how
grateful should the United States be in return? Impressed by Saratoga,
France had signed a treaty of recognition and alliance in early February
1778, days before Adams had set sail. The first goal of America's European diplomacy was thus accomplished before Adams set foot in Europe. It remained to be seen, however, what the French alliance would
amount to. France's foreign minister, the Comte de Vergennes, was a career diplomat who longed to roll back Britain's gains in the last round of
Anglo-French warfare. "[H]is fear of England makes him value us a
makeweight," a later American diplomat would observe.[17] But how
much did Vergennes value his makeweights? France was engaged in ambitious worldwide projects in Europe, India, and the West Indies. The
American Revolution tied Britain down in one theater, but if the result
could be accomplished with minimal French effort, and without a strong
United States, Vergennes might hazard it.

Franklin wanted to bring the French along with patience, cunning,
and tact—a strategy he described as one of "decency and delicacy."
Adams believed that a new and weak nation had all the more reason to
insist on its own ends. He found Franklin too accommodating: "as good
an index" of official French opinion "as I know." "Let us," he wrote on

another occasion, "avoid, as much as possible, entangling ourselves with their wars or politics."[18] The politics of America's diplomats intersected with their personalities. Franklin, celebrity and *bon vivant*, was a glittering example of a diplomat going native. Adams's principles and his temperament, reinforced by the small social figure he cut, spared him that temptation.

Adams went home for seven weeks in 1779, keeping himself occupied by writing the Massachusetts state constitution. Congress sent him back with John Quincy and his second son, Charles, and a commission to negotiate a peace treaty with Britain. Since this was a remote contingency, Adams settled himself in Paris and engaged in propaganda for the American cause. Franklin had set up a press in his residence, and had been writing pro-American squibs: humorous fables and hoaxes about the bloodthirstiness of Britain's Indian allies. Adams submitted long and spirited arguments to a French newspaper, whose editor asked that they be made shorter. Adams also pressed Vergennes for naval assistance and hinted that America might be willing to make a separate peace with Britain. Vergennes, for his part, tried to get Adams recalled for being too confrontational. This was a real possibility: The lightweights who remained in Congress included some who took French bribes. Adams stayed on but accomplished little.

In the summer of 1780, Congress reassigned him to Holland (their first choice for the Dutch mission had been captured at sea and was being held in the Tower of London). Adams interpreted his credentials aggressively, as allowing him to open a new diplomatic front. The country, diminished from the days when it owned New Amsterdam and fought the British navy in the Thames, was still a capital of international finance. Adams hoped to secure a loan, diplomatic recognition, and a commercial treaty, and thus show both France and Britain that the United States had a range of resources available to it.

Away from Franklin and Vergennes, Adams had a better sense of his own resources. His establishments in Amsterdam and The Hague, the two major Dutch cities, furnished with gilt, mahogany, and damask, and equipped with horses and chefs, were designed to impress Dutch money men, in the same way that Franklin's banter impressed *philosophes* and bluestockings. When his Dutch diplomacy was finally rewarded, in

1782, with everything Adams had sought, a Spanish diplomat told him, with professional hyperbole, that he had accomplished the greatest diplomatic coup in all of Europe. This, he told Abigail with pardonable pride, was "but the litteral truth."[19]

All the labors of America's diplomats were designed to assist her soldiers. Seventeen eighty was perhaps the worst year of the war, marked by Benedict Arnold's treason and the loss of the Carolinas; 1781 was the best, with success in the south and Franco-American triumph at Yorktown. America's victory, six years after Adams told his wife to fly to the woods with their children if the British attacked Braintree, struck him as almost miraculous, and perhaps an example to the world. "Light spreads from the day spring in the west," he wrote at year's end, "and may it shine more and more until the perfect day."[20]

But now was the time for diplomats to bear down. Congress had assigned Franklin and John Jay of New York to join Adams in negotiating the treaty with England. When Adams returned to Paris from Amsterdam, there were some awkward moments between him and Franklin: He remembered the older man as "solemn" and "frigid" on public affairs, though "merry and pleasant enough about trifles and tittle-tattle." The state of public affairs was serious. Spain, which had joined France and Holland in backing the Revolution, wanted all British land west of the Alleghenies and south of the Ohio. France agreed, preferring a United States that would be small and weak, and dependent on itself. Responding to French influence, Congress had directed Adams, Franklin, and Jay to be guided by the "advice and opinion" of America's overbearing ally.[21]

The American diplomats, even including the Francophile Franklin, agreed among themselves to do no such thing, and the British, eager to finish a bad job, were generous. The United States got a western border on the Mississippi. Adams insisted that New Englanders be able to fish the Grand Banks off Newfoundland and dry their catches on the Canadian coast: "a constant scuffle," as he put it, "morning, noon and night about cod and haddock." This was more than a commercial proposition, for fishermen were potential sailors in a future American navy. Ruefully he told Abigail that "all the fortune that I have been able to make for myself" and his children amounted only to "liberty, and the right to catch fish."[22] But the second would help guarantee the first. The success of the negotiations taught a lesson about diplomacy that would be taught again to a later generation of the Adams family. Diplomatic missions composed of men as disparate as Franklin and Adams can produce rancor and cross-purposes, but they can also draw on a range of talents that may achieve a better result than any single diplomat could have. The final treaty was signed in September 1783.

Adams was in no mood to concede the virtues of others. The stress of his work; the stakes involved, patriotic and personal; the opposition of Vergennes; and the adulation accorded to Franklin had all taken their toll. He suffered from bulging eyes, eruptions, and aching joints; he was subject to melancholy and rages. He declared that he had suffered more than Job, more than Joseph Warren, who had died at Bunker Hill. In a grandiose moment, he sent Congress a description of an ideal minister to London: "his own likeness," wrote James Madison of Virginia, "is ridiculously and palpably studied." He sniped at Franklin behind his back—unwisely, for Franklin, hearing of it, replied with a crack that has stuck to Adams for centuries: He "is always an honest man, often a wise one, but sometimes, and in some things, absolutely out of his senses." Adams's hair-trigger reaction, when he learned of Franklin's judgments, only confirmed them: "the most unprovoked, the most cruel, and the most malicious representations that were ever put upon paper."[23]

Adams got the appointment to London. He was also reunited with his wife and all his children. In 1782, Abigail had written him that he had been absent "near half the term of years" that Ulysses "was encountering Neptune, Calipso, the Circes and Syrens." They met in London in August 1784, and the wonderful letters between them cease, though Abigail sent her friends pungent descriptions of what she saw in Britain and on the continent. "After dinner [Mme. Helvetius, a French friend of Franklin's] threw herself upon a settee where she showed more than her feet. She had a little lap-dog, who was, next to the Doctor, her favorite. This she kissed, and when he wet the floor she wiped it up with her chemise. . . . I own I was highly disgusted."[24] Franklin, for his part, sized Mrs. Adams up and gave her a book of sermons.

After a gracious initial interview with George III, Adams discovered something that generations of his family and other diplomats would experience, until the end of the next century: The United States was low on the list of Britain's concerns, and details of American policy shifted with the ebb and flow of extraneous factors, personalities, and party politics. Since Congress had no power to offer Britain economic advantages, or to threaten economic retaliation, Britain felt no obligation to be friendly. This imbalance, combined with British charm, confirmed Adams's basic Anglophobia. If John Bull "don't see a thing at first," he wrote, "you know it is a rule with him ever after wards to swear that it don't exist." Abigail, as she often was where politics was concerned, was sharper than her husband, calling a story in the newspapers "false as Hell," or if that was "too rough a term for a lady to use . . . false as the English." [25]

Adams stayed in England until the spring of 1788. Thus he saw only at a distance the United States' struggles with debt and taxes; Shays's Rebellion in his native Massachusetts ("ignorant, wrestless desperadoes," Abigail called its leaders); and above all the writing of the Constitution. Coincidentally, Adams's thoughts had turned to constitutional questions. In early 1787, he began publishing a three-volume *Defence of the Constitutions of the Governments of the United States*. His bugbear was unicameralism, or the one-house legislature, a system—supposedly more democratic than a two-house legislature—that was a favorite of Franklin. Adams wanted two legislative houses and an executive, each checking the other, and inveighed against the "outrages of unbalanced parties." His first volume was reprinted in Philadelphia as the delegates to the Constitutional Convention gathered, and years later he wrote that it had such an impact on them that Franklin could not sign the final document "without shedding tears." [26] This was a self-aggrandizing fantasy. But Adams's preferences matched those of most of the delegates, and the *Defence* reintroduced him to a home audience. Soon after he landed in Boston in June 1788, he concluded that he should be the first vice president.

The nation shared this opinion. Adams had been a leading figure at home and abroad for fourteen years. Franklin, a gouty octogenarian, was past consideration: His speeches at the Constitutional Convention had been read for him by others; Samuel Adams was occupied with state politics. Only one man had a claim on the presidency. George Washington, at war's end, had surrendered his commission as commander-in-chief with republican alacrity. Four years later he had presided over the Constitutional Convention. The office of president had been designed in his presence, with him in mind, and the document was ratified, in large part, because he approved of it.

Adams resettled in Braintree, in a larger house—which nevertheless, after their years in European metropolises, struck Abigail as a "wren's house"[27]—then came to New York City, the capital, in April 1789 to be sworn in.

Adams was moving back into the aura of the man he had nominated in 1775. Then Congress had sent Washington off to lead the military, and Adams had observed him, sometimes critically, from afar. Now he and Washington stood together at the top of the civilian structure, though Adams acknowledged Washington's pre-eminence, and even uniqueness. When the president came down with a near-fatal case of influenza and pneumonia during his first year in office, the Adams household went into shock. The government, wrote Abigail, depends "under Providence upon his life. At this early day . . . his death would I fear have had most disasterous concequences." "I am nothing, but I may be everything," Adams tersely described his own situation.[28] He was not psychologically prepared to become everything—certainly not with Washington's responsibilities—just yet.

Adams's subordinate position was confirmed by his distance from the president and by the nature of his office. Everyone else in the Executive Branch knew Washington better than he did. Thomas Jefferson, the secretary of state, had met him in the Virginia legislature in 1769. Henry Knox, secretary of war, had been his artillery commander, and Alexander Hamilton, the thirty-two-year-old secretary of the treasury, had been a colonel on his staff. Unlike these men, Adams had almost nothing to do. Not that anyone, except the busy Hamilton, had much. Jefferson airily wrote that the less he communicated with his ministers abroad, the better. Adams had no one with whom he had to communicate at all. His only constitutionally prescribed duties were to be available, in case the president died, and to preside over the Senate.

His behavior there got him into trouble. During his first months in New York, the Senate debated how it should respond to presidential addresses, and what the president should be called. Politeness, like war, is politics by other means, and the Senate correctly took these questions of

etiquette seriously—none more so than its presiding officer. Adams
spoke to the substance of motions from the chair, arguing that the Senate should thank the president for his "most gracious" speeches—the
very words Parliament used to thank the king—and that the president
be given some sonorous title. His perspective had been shaped, and
warped, by his years away. "What will the people of foreign countries,
what will the soldiers and sailors say? 'George Washington, President of
the United States'—they will despise him *to all eternity*." Revealingly, he
admitted during another discussion that "he had been long abroad, and
did not know how the tempers of the [American] people might be now."
Still he persisted in delivering his opinions, buttonholing senators on the
floor. "He got on the subject of checks to government, and the balances
of power," wrote one whom he accosted. "His tale was long."[29] The
Senate's deliberations at that time were not public, but word of Adams's
stance got out, at least among the political class.

He made his next mistake in plain sight. In the fall of 1790, the capital moved to Philadelphia; from then until the spring of 1791 Adams
published a series of essays for the *Gazette of the United States,* a semi-
official newspaper favored with federal advertising. Recent events in two
of the countries in which he had served prompted him to write once
more. In 1787 Holland—a quasi-republican government, one of the few
in the world—suffered a civil war and a foreign invasion. In 1789,
months after Washington and Adams took office, France entered its
own time of troubles. Vergennes's globalist strategy had bankrupted the
state; financial reform led to political upheaval, including violence and
mobs. Thomas Paine, who had moved to France, brought Washington a
key to the Bastille: "a share in two revolutions," he exulted, "is living to
some purpose."[30] America's ally, and one of the few nations with a similar form of government, had slid into chaos. Might America suffer the
same fate? Adams sidled into these issues with a series of essays—he
called them "Discourses"—on French civil wars of an earlier epoch. But
the relevance to contemporary Holland, France, and possibly America,
was clear.

Adams, as he had before, urged a "well-balanced government" as the
only "effectual control of rivalries." Balance would come from a two-
house legislature and a strong executive. But in his last essay, he broke

new ground on the subject of how executives should be picked: "hereditary succession was attended with fewer evils than frequent elections."[31] In other words, the system that produced George III would produce less tumult over the long run than the system that produced George Washington.

Adams had explained these sentiments more thoroughly in a letter to Benjamin Rush, a Philadelphia doctor who had served with him in the Continental Congress. Hereditary monarchy or aristocracy were "admirable" institutions "in a certain stage of society in a great nation. . . . I am clear that America must resort to them as an asylum against discord, seditions, and civil war, and that at no very distant period of time. I shall not live to see it—but you may. [Rush was ten years younger than Adams.] . . . Our country is not yet ripe for it in many respects, and it is not yet necessary, but our ship must ultimately land on that shore or be cast away." Adams was not the only American to have had such thoughts in the tense aftermath of the Revolution. Several delegates to the Constitutional Convention had supported an executive chosen for life, and one had remarked privately that "the sooner we take [a king], while we are able to make a bargain with him, the better."[32] But the deliberations of the convention, and the speculations of its delegates, had been private. Adams was doing his speculating in public, while he was vice president.

The reaction to his "Discourses" was sharp. Madison, a representative in the new Congress, wrote that Adams was getting "into difficulties" for "obnoxious principles." Paine had written a fervent defense of the French Revolution, *The Rights of Man*, which, when it was reprinted in Philadelphia in April 1791, appeared with a glowing blurb from Jefferson, who praised it as an antidote to "political heresies which have sprung up among us."[33] By "heresies," Jefferson meant the "Discourses," which were still appearing in the *Gazette of the United States*. In July, after the controversy was well-launched, the secretary of state assured the vice president, unconvincingly, that his words were a private note, published without his permission. Adams accepted Jefferson's explanation and explained in turn that he was not responsible for a counterattack on Jefferson and Paine, signed "Publicola," which had been attributed to him. He was telling the truth, though not the whole truth: "Publicola" was by John Quincy Adams, then a twenty-four-year-old lawyer in Boston.

As the Washington administration went on, Americans would con-
tend over larger matters than titles and French history: Hamilton's financial program; the Whiskey Rebellion; the wars arising from the
French Revolution. But the first controversies had fixed Adams in the
popular mind as a partisan, and when the first party system coalesced—
Federalists, led by Washington and Hamilton, defending the government, versus Republicans, led by Jefferson and Madison, attacking
it—Adams was classed with the former.

Adams lacked a trait possessed, in different ways, by both Franklin
and Washington. Though all three men had strong beliefs and hot tempers, the older men could conceal their opinions and emotions, Franklin
behind a screen of banter, Washington behind a mask of reserve. When
Washington did speak or act, it was always decisively: Faced with a frontier tax revolt, he personally led an army five times larger than the one he
had taken across the Delaware for the battle of Trenton to the foothills of
the Alleghenies. But when it was not necessary to act, he knew that it
was necessary not to act. He possessed, as Adams would acknowledge
years later, "the gift of silence."[34] Silence was prudence; it could also con-
vey strength. Adams had argued that Washington would be despised in
Europe if he lacked a title. But Washington had already earned the
world's respect; he didn't need one.

Ironically, considering his reputation, Adams was the most unde-
pendable party man in the country. Following the political theory of the
day, he deplored parties, as embodiments of the very "rivalries" that a
"well-balanced government" should control. Everyone agreed with him,
though everyone behaved otherwise where his own party was concerned. Only Adams remained true to his professed beliefs, willing, as he
had been two decades earlier, to "quarrel with both parties and with
every individual of each," rather than diminish his independence.[35]
What he did not understand was that if he acted entirely alone, he would
not stand above the parties, but be blown between them.

When Washington announced that he would not run for a third
term, Adams believed that the presidency should come to him, not because he was a Federalist champion, but because seniority and service
entitled him to serve. He won, narrowly; Jefferson finished three votes
behind him in the Electoral College and became, according to the laws

of the day, vice president. Adams described his own inauguration, in Philadelphia in March 1797, with becoming modesty, and with appreciation for the system he had criticized in his "Discourses": one "sun setting full-orbit, and another rising (though less splendid)."[36]

Adams won because he had done several important things well, while all the things he had done badly had been minor. He was a bad president, however, though his partisans, beginning with himself, have labored to obscure the fact.

In fairness, he faced difficult problems, some of them unique. As the second president, he was the first who had to deal with a predecessor's cabinet. When Washington left office, all his original cabinet had long since retired, and the current secretaries—Timothy Pickering (State), Oliver Wolcott (Treasury) and James McHenry (War)—were both undistinguished and little known to Adams. Worse, they were well-known to Alexander Hamilton, who continued to play the role of a youthful wise man. When Adams made appointments of his own— Benjamin Stoddert, for the newly created Navy Department, and John Marshall, for Chief Justice—he made excellent ones, but he kept Washington's leftovers for more than three years.

Adams suffered from comparison to the old, more splendid sun he had replaced. George Washington had been Father of His Country. What did that make John Adams at the moment of his inauguration? Step-father? Sixty-one-year-old son? Adams and America were bewitched by a theory of leadership expounded by one of the most popular British polemicists of the early eighteenth century, Henry St. John, Viscount Bolingbroke. Bolingbroke was a shifty opportunist and brilliant journalist, whose eloquent spin had a great impact, especially on Americans, who had never experienced the disillusionment of dealing with him directly. One of Bolingbroke's most compelling notions was the idea of the Patriot King—the leader beyond politics, who enters the political arena from outside and rebukes the squabbling partisans for the benefit of the nation. George III, who had studied Bolingbroke as a boy, tried to be a Patriot King. George Washington, the citizen-soldier, came closest to enacting the ideal. But his success was a tribute to the people's need for such a figure; to his remarkable prepresidential record; and to his talents as a leader and an actor (Washington knew perfectly well that Abi-

gail Adams and others saw him as a divine temple, and he labored to ful-
fill their expectations). It was an impossible act to follow.

But Adams brought many problems on himself. He had no executive
experience—Washington was a former commander-in-chief and plantation owner; Jefferson was getting valuable training as chief wirepuller
of an opposition party. Adams had spoken, written, worked on committees, and wrangled with Franklin and Vergennes. But he hadn't led
anything. He also, it turned out, lacked political skill. He ran his administration from long distance, spending as many as six months at a time in
Quincy, as northern Braintree had been called since 1792. Travel to and
from Quincy was slow; on one trip south, Abigail and her coachman got
lost outside Baltimore. Adams's long furloughs were politically dangerous for him. Stoddert urged him to spend more time in the capital, and
Washington fretted about his absence: It "gives much discontent to the
friends of government, while its enemies chuckle at it."[37] In the Continental Congress and in Paris, Adams had thrown himself into work;
now, when he was at the summit of power, he threw himself into being
out of town. The motive, in both cases, was the same: to avoid potentially
awkward confrontations.

At home or away, he was personally and politically isolated. His wife's
advice was noxious—she called Adams's Republican enemies "traitors to
their country"—an amplification of his own prejudices. He listened to
his eldest son, who had better judgment, and who had been given a
diplomatic post by George Washington (his father kept him on the job).
But John Adams also listened to Elbridge Gerry, a Marblehead merchant who had served in Congress and the Constitutional Convention
(he had refused to sign). Gerry was querulous, long-winded and eccen-
tric; he thought the country should have two capitals and a traveling
Congress. "Poor Gerry," said Abigail, "always had a wrong kink in his
head." Adams thought him one of the "two most impartial men" in
America.[38] Probably Gerry was the only man more peculiar and prickly
than Adams himself; Adams took this to be a sign of wisdom and virtue.

Listening to his mostly odd soulmates, Adams could not deal effectively with his cabinet. It is a staple of Adams defenders that his cabinet
plotted against him, by consulting with other Federalist leaders more
than with him; certainly Pickering and Wolcott did. "I wish," Pickering

wrote Hamilton, "you were in a situation not only to 'see all the cards,' but to play them; with all my soul I would give you my *hand*."[39] But many leaders face plots; Washington had to face down Gates, Conway, and Lee. Good leaders identify plotters, isolate the ringleaders, and neutralize or win over the followers. Adams let his cabinet fester while he sat in Quincy.

Most seriously, he stirred up a war fever that he later decided must be broken. The state of the world was dangerous. The wars of the French Revolution were, in one sense, the last of the Anglo-French wars that had begun in the late seventeenth century; in another sense, they were the first of the modern world wars, driven by utopian hopes and totalitarian ideologies. In this situation, the young country floated like a chip in a whirlpool. During the Washington administration, France had made bumptious demands that the United States maintain the wartime alliance of the two countries. After Adams took office, a new phase of the revolutionary government, the Directory, embarked on an ambitious foreign policy, invading Italy and bullying American shipping. When Adams sent three ministers to Paris to negotiate, including Gerry, the Directory insulted them and tried to extort *douceurs*—bribes—from them. The country blazed in anger at French high-handedness and rallied round the government. A Federalist majority in Congress, swept into office in the midterm elections of 1798, passed a Sedition Act allowing the federal government to prosecute editors who libeled the president and other federal officials. "In any other country," wrote Abigail, they "would have been sezd long ago."[40] Adams fed the flames, giving bellicose speeches and writing warlike letters to citizens' groups. Biographer John Ferling shrewdly notes that Adams's lifelong insecurity about never having borne arms fed his rhetoric now.

Yet Adams soon cooled on the war fever he had helped create. Gerry and John Quincy assured him that the French might be willing to negotiate in earnest. Meanwhile Congress proposed to raise an army of fifty thousand men—larger than anything the country had fielded during the Revolution—and all of Adams's classical republican suspicions of military establishments were activated. Since the means were distasteful, he began to question the ends. The psychological turning point came in February 1799 when he received a letter from George Washington. The

Father of His Country had come out of retirement to serve as commander-in-chief, in case the French invaded. In the last year of his life, he sent Adams a letter from Joel Barlow, an American poetaster living in Paris, who argued that French peace feelers were genuine. Washington hoped that Barlow's letter might be an opening, "however small," for "restoring peace and tranquillity," which was "the ardent desire of all the friends of this rising empire." As Ferling put it, the letter "released Adams from the emotional shackles" of the war crisis.[41] If the greatest warrior in America was for peace, Adams could pursue it without risk to his own self-esteem.

He pursued it, unfortunately, in a slapdash way. He announced that he would send a new minister to Paris, without consulting anyone in "his" party. Since he was above parties, with whom would he consult? In the spring of 1800 he finally cleaned out his cabinet, firing the guilty Pickering and the innocent McHenry (the latter in a screaming fit), but leaving the guilty Wolcott in place. He mocked Hamilton as a British toady; in return, Hamilton called him "as wicked as he is mad."[42]

Adams would go to his grave believing that he had sacrificed himself for peace. A more realistic view is that he did the right thing in the worst possible way. A sterner view is that he did the wrong thing, making a hasty peace with untrustworthy negotiators. The day after the Franco-American treaty was signed, Napoleon Bonaparte, the young general who had succeeded the Directory, bullied Spain into giving him the Louisiana Territory. The United States now shared a defenseless border with the world's most successful aggressor.

In the election of 1800, the Federalists hemorrhaged in Congress, and although only one state switched its electoral vote from 1796, that was New York, one of the largest. Adams found himself in another new situation—the first loser in American presidential history.

CHAPTER 4

ADAMS RETURNED TO Quincy in March 1801, never to leave it except for brief trips, and never to take an active role in politics. His retirement, which lasted from 1801 to his death in 1826, was almost as long as his national career (1774–1801).

During Adams's last days in office he received a consoling letter from his youngest son, Thomas. If his presidency were "the only inheritance left your family they might esteem themselves rich in possessing" it. Adams's family had been tried as much as the paterfamilias. Thomas was an ineffectual Philadelphia lawyer who would soon move, at age thirty-one, back to Quincy, to live with his parents and drink. Abigail, the eldest child, had married a ne'er-do-well whom Adams had given a patronage job; after the Republicans chivvied him out of it, he would take part in a failed effort to liberate Venezuela. Charles, the middle son, had died in November 1800, of liver failure, at the age of thirty; homosexuality, and his parents' disapproval, may have accelerated his alcoholism. "Happy Washington!" Adams exclaimed bitterly as Charles was going down. "Happy to be childless!"[1] Only John Quincy, who returned from Europe in 1801, was well-launched.

Jefferson had lost the first contested presidential election in 1796, but then he had won. Adams had won in 1796, but then he had lost. He was the first loser, and his loss, coming at the end of a busy, laborious and in many ways great career, seemed to negate it. He brooded; he remembered; he justified himself. In 1802, he began an autobiography. He told John Quincy, who encouraged him, that he needed a "bucket of water" at his side, to douse the passions that "set me on fire." Five years later, he abandoned it. When he later read Franklin's *Autobiography,* his own struck him as "dull" and "dreary." In 1806, Mercy Otis Warren, sister of James Otis and a former neighbor, published a history of the Revolution, which criticized Adams as a backslider from republicanism, tainted "by living long near the splendor of courts and courtiers." He wrote her ten long letters in thirty days, expostulating against her "severity," which had "reduced him to the necessity of pouring out all myself." She sent six replies, then ended the correspondence, chiding him for his "rancor."[2] Some years after that, he contributed over a hundred essays to a Boston newspaper, rehashing his diplomatic career. Only as he moved into his late seventies did he let the old controversies go.

Yet polemics took only a part of his time. Out of office, and largely out of the public eye, other traits of his character asserted themselves. He could no longer serve his country in Paris, or create it in Philadelphia; he did not have to work like a drayhorse; he was beyond his mistakes. So he could give more play to his curiosity, to his quick and appreciative senses. "[A]rose by four o'clock and enjoyed the charm of earliest birds. Their songs were never more various, universal, animating or delightful." He had written that in 1796, during a visit to Quincy; almost twenty years later, he was still avid to observe. "When one of the comets was here in our neighborhood I went out one evening into my garden to look at the wandering star. . . . In the dark I blundered against [a] stake. . . . I felt a sharp cut but thought it had only broke the skin. I scampered up and returned to the house. . . . My daughter . . . cryed out, Sir, what has happened to you, your leg is all bloody. I striped off the stocking and lo! A gash from half an inch, to an inch deep." He read books of history, philosophy, memoir, and theology, until his sight failed, then had family members read to him. "I wished I owned this book," he wrote of some tome when he was seventy-eight, "and 100,000 more." He also showed interest in and affection for in-laws, grandchildren, old acquaintances, and new correspondents. He gave a (perhaps unintentionally) comic explanation of his sociability in one of his letters. "My temper in general has been tranquil except when any instance of extraordinary madness, deceit, hypocrisy, ingratitude, treachery or perfidy has suddenly struck me. Then I have always been irascible enough."[3] He could still be irascible, as the parade of instances showed. But now that he was away from the stress of action, the intervals of tranquility could lengthen.

But politics still interested him, on the levels of personality and philosophy: Who were the great men he had known? How great were they?

And how should men be governed? These were old questions. He continued to sift the reputations of Franklin (dead in 1790) and Washington (dead in 1799). His old mentors, James Otis and Samuel Adams, who died in 1803, he believed, were greater. He had encountered them at a more impressionable age; Otis, by going mad, and cousin Samuel, by concentrating on state politics, had not competed with him at the peak of his career. Of himself, he wrote harshly, "I am not, never was, and never shall be a great man."[4] When, in his letters to Mrs. Warren, he wasn't sputtering, he defended the works, particularly the "Discourses," that seemed to justify her charges.

The question of personality and the question of philosophy joined in his late correspondence with the man who beat him. Adams had met Jefferson at the Second Continental Congress and served with him on the committee charged with explaining the reasons for declaring independence; Jefferson drafted the document. The two became still closer a decade later, when Congress sent Jefferson abroad to fill Franklin's slot as ambassador to France. "No one can replace" Franklin, said Jefferson modestly, "I am only his successor." But Adams had found him a great change for the better. Jefferson was eight years younger than Adams and had no desire to be the toast of the town; he charmed and delighted Abigail. These experiences gave Jefferson a shrewd and measured view of Adams. "You will love him," he wrote Madison, "if you ever become acquainted with him," and on another occasion, more keenly, he wrote that Adams's "dislike of all parties" gives "the same fair play to his reason as would a general benevolence of temper." Adams was fair because he was difficult; once you got past the difficulty, he was warm. Adams took much longer to understand Jefferson, because he was a harder case: "like the great rivers," as Adams told John Quincy, "whose bottoms we cannot see and make no noise."[5]

Politics drove them apart. If Jefferson was to defeat the unwholesome schemes of Federalism and win office himself, he had to supplant John Adams, and he did it as coolly as one would put down a dog. The blurb for Paine's *Rights of Man* in which he criticized Adams's "heresies" was his opening shot. He was, on the whole, relieved to have finished second in the election of 1796, foreseeing the foreign policy storm that the victor would have to navigate. When Adams, on the eve of his inauguration, asked Jefferson if he would be part of a diplomatic mission to Paris, the vice president–elect was polite, but had no intention of helping him out of his coming troubles. During Adams's administration, the Republican press savaged him, with Jefferson's encouragement and subsidies; Adams did not attend his successor's inauguration. When one of Jefferson's hacks switched sides and published the first account of the Sally Hemings story, Abigail wrote her former friend triumphantly, "The serpent you cherished and warmed, bit the hand that nourished him."[6]

In 1809, Benjamin Rush, the Philadelphia doctor who had served with both of them in Congress, tried to bring the estranged founders back together. Jefferson by then was out of office, having had a second term almost as grim as Adams's only one. After more than two years' persistence, Rush finally succeeded. Adams sent Jefferson a book on rhetoric, recently published by John Quincy; he offered his child as a connection, but the larger connection between them was their common legacy to their country.

In his first letter Jefferson made a slip of the pen. "We shall continue," he wrote of the country, "to growl," meaning, "to grow"—but his unconscious, writing of himself and Adams, supplied the *l*. Yet for fourteen years they kept up a friendly exchange. Adams supplied more than two-thirds of the letters, 109 to Jefferson's 49. There is often a slight feeling of refrigeration in Jefferson's, such as one exudes in the presence of a dear, but boisterous, and somewhat-below-the-salt friend. Occasionally, Jefferson writes from the heart, as when, after a long letter of theology, he hopes that, when they die, they may "meet . . . again, in Congress, with our antient colleagues, and receive with them the seal of approbation, 'Well done, good and faithful servants.' "[7]

Adams agreed that their afterlife, certainly in the minds of men, would depend upon their deeds in 1776. That was how his career had taken shape in his own mind. We are the ancestors of "liberty and independence," he wrote in 1813; "I look back with rapture," he wrote in 1825, "to those golden days when Virginia and Massachusetts lived and acted together like a band of brothers."[8] He wrote more often than Jefferson, and more vehemently, not only because it was his nature, but because he had more to prove. Although Jefferson's presidency had ended badly, it had not ended in repudiation; Jefferson was followed in the White House by his longtime disciple and counselor, James Madison, and Madison was followed by yet another Virginia Republican, James Monroe. Jefferson was first in political war, and first in political peace. His later career seemed continuous with his more glorious early one. Adams's participation in the golden days had been darkened by failure. Reconnecting with Jefferson was one way of refurbishing himself. Both men needed the past, but Adams needed Jefferson to get back to it.

But there was an irony in Jefferson's role as Adams's rehabilitator. At the center of the golden days was the Declaration that their congressional committee had produced, and that was Jefferson's handiwork. Years later, Adams remembered talking Jefferson into taking the assignment ("you can write ten times better than I can"). If he did, he was expressing, as he had with his nomination of Washington to be commander-in-chief, an obvious choice, for Jefferson had come to Congress renowned for a lucid and supple pen. He wrote the Declaration, Adams recalled, in "a day or two."[9]

In 1819, after Abigail had died (Jefferson sent a moving letter of condolence), Adams went to Boston to see John Trumbull's painting of the Declaration of Independence. Trumbull had begun a small version in 1786, at Jefferson's residence in Paris, using a floorplan of Congress's meeting place drawn from memory by Jefferson himself. The following year, Trumbull caught Adams as he was about to leave London. Adams had just had "the powder combed out of his hair," Trumbull recalled. "Its color and natural curl were beautiful, and I took that opportunity to paint his portrait."[10] A large version, finished in 1818, toured the country before being installed in the rotunda of the Capitol. Adams stands almost dead center; to the right of him are the drafting committee's other members—Roger Sherman, Robert Livingston, Jefferson, Franklin. Before them sits the president of Congress, John Hancock. But the act that they, and all their "antient colleagues," ranged behind them like pins on a crowded bowling green, are watching—and that Adams saw for himself when he viewed the painting in Boston—is Jefferson's gesture of handing over a piece of paper.

That piece of paper and its prominence came to vex Adams. He dismissed the Declaration to correspondents as a "coup de theatre"; to Jefferson himself he wrote that he had dismissed all Congress's declarations at the time as mere "ornament[s]" ("I was in a great error, no doubt," he added sheepishly). Writing to himself, in the margin of his own copy of his "Discourses," he expressed the feeling of being cheated. "The mighty Jefferson, by the Declaration of Independence 4 July 1776, carried away the glory both of the great and the little. . . . Such are the caprices of fortune." [11]

Adams's caveats and carpings about the Declaration recall the arguments of present-day scholars who solemnly point out that Jefferson's draft was lightly edited by his fellow committee members and heavily edited by Congress. Jefferson thought they ruined it, and ever after thrust his original on correspondents, like an aggrieved party pursuing an old lawsuit. In fact Congress improved it, removing absurd charges (that George III, not American slaveowners, was responsible for the slave trade) and doubtful theories. Yet the critics try to prove too much. Many good editors cannot write themselves, and the best editors do well only when they work with great writers. What other members of the drafting committee—or of Congress—left us anything we now read? Roger Sherman? Robert Livingston? John Adams? Franklin left plenty, but it is all funny or proverbial, qualities hardly suited to such a moment. Five days after the Declaration was approved, Washington had it read to his soldiers in New York City. Seven weeks after that, fifteen hundred of these soldiers were killed or captured in the battle of Long Island. When you ask men to risk their lives, fortunes, and sacred honor, you should tell them why, and you had better tell them well.

Adams had a problem with the Declaration, however, more serious than bruised ego. He disagreed with it. His problem was with the immortal opening (which Congress hardly edited at all). The first of the self-evident truths—"All men are created equal"—was a truism of American political thought. Jefferson claimed no originality for writing it: "it was intended," he told another correspondent in his old age, "to be an expression of the American mind." Adams himself, when he drafted the Massachusetts constitution in 1779, wrote that "All men are born equally free and independent." [12] Like many a truism, however, it concealed unexamined shades of meanings. As a statement of personal

rights—that all men are equally entitled to enjoy their possessions, and
the fruit of their labor—Adams accepted it. But another possible meaning is that all men are approximately, or potentially, equal in condition,
and therefore equal in their political rights. Adams thought that was
fantastic. Some people had advantages at birth, or in their character,
which raised them above their fellows, in prestige and power. This was a
universal and indestructible feature of human society. Some men are created aristocrats; all societies are aristocratic.

"The five pillars of aristocracy," he lectured Jefferson in 1813, "are
beauty, wealth, birth, genius and virtues. Any one of the three first"—
that is, the very three he lacked—"can, at any time, over bear . . . both of
the two last." This prompted the sage of Monticello to make a famous
demurral. There was, he conceded, an "artificial aristocracy" of wealth
and birth, digging itself into power by hereditary offices or corruption.
But there was also a "natural aristocracy," composed of the virtuous and
the talented, who rise to the top by their own efforts. Jefferson's solution:
"to leave to the citizens" the job of separating "the aristoi from the
pseudo-aristoi . . . the wheat from the chaff. In general," he added with
the sunny confidence of the winner, "they will elect the real good and
wise." All men were equal enough to vote well. In some benighted communities—Jefferson mentioned Connecticut, one of the few states he
never carried—established families retained their pre-eminence. But
"[i]n Virginia we have nothing of this." [13]

Adams would not be put off. He focused on the pillar of birth. The
well-born had power because people admired them; elections expressed
that regard, and fortified the power. Adams was too tactful to dwell on
the absurdity of considering Virginia—a cat's cradle of first families,
from Byrds to Randolphs to Lees, in which Jefferson was enmeshed (his
mother was a Randolph)—as a land of egalitarianism and opportunity.
But he discoursed on his own region. He remembered a conversation
from the 1760s with a senior judge in Worcester. "The old sage asked me
to look for the news from Rhode Island and see how the elections had
gone there." Adams read out the winners. "I expected as much," the
judge said; ". . . in the most popular governments, the elections will generally go in favour of the most ancient families." The Bowdoins were an
old Massachusetts political family, descended from French crusaders.

"You," he added pertly, "have immortalized the name by making an ambassador of it" (James Bowdoin, one of Jefferson's ambassadors to Spain). "Aristocracy, like waterfowl, dives for ages and then rises with brighter plumage."[14]

These were old observations of his. In his *Defence* of the American constitutions, Adams had asked if "the name of Andros [a hated colonial governor] and that of Winthrop [founder of the Massachusetts Bay Colony] are heard with the same sensations in any village in New England? Is not gratitude the sentiment that attends the latter, and disgust the feeling excited by the former?"[15]

Family prestige had its dangers and its uses. It could afflict a community with vices, which were as likely to be inherited as talents. It could be a bulwark against the rise of despots or political chaos, which is why Adams had once thought the fragile American republic might have to turn to hereditary offices in Benjamin Rush's lifetime. Rush died in May 1813, the very year Adams and Jefferson were disputing about aristocracy, and hereditary offices had not yet come. But family prestige still existed. Adams thought it was folly for political philosophers blandly to dismiss it from their calculations or their declarations.

In all these discussions of New England families, there is a conspicuous omission. Go into any village in New England, and ask how people regarded the name of Adams (Adams had carried every New England state in both 1796 and 1800). What effect would that prestige have? In his "Discourses," Adams had written that nations are "in the habit of respecting" surnames and "race[s]" (Adams here means families). Positive emotions are "so long associated" with certain families that they "become national habits. National gratitude descends from the father to the son, and is often stronger to the latter than the former." When Adams wrote that, Charles was alive, Thomas was not a failure, and John Quincy, young as he was, had already performed diplomatic services for his country. By the time Adams and Jefferson resumed their friendship, Charles and Thomas had fallen by the wayside, but John Quincy had been a congressman, a senator, and minister to Russia. He went on to serve in his father's old post, minister to Great Britain; as secretary of state; and finally, in 1825, in his father's highest post, the presidency. "It must excite ineffable feelings in the breast of a father," Jefferson wrote in congratulation, "to have lived to see a son . . . so eminently distinguished by the voice of his country." [16]

John Quincy Adams was not his father's claim to greatness, but he was his father's heir, and could be, more than any outbursts to Mrs. Warren or even exchanges with Jefferson, his father's justification.

John Quincy Adams

---

*E*ARLY IN HIS diplomatic career, John Quincy was asked by a British official if he wouldn't like being minister to London. After all, his father had held the post before him. "That may do very well for you," he replied, ". . . but in my country, you know, there is nothing hereditary in public offices."[1] That may have done very well for a patriotic flourish, but the desire for public offices may be inherited. Certainly John and Abigail Adams tried to cultivate it in their sons.

When John first went to the Continental Congress, Abigail wrote him that she had persuaded "little Johnny," age seven, to read her a page or two a day from Charles Rollin's *Ancient History,* a popular work that served as a textbook for patriots who wanted to make modern history; she hoped that he would develop "a fondness for it." "Fix their ambition upon great and solid objects," her husband wrote back approvingly, "and their contempt upon little, frivolous and useless ones." The Adams boys were immersed in congressional politics. When John's letters from Philadelphia arrived, they ran for them "like chickens to a crum," and asked, "who is for us and who against us."[2]

John took little Johnny to Europe when he was ten, and again when he was twelve. By that time, parental exhortations were addressed to him directly. "These are times in which a genious should wish to live," Abigail wrote her eldest son. "It is not in the still calm of life, or the repose of a pacific station, that great characters are formed. . . . Great necessities call out great virtues." John Quincy had a second incentive to greatness, for he had "a parent who has taken so large and active a share in this contest." The double stimulus of the age and John Adams should produce results. "It will be expected of you, my son . . . that your improvements should bear some proportion to your advantages."[3]

Some of the advice that John Quincy's two intelligent and ambitious parents gave him was deeply wise, suitable for any stage or condition of life: "You will never be alone with a poet in your pocket," his father once wrote him. All their tutoring that was purely hortatory—designed to make their son a replica of themselves—must have both stimulated and flattered him. But what were the penalties of failure in the Adams household? When he was in his sixties, John Quincy confided to his diary a childhood memory, of discovering, "in a closet of my mother's bed-chamber," a two-volume edition of *Paradise Lost*, "which, I believe, I attempted ten times to read, and never could get through half a book." Milton's winding sentences, dense with allusions, can puzzle adults who do not catch the tempo of his music. Little Johnny was more than puzzled: "I was mortified, even to the shedding of solitary tears, that I could not even conceive what it was that my father and mother admired so much in that book, and yet I was ashamed to ask them an explanation."[4] A precocious, pressured child might well weep with frustration at encountering something he could not understand, but the shame that prevented John Quincy from asking his parents came from the parents. As long as he did everything right, they admired and encouraged him. Whenever he failed, they must have withdrawn their favor.

John tutored his son in Europe; they read Plutarch aloud to each other over breakfast. John Quincy learned French faster than his father, and on his third Atlantic crossing, taught the French diplomats traveling with them English. In 1781, Francis Dana, a thirty-eight-year-old ex-congressman who was serving as secretary to the Paris legation, was sent to St. Petersburg to try to negotiate a treaty with Russia; since Dana was weak in French, the language of the imperial court, fourteen-year-old John Quincy accompanied him as a translator. Back in Paris, he hobnobbed with Franklin, Lafayette, and "Mr. Jefferson" ("I love to be with [him] because he is a man of very extensive learning and pleasing manners"). In London, he heard Pitt and Fox debate in Parliament. John Quincy seemed "so far beyond his years," John wrote, that he was "admired by all who have conversed with him. . . . The world says they should take him for my younger brother."[5]

John Quincy's childhood, which looked like a successful adulthood, had been charmed. But he needed a college education. Jefferson had suggested he go to William and Mary, but John Adams's son was going to go to Harvard. John Quincy returned to Massachusetts a month after turning eighteen.

Naturally it was a letdown. He had plummeted, from the capitals of the world—Paris, St. Petersburg, London—not even to Boston, but to the rural village of Cambridge. He was exchanging the company of some of the greatest men of the age, his personal friends, for that of pedantic Unitarian clergymen. What was worse, they were in a position to correct him because his classical education, provided by his father, had deficiencies. Perhaps, he consoled himself, being "subjected to the commands" of people "that I must despise" would teach him "humility" (there was little humility in that reflection).[6] After Harvard, he read law and opened a practice in Boston. This was even worse. He had no interest in the field; he played the flute and drank. (All his life he would be a serious drinker—as an old man he would correctly identify eleven out of fourteen Madeiras in a blind tasting—though unlike his brothers he stayed this side of alcoholism.) He roused himself to defend his father in his 1791 quarrel with Jefferson; James Madison shrewdly guessed that the "Publicola" essay, commonly attributed to John, was actually by John Quincy, because the style was too good to be John's.

His father responded to his depression by hectoring him. "You come into life with advantages which will disgrace you if your success is mediocre. And if you do not rise to the head not only of your profession, but of your country, it will be owing to your own *lasiness, slovenliness* and *obstinacy.*"[7] Many parents tell their floundering children to pull themselves together and work; few tell them to pull themselves together and become president.

John Quincy was plucked from his rut by the father of his country. Washington appointed him minister to Holland in 1794, because John Quincy had lived there; because he had diplomatic experience, however lowly; and because his journalism was sound (his father had been showing it to the president). He prepared himself by reading the diplomatic records of the 1780s, including his father's struggles with Franklin, and by buying a new diary, which would become the most detailed political record of the next half-century. Passing through London, he had his portrait painted by John Singleton Copley, the transplanted Bostonian whose luscious brush loved the faces, and fabrics, of the Anglo-

American upper class. Copley depicted an attractive, genial young man, now radiating confidence, with a trace of romantic dishevelment. His performance in Holland justified Washington's judgment. "I shall be much mistaken," the president wrote, "if, in as short a period of time as may well be expected, he is not found at the head of the diplomatic corps."[8] During his first posting, he married Louisa Johnson, the pretty daughter of a Maryland merchant and an Englishwoman. Louisa, raised in Europe, was intelligent and strong-willed, like her husband, and like him, had a vein of melancholy.

When John Adams became president, one of his first actions was to send his son to Prussia. John Quincy, who had been expecting Washington to transfer him to Portugal, felt crushed by paternal favor; the reassignment, he complained, destroyed "all the satisfaction which I have enjoyed hitherto" at being a public servant. He had earned Washington's good opinion; the world would say his father's good opinion was pure nepotism. The Republican press indeed said that the American mission to Prussia, which was new, had been created to line the Adams family's pockets. When he first arrived at the gates of Berlin, the "dapper lieutenant" in charge "did not know, until one of his private soldiers explained to him, who the United States were."[9]

In his years as a diplomat he established the outline of the routine he would maintain for the rest of his life. Rising early, at six, five, or even four in the morning, he would read several chapters of the Bible, sometimes in Greek. It generally took him a year to finish, whereupon he would begin again. Later in life, to broaden his understanding of the text, he read the Scriptures in French and German, comparing the translations. "[T]he German, I think, has the fewest . . . obscurities. But the eloquence of St. Paul strikes me as more elevated and sublime in the English." For exercise, he walked; he knew the length of his stride—two feet six inches "and eighty-eight one hundreds of an inch"—and kept track of the distances he covered and the time he made. When he lived in warm climates, he swam. When official business permitted, he read modern literature and classics, and composed or translated poetry. One batch of versified Psalms, he wrote sadly, was "all bad, but as good as I could make them."[10] Often he shifted from project to project, in silent protest at the number of projects he loaded himself with. In the midafternoon, he might collapse into vacancy—other people would call it resting—which made him push himself all the more. A man who was not as intelligent, talented, and healthy as he was would have destroyed himself. He did his best.

John Quincy represented a stage in the evolution of Puritanism into strenuousness. Calvin's followers, committed to a belief in predestination, had always scanned their lives for signs of grace. Luther had preached justification by faith, not works; Puritans sought proof of justification in hard work, labor relieving them from intolerable theological anxieties. But as the religious faith of post-Puritans changed—in the generation after John Quincy's, it would begin to disappear altogether—the focus, and the anxiety, shifted to labor itself.

Mr. Jefferson's election in 1800 was attributed by John Quincy to "pimping to the popular passions." He wrote his father a letter expressing the Adams family explanation of defeat: "you were not the man of any party, but the man of the whole nation."[11] He hoped to transmit that ideal by naming his and Louisa's first child, born in April 1801, George Washington. Two weeks later, John Quincy received notice that his father had recalled him, to deprive the new president of the opportunity of doing so.

Back home he resumed the practice of law, which he found as boring as he had found it before. He did not stay in it long. Within eighteen months, he had run for the state Senate (successfully) and Congress (unsuccessfully). When Massachusetts's two United States senators resigned early in 1803, the legislature (which then picked U.S. senators) turned to him, and he became senior senator from his state at age thirty-six.

Like all the leaders of the founding generation, John Quincy's father had ambition, yet, like all of them, he was leery of expressing it, lest he be seen as overreaching. Still there was a measure of frankness in his dealings with the trait. John Adams was keenly aware of the ambition of others (Jefferson, he had written, was "eaten to a honeycomb" with it), and he certainly complained openly when his own ambition was thwarted. No forts had been named after him during his administration, he wrote, "except perhaps a diminutive work at Rhode Island."[12] He might be blinded in specific cases, but he was not systematically self-deceiving.

John Quincy kept himself in ignorance. The notion that he would extend his hand to reach for public office was unacceptable to him. He had
to be summoned, he could not seek; he had to be called, he must never
campaign. Since he often sought and campaigned, generally successfully, he could never acknowledge what he was doing. His enemies
pointed it out to him, as did his loved ones. "[H]owever free you may
fancy yourself from ambition," his wife-to-be Louisa wrote when they
were courting, "you would feel infinite mortification" in giving up the
"flattering positions" for which he had "insensibly acquired a taste" in his
glittering youth.[13] Unable to be so frank, John Quincy dissembled whenever the subject loomed, or said nothing at all. His elevation to the Senate was not automatic, for his father's old enemy, Timothy Pickering,
also wanted to go to Washington, and pro- and anti-Adams factions in
the Federalist party had to strike a bargain that gave John Quincy the
senior seat and Pickering the junior one. But John Quincy's diary is
silent on these maneuvers—the first of several such omissions.

Another feature of his political career seemed to recall his father. John
Adams had been a man above parties. Republicans and Federalists, he
said of his blighted term, each had a party, "but the commonwealth had
none." In his own mind, John Adams supplied the lack. John Quincy entered politics proclaiming the same doctrine. "A politician in this country," he wrote his brother Thomas, "must be a man of a party." But "I
would fain be the man of my whole country."[14]

The party situation in the country at the start of the new century was
both confused and acrid. The Federalists, who had defined themselves as
the friends of government when Washington and John Adams ran it,
had to decide how to conduct themselves now that they were out of
power. Federalism in the south and middle states, except for a few pockets, withered away, leaving a New England base. The party wanted a
strong military establishment, and the taxes necessary to pay for it, and it
continued to fear the ambitions of France. These were real. Though
Napoleon Bonaparte had declared that the Revolution was complete, he
was extending France's power farther than his radical predecessors. The
most alarming example of his reach, to Americans, was his acquisition of
Louisiana—the inner third of the continent, including New Orleans at
the mouth of the Mississippi River, its economic spigot. The nation's re-

jection of the policies and fears of the Federalists filled them with gloom. America, wrote one, was "infamous and contented." [15]

The leading Federalist in New England became Timothy Pickering, the former secretary of state whom John Adams had fired. Pickering's rise to national power had been a function of the reluctance of better men to hold office: He had been Washington's seventh choice as secretary of state. Nevertheless, there were many in New England who admired him for his upright manner and firm principle. When he was an old man, sharing a stagecoach to Washington with Elbridge Gerry, he loaned Gerry his cloak. "The mantle of Timothy the prophet hath fallen upon me," Gerry joked. "The mantle of charity, rather," Pickering replied, " 'for charity shall cover the multitude of sins.' " [16] This sounds like curmudgeonly quickness. The problem was, Pickering meant it. His enemies were wretches; he was virtuous; anyone who did not agree entirely with him was an enemy. He was a parody Adams; he had their intelligence, self-righteousness, and wrath, without their humor, humanity, or talent.

The Republicans had little to fear from Pickering or the Federalists, whom they outnumbered in Congress by almost three to one when Adams took his seat. Their spokesman in the House of Representatives was the chairman of the Ways and Means Committee, John Randolph. A thirty-year-old cousin of Jefferson's, Randolph had a beardless face, a high unbroken voice, and an eloquent, uncontrollable tongue. He expressed the principles of Republicanism in their purest form: pay down the national debt; break up the army; cut back the navy and defend the country with gunboats; and give the states maximum liberty. Randolph thought Georgetown, in the District of Columbia, could not clear the Potomac because the river was jointly owned by Maryland and Virginia; he doubted whether the federal government should coin its own money (Spanish dollars would serve as well). Adams came to detest him. "Virginian aristocracy, slave-scourging liberty . . . generous feelings, and malignant passions constitute a chaos in his mind, from which nothing orderly can ever flow." Randolph loathed all Adamses; he called the family the American House of Stuart, and said that John Quincy, "the cub," was worse than the old bear. [17]

Ruling the political world with the distant efficacy of a Deist God was the friend of John Quincy's youth, Thomas Jefferson. Jefferson had abolished the pomp of the presidency, which John Adams had made himself so unpopular trying to define; he received visitors at the White House in worn old clothes and let his dinner guests seat themselves without protocol. The wines and the conversation, however, were excellent. Jefferson used such occasions to win politicians with his charm; he let Randolph and other congressional leaders appear to take the lead in lawmaking, though he gave them their marching orders privately; when they went too far for his convenience or his temperament, he paid them no mind. Randolph's discourses on the Potomac, he told one guest, were "mere metaphysical subtleties." John Quincy, periodically invited (as were all members of Congress) to his table, studied him with fascination. One night Jefferson said "he had seen Fahrenheit's thermometer, in *Paris*, at twenty degrees below zero, and that . . . for six weeks together it stood *thereabouts*." John Quincy, unhappily for the credit of his host, had lived in Paris. "Fahrenheit's thermometer," he wrote in his diary, "never since Mr. Jefferson existed was at twenty degrees below zero in Paris. . . . He knows better than all this; but he loves to excite wonder." Jefferson could be untrustworthy about matters more important than the weather; years later, John Quincy wrote, with epigrammatic savagery, he had "a memory so pandering to the will that in deceiving others he seems to have begun by deceiving himself." [18]

In his first inaugural address, Jefferson had generously declared that Americans were now "all federalists" and "all republicans." What he meant by this was that he wanted all men of good will to join his party; meanwhile, he would crush Federalism as an independent force. One important advantage was given to him by the Constitution—the 3/5 rule of Article I, Section 2, whereby every slave was counted as three-fifths of a free person for the purposes of representation, although only free white men could vote, thus swelling the political power of the slaves' masters. At the Constitutional Convention the slave states had wanted slaves counted as whole persons, but the free states had beaten them down to a fraction. Still the slave states, which were mostly Republican, were overrepresented in the Electoral College and the House. Timothy Pickering spoke with characteristic pith of "Negro Presidents and Negro Congresses" [19]—except for John Adams, four of the first five presidents would be southerners—and John Quincy supported a failed Federalist attempt to amend the rule.

The Republican electoral lock grew potentially tighter when Napoleon, abruptly switching course, sold Louisiana to Jefferson in 1803 for $15 million. (Jefferson got his bargain because a slave revolt in Haiti made it impractical for France to supply a colony on the mainland.) Most Federalists thought the acquisition was illegal; the Constitution, they argued, was meant to cover only the territory that Franklin, Jay, and John Adams had negotiated for in Paris in 1783. They clearly saw that states carved from the new frontier would be as Republican as Kentucky and Tennessee. John Quincy alone of his party supported the purchase. Unlike most Federalists, he favored expansion. In a speech commemorating the Pilgrims, he had adapted a line from George Berkeley's eighteenth-century poem, "On the Prospect of Planting Arts and Learning in America": "Westward the course of empire takes its way" (Adams, more poetic, changed *course* to *star*). As the English had come to the New World, so New Englanders and other Americans should cross it. John Quincy did believe, however, that a constitutional amendment was needed to determine the government of the new territory. The Republicans, and the nation, swept away such scruples, and the party that hesitated to clear a river bought 828,000 square miles, including the Mississippi.

Jefferson's re-election in 1804 was so smashing—he even carried Massachusetts—that he needed no help from the 3/5 rule. Flush with triumph, he moved against the one branch of government Federalists dominated, the Supreme Court. Congress impeached Justice Samuel Chase, a bumptious and dogmatic Federalist who gave political lectures from the bench. If they had removed him from office, their next target would have been Chief Justice John Marshall, John Adams's greatest appointee. John Quincy thought only "the dispensation of Providence" could save the judiciary.[20] But John Randolph, the House manager, so bungled the prosecution that even the Republican Senate would not vote to convict, and Chase and Marshall were spared.

These public clashes were engrossing, but behind the scenes were political movements that were potentially more momentous. Pickering wanted to leave the union. In March 1804, John Quincy, visiting a moderate New York Federalist, Rufus King, ran into Pickering on the way out. King told Adams that his fellow senator had been talking up a northern confederacy. Pickering already had the support of Federalist politicians in New England. Another plotter he reached out to was Vice President Aaron Burr, elected as a Republican, but in fact a self-interested freelance. Burr had a web of contacts, from northern Federalists to western frontiersmen, to whom he proposed either invading Mexico or seceding from the union (two men marginally interested in his schemes were the Tennessee warrior-politician Andrew Jackson and a young Kentucky lawyer, Henry Clay). When Burr was finally arrested and indicted for treason, Chief Justice Marshall, who tried the case, made sure he was acquitted, at least in part to spite President Jefferson.

Talk of disunion and disloyalty was not uncommon in the early republic. In the Washington administration, the Whiskey rebels raised their own flag; in the Adams administration, Virginia questioned federal law and readied the armory at Richmond for self-defense; Gouverneur Morris, the peglegged aristocrat who drafted the Constitution in 1787, scornfully called, a quarter of a century later, for a secession of the north, even at the risk of civil war. The country was still newly made; men who believed that it was not well-made were willing to start again. At this point in his career, John Quincy Adams was not one of them. Just as he wanted the country to make its way westward, he wanted it to stay in one piece. *"Union,"* he wrote his father, "is to me what the *balance*" of bicameral legislatures "is to you."[21]

The greatest stresses on the union came from foreign affairs. After a brief peace, France and Britain resumed their war, and each sought to restrict American trade with the enemy. Britain additionally claimed the right to stop American ships on the high seas and search them for deserters from its navy. In 1807, the *Chesapeake*, an American frigate cruising off the Virginia coast, was attacked and disabled by a British warship, on the prowl for deserters. If Congress had been in session when the attack happened, it would surely have declared war. London grudgingly disavowed the act, but passed a regulation forbidding neutrals to trade with France and its allies. Congress might feel warlike, but America, by Republican policy, lacked sufficient means of punishing insults or defending itself. If American merchant ships were bound to be taken as soon as they left port, "is it not better," Jefferson asked, "to keep them at home?"[22] He decided to coerce the hostile superpowers by depriving them of American trade altogether. He would spite their faces by cutting off his nose.

Jefferson's embargo enraged New England, for it destroyed its commerce. New England Federalists were doubly enraged on account of their Anglophilia. In the spring of 1808, John Quincy had a talk with Theophilus Parsons, the man who had taught him law twenty-five years earlier, and who was now chief justice of Massachusetts. "I found him, as I expected, totally devoted to the British policy." Adams's mentor thought the American people had been "corrupted," and that "the only protection of our liberties . . . is the British navy."[23] The British navy could fire on American frigates, but as long as it fought Napoleon, it could do no wrong in Federalist eyes. The two-party system amounted to patriots who couldn't defend themselves, and statists who weren't patriots.

John Quincy had already changed parties. His father had angered Federalists by negotiating for peace; John Quincy angered them by his willingness to risk war. In January 1808 he caucused with Republican congressmen, who nominated James Madison to succeed Thomas Jefferson. Adams, wrote a Massachusetts newspaper, was "one of those amphibious politicians, who lives both on land and water, and occasionally resorts to each, but who finally settles down into the mud." Republicans and Federalists alike speculated what his reward for defecting would be, though Adams disclaimed any desire for one, insisting, when a Virginia Republican buttered him up, that he had been "governed solely by public considerations." In June 1808, the Massachusetts legislature, run by Federalists, voted eight months ahead of time that it would not re-elect him to the Senate. While the balloting was under way at the State House in Boston, Adams ostentatiously read in the library of the Athenaeum. He resigned his seat at the insult, and entrusted his "future prospects" to "the Disposer of Events."[24] The newly elected president Madison disposed of his future early in 1809 by appointing him minister to Russia.

John Quincy could see that Federalism's passion was only the efflorescence of decay, and that the party's power was collapsing along with the morals of its dominant faction. There was nothing wrong in acting on such perceptions. Nor was there anything wrong with Madison rewarding a convert, or even dangling the promise of a reward ahead of time to encourage a change of heart. But, as with the winning of his Senate seat six years ago, John Quincy maintained, even in his diary, that he had made no calculations and given no signals. The offer from Madison, he wrote, was "totally unsolicited."[25] Thomas Jefferson was not the only politician who deceived himself.

The Adamses had had two children during John Quincy's Senate career—John II, and Charles Francis, named for John Quincy's dead brother and for Francis Dana, his superior on his first assignment to St. Petersburg. John Quincy took his wife and Charles Francis, age two, with him to Russia, leaving the older boys with relatives.

Travel in America was somewhat improved since the Revolution—it took only forty-nine hours to go from Quincy to New York on turnpikes—but sailing to Russia took eighty days. When John Quincy went there as a teenager, the empress was the elderly Catherine the Great. Now the emperor was young Alexander I, a romantic whose idealism fancied itself to be liberal. John Quincy would run into him on his daily walks and talk about the weather, which often did produce temperatures of twenty degrees below zero. "I met the Emperor upon the Fontanka [the embankment of a St. Petersburg canal]. He observed I had no gloves on my hands, and asked me if I were not cold without them. . . . In general, the Emperor is extremely quick and particular in observing slight peculiarities in dress." In his diaries, John Quincy observed everything, from the christening of his footman's daughter—the priest "cut off three locks of the child's hair, which, with wax, he rolled up into a little ball, and threw into the water in which the child was baptized"—to the princess Woldemar Galitzin, "venerable by the length and thickness of her beard."[26] There was little intellectual stimulation, except what was provided by Joseph de Maistre, a fellow diplomat who would become the *philosophe* of European reaction; Adams chatted with him about divine retribution and Molière. Adams stimulated himself by reading, by studying the American Census of 1810, and by comparing systems of weights and measures—a hot topic since France had adopted the metric system, but not one that needed to be researched in Russia.

He did not in fact have much to do. The future of America was being determined in Washington and on the battlefield. In 1811 a freshman class entered the House of Representatives, overwhelmingly Republicans, who were younger than Adams, and even more expansionist. John C. Calhoun of South Carolina had just turned twenty-nine; Henry Clay became Speaker at thirty-four. They wanted to take what was still untaken in the eastern half of the continent—Spanish Florida and British Canada. Calhoun thought most of Canada could be conquered in four weeks; former president Jefferson thought it would be "a mere matter of marching."[27] Such airy bellicosity alarmed John Randolph; he called his new young colleagues "War Hawks" because they talked of *Canada* with the repetitive insistence of a birdcall. New England Federalists were sullen (in 1813, they sent a promising young man of their own, Daniel Webster of New Hampshire, to Congress).

America prepared to fight Britain with a pathetic army, a small navy, and no means to build them up ahead of time, since, when the charter of Alexander Hamilton's Bank of the United States came up for renewal in 1811, Congress let it lapse as a relic of Federalist statecraft. By war's end, the federal government would have to rely on loans from Stephen Girard, a one-eyed Philadelphia merchant, to avoid bankruptcy. In time, American soldiers and sailors proved their mettle. But there were many debacles along the way. Failure encouraged Timothy Pickering, who revived his secessionist plots.

When news of one American defeat reached John Quincy in his icy outpost, he prayed "that these disasters instead of sinking may rouse the spirit of the nation."[28] But he missed all of it; he had been in greater danger during the Battle of Bunker Hill than he was during the entire War of 1812. John Adams spent his life ashamed that he had never been a soldier, but he had done his country essential service in Congress, and in Paris and Holland, the focal points of its diplomacy. John Quincy Adams stayed in the wings. His position was politically profitable to him: The country was showing, however clumsily, that it shared his expansionist ideas, but by watching its efforts all the way from Russia, he escaped responsibility for Republican mistakes, as well as the labor of fighting desperate Federalism on its home ground. He suffered, perhaps, over the long run by not seeing the next generation of leaders at their first appearance, though he would soon meet the most flamboyant of them.

In 1813, President Madison gave his protégé the chance to perform significant service, by appointing Adams to a commission to negotiate peace. One Adams had helped end the first war with Britain in 1783; another would now try to help end the second. After a thirty-year apprenticeship, beginning in his teens, John Quincy would finally have the opportunity to perform at the level of his father. John Quincy got the opportunity because he had a skill John never mastered: success at playing the game of partisan politics—a skill limited only by his unwillingness to acknowledge it.

CHAPTER 6

I T TOOK ALMOST a year for peace negotiations to begin. The venue changed from Russia to Sweden to the Netherlands; the number of American peace commissioners rose from three to five; they spent weeks in different European cities trying to find each other, and weeks more, after finally settling in Ghent, waiting for the British commissioners to arrive. Discussions began in August 1814.

Besides Adams, the Americans were Jonathan Russell, a merchant; James Bayard, a Federalist congressman; Albert Gallatin, who had served both Jefferson and Madison as treasury secretary and given up the job to make peace; and Henry Clay. Adams was nominal head of the delegation and drafted all its communications to the British side, though he complained bitterly of his colleagues' editing: Gallatin "is for striking out every expression that may be offensive"; Clay "is displeased with figurative language"; Russell wanted to "amend . . . the construction of every sentence"; Bayard, "even when agreeing to say precisely the same thing, chooses to say it only in his own language." The other commissioners found Adams stiff and unbending; Gallatin called him "a thorn."[1] The former treasury secretary became the peacemaker among the peacemakers.

Of all the Americans, the one least like Adams, by background and temperament, was Henry Clay. In appearance he looked like a tall, thin farmer, with sly gray eyes; when he spoke, he was transformed. His voice could be "soft as a lute, or full as a trumpet"; in conversation, he talked fast, told stories, and swore. His talents and vices were not in the New England mold: He was a fiddler, and a ladies' man. Kissing, he claimed, was like the presidency, "not to be sought, and not to be *declined*"—a remark that must be understood in light of the fact that he would run for president three times and would have run even more times if his party had let him. The vice of Clay that Adams encountered in Ghent was gambling. "I have always paid peculiar homage to the fickle goddess," Clay admitted. When Adams rose at his usual predawn hour, he would hear card parties breaking up in Clay's room. Clay's favorite game was poker, then called brag. "He asked me," Adams wrote in his diary, "if I knew how to play *brag*. I had forgotten how. He said the art of it was to beat your adversary by holding your hand, with a solemn and confident phiz [face], and outbragging him. He appealed to Mr. Bayard if it was not. 'Ay,' said Bayard: 'but you may lose the game by bragging until the adversary sees the weakness of your hand.' And Bayard added to me, 'Mr. Clay is for bragging a million against a cent.' "[2]

Clay's poker experience served the delegation well early on. The first British offers were unyielding. Britain wanted to fortify the Great Lakes and navigate the Mississippi as freely as if it were the English Channel; it demanded a route across Maine, from Nova Scotia to Quebec; and it proposed an independent state for its Indian allies, which covered much of the midwest. Adams characterized these proposals as "arrogant, dictatorial, insulting." Clay thought he recognized a bluff. "Mr. Clay," Adams wrote in his diary, "has an inconceivable idea, that they will finish by receding from the ground they have taken."[3]

Clay was right. British intentions varied with the fortunes of war— the British commander who captured and burned Washington, D.C., in the summer of 1814 was repulsed and killed outside Baltimore in the fall—besides which, the British government had matters more important than America to deal with. Britain and its allies had beaten Napoleon, seemingly for the last time, early in 1814; but tensions had arisen among the victors, and London wanted the American war settled so it could focus on them. John Quincy discovered, as his father had before him, that American affairs were not Britain's top priority.

As the British commissioners in Ghent retreated from fortifying the Great Lakes and defending the Indians, the Americans had to decide what was essential to them. Clay and Adams fell into a passion. Clay would not consider granting a British right to navigate the Mississippi, and he did not care whether New Englanders retained the right "of drying fish upon a desert."[4] For Adams the North Atlantic fisheries were crucial. Three-quarters of the dried fish his state exported came from Canadian waters; New England fishermen ran a flourishing black market by selling goods off their boats. The right to fish, finally, was a matter of family pride. John Adams had contended for it in Paris thirty-two years earlier; his son was determined to keep it now. Satisfying both men and the interests they represented, the British and the Americans finally agreed simply to leave the river and the fisheries out of the treaty altogether.

When the two delegations signed a final text on Christmas Eve, 1814, John Quincy told his British counterpart that he "hoped it would be the last treaty of peace between Great Britain and the United States."[5] It was; it was also the last American negotiation for more than a century that looked so steadily eastward. Britain and other European powers would always figure in America's calculations, but America would fear them, on the rare occasions that it did so, as rivals and meddlers, not conquerors. The War of 1812 ended an era of American involvement in Anglo-French imperial wars; the country would follow the star of its own empire westward.

New England was not grateful to Adams for his labors in its behalf. While the commissioners were considering their final counteroffers in Ghent, delegates convened at Hartford, Connecticut, to consider secession. The convention stopped short of that, but Timothy Pickering expected disunion soon. Before the peace treaty was signed, Britain sent a last expeditionary force from Jamaica to New Orleans; if it took the mouth of the Mississippi, Pickering believed, the west would make a separate peace, and then so would New England: "I shall consider the Union as severed."[6] New Orleans, and the union, was saved by Major General Andrew Jackson, and the most ill-planned and incompetently waged war in American history ended in something like success. James Madison, the second Virginia Republican president, would be able to pass his office on to a third, James Monroe. Federalism collapsed into dying embers, though some of its concerns would return to agitate Adams, and the nation.

Madison rewarded Adams by making him minister to Great Britain. While in London, Adams saw his first gas-light, and heard Beethoven's Battle Symphony ("Bad music, but patriotic," he said). A greater reward was in the offing. As usual, Adams claimed not to notice its approach. In the fall of 1816, a message came to him from President-elect Monroe that he would be offered the position of secretary of state. John Quincy forgot about it until reminded by a letter from his mother. He would not take "any step whatever," he wrote anxiously in his diary, to seek the job.[7] He had already taken the steps, in eight years of politicking and diplomatic work; now the job sought him.

The new president, like Adams himself, was a transitional figure, an aging holdover from the revolutionary era. Only nine years older than Adams, James Monroe had been shot through the lung as a lieutenant at the battle of Trenton. Though he went to the Continental Congress in his mid-twenties, he was always a lightweight. In the early decades of the Republican party, he was known as an extreme partisan and Francophile. Time and experience had ripened him, without giving anyone a very high opinion of him.

The race to succeed him began instantly. The phrase "the permanent campaign" lay far in the future, but the campaign to follow President Monroe in the White House lasted four years, then since he won re-election in 1820, lasted four years more. Every major politician made a bid. The fact that they were all Republicans, without any ostensible ideological differences, only made them struggle all the harder.

Henry Clay, using the Speakership as his platform, tried to run foreign policy from the House. Adams wavered between admiration for his abilities and irritation with his personality. Sometimes it was Clay's emotions that were irksome—Adams called him "warm, vehement, and absurd . . . ardent, dogmatical and overbearing"—sometimes it was Clay's crassness: one Sunday, after the two men had attended a Unitarian church service, Clay brightly remarked that he was "much pleased" with the religion "the clergymen of the Boston are now *getting up*."[8] Adams was not pleased when Clay got up a published attack on his role at Ghent, using their former colleague Jonathan Russell as his mouthpiece. Russell accused Adams of caving in to the British on navigation of the Mississippi and use of the fisheries. Adams wrote a book-length rebuttal.

William Crawford, secretary of the treasury, had been the strong second choice of the Republican party to succeed Madison; he disposed of the ample patronage of his department to bolster his chances the next time. Adams sourly called him "a worm preying upon the vitals of the

Administration within its own body." A stroke caused by an overdose of lobelia damaged his prospects. Crawford's ambitions and his fear that they might be thwarted caused a nasty scene at the White House at the end of Monroe's second term. During a quarrel over the appointment of customs officers, Crawford raised his cane to Monroe and called him a "damned infernal old scoundrel!"[9] The president grabbed the fireplace tongs and threatened to have the treasury secretary thrown out. Crawford left under his own power, but the two never spoke again.

John C. Calhoun, the war hawk, had become secretary of war. Calhoun's home and constituency was rural South Carolina, but he had been educated at Yale and trained as a lawyer in Connecticut. At this stage in his career, he was, as Adams said, "above all sectional and factious prejudices"—an expansionist, a nationalist, a supporter of vigorous federal government. He was also the only man in public life whose intelligence Adams rated as highly as his own. Calhoun's thoughts were terse, tightly woven, and forceful. There is a story, probably apocryphal, that the only poem he ever tried to write began, "Whereas . . ." It is true that his speaking style was dry, staccato, and unadorned, relying on substance to persuade—substance, and a pair of blazing black eyes. Calhoun shared with Adams an interest in history. One day in 1820, after a funeral, they discussed the meager Washington graveyard for public figures who had died in the capital. "[T]he nature and genius of our institutions," they agreed, "confine[s] all our thoughts and cares to present time." Americans behaved, and built, as if they had "neither forefathers nor posterity."[10] Adams suggested an American version of Westminster Abbey or the Pantheon. Both men intended to be in it.

Hovering beyond this system of office and intrigue was the comet of Andrew Jackson, hero of New Orleans. Later his enemies would depict him as a ranting spitfire, and he could rage for effect. "They thought I was mad," he told an associate after the audience for one feigned tantrum had fled. Most of the time he was courteous and self-possessed. One visitor described the "melancholy gravity" of his face, his "slow and quiet" speech, and phrases that showed "his time has not been passed among books."[11] Jackson's medium was action. Like Alexander, he cut knots instead of studying to untie them.

He had been born to Scotch-Irish immigrants on the North Carolina

frontier. Serving briefly in Congress in the mid-1790s, he was a Republican so extreme that he was one of only twelve to oppose a motion
thanking President Washington for his Farewell Address. In Jefferson's
administration, he supported Aaron Burr's plots on the assumption that
they were directed against the Spanish empire. In Madison's administration, he maintained America's new western empire against Britain and
the Indians whose lands Americans coveted. When Monroe became
president, he told Jefferson he thought of sending Jackson as minister to
Russia. "Good God!" the former president exclaimed, "he would breed
you a quarrel before he had been there a month!"[12]

In 1818, Jackson, who had stayed in the army, threw three countries
into confusion by invading Spanish Florida, killing Seminole Indians
who had raided across the border, and hanging two British subjects who
had stirred them up. Clay wanted Congress to punish Jackson, in order
to embarrass the administration, and Calhoun claimed he had exceeded
orders. Adams, alone in the cabinet, defended him. Invading had been
"justified" by the "misconduct" of Spaniards who could not police their
own territory. As for the dead Britons, they had "degrade[d] themselves
beneath the savage character by voluntarily descending to its level."[13]

The emergence of a figure like Jackson was a paradoxical consequence
of suspicion of the military. American politicians had long feared generals. But since neither the need for armies nor the love of glory could be
extinguished, generals would keep appearing on the scene. In George
Washington they had found one calmly obedient to their authority. But
after he retired, the military, isolated from mainstream currents of political thought, produced officers of a different stripe. Jefferson and
Madison found themselves relying on General James Wilkinson, a Revolutionary War veteran who helped Aaron Burr, loved medals, uniforms,
and leopard-skin saddle blankets, and was a secret agent of the king of
Spain. The War of 1812 proved Wilkinson to be as incompetent as he
was untrustworthy, and he ended his life selling Bibles in Mexico. General Jackson was honest and able, but he did tend, as one congressman
put it, to "consider the law, and his own notions of justice, as synony-
mous."[14]

Adams admired him throughout the Monroe administration. In
1822, when Jackson had become governor of the Florida territory, newly

purchased from Spain, he caused another fracas by quarreling with his Spanish predecessor and locking him up. Once again Adams backed him up. It is "impossible," he wrote, "for me to contemplate his character or conduct without veneration."[15]

John Quincy's younger peers were a talented group. Clay would have ornamented the First Continental Congress, and Calhoun was as sharp as any of the framers of the Constitution. Yet there was a sense of dwindling from the founding generation, of which they themselves were conscious. Their status as men no longer of gold, maybe of silver, bred in them (if it was not partly caused by) a certain violence of temper: Clay's emotions were violent, Calhoun's reasoning was violent; Crawford and Jackson were violent, each man having killed a rival in a duel (Jackson nursed a wounded shoulder the rest of his life). A portrait of Jackson by Charles Willson Peale a year after his invasion of Florida shows a domineering air and a superior smirk, as if saying to Congress, "Punish me if you dare." A portrait of Calhoun by Peale's son, Rembrandt, painted fifteen years later, shows the same air and the same smirk. Lesser figures displayed the national temper as markedly as their leaders. The ranting American, who amused and alarmed British visitors, dates from this period.

John Quincy Adams was running for president as hard as any of his colleagues. His job, the great stepstool of promotion to the presidency—Jefferson, Madison, and Monroe had all been secretaries of state—practically required it of him. Adams observed all the maneuvering around him with cat's eyes, and recorded it in his diary. Eighteen twenty-two found him reading a volume of eighteenth-century British political memoirs. "The interior working" of any government, he noted, "must be foul. There is as much mining and countermining for power, as many fluctuations of friendship and enmity, as many attractions and repulsions, bargains and oppositions" narrated in the book he was reading "as might be told of our own times. . . . And shall not I, too, have a tale to tell?" His own activities included throwing balls—the capital, a grim and squalid nowhere that had recently been burned, was badly in need of social life—and proposing to shunt his rivals to foreign missions. At various times he considered sending Calhoun to France, and Clay or Jackson to Latin America (Monroe nixed Jackson for the same reason Jefferson had: "he was afraid of his getting us into a quarrel").[16]

But as before, he had to avoid self-knowledge. When supporters called to consult on his campaign, he denied that there was one. A visitor in 1818, told that Adams would do "absolutely nothing," observed that "others would not be so scrupulous." "[T]hat was not my fault," Adams answered, "my business was to serve the public . . . and not to intrigue for further advancement." Three years later, he analyzed the politics of the northeast with another ally, then announced that he "would take no one step to advance or promote" himself. "If [the presidency] was to be the prize of cabal and intrigue, of purchasing newspapers, bribing by appointments, or bargaining for foreign missions, I had no ticket in that lottery." His ally called this the "Macbeth policy": "If chance will have me king, why chance may crown me, / Without my stir" (*Macbeth*, Act I, scene iii).[17] Adams observed that Macbeth changed this policy and served an unhappy term.

Adams's post allowed him to avoid issues that would vex American politics for years. Being secretary of state was not like being stationed in St. Petersburg, but it could be a form of internal exile from prickly domestic problems. An economic crash in 1819 highlighted the related issues of tariffs and monetary policy, which would ultimately impel Calhoun to abandon nationalism, and to defy the federal government in the name of his home state almost as boldly as Timothy Pickering had done (he asserted a state's right to defy federal laws, in this case a tariff, that it found onerous). Adams took no conspicuous stand on either issue.

More troubling than economic arguments was the crisis caused by Missouri's application for statehood. Missouri was the first state to be created entirely west of the Mississippi. Early in 1819 the House passed a bill to make Missouri a state, provided it guarantee eventual emancipation to its slaves, but the Senate blocked it. The debate that followed was long and acrid because Missouri, and the rest of the Louisiana Territory, seemed like a blank slate (Indians were not considered). As empire moved westward, what kind of empire would it be? The clash was no longer partisan in the old sense, since New England Federalism and its resentment of the 3/5 rule scarcely existed; it was sectional, a matter of mores and morals.

The scruples of an older generation of slaveholders were wearing

away. Slaveowning founders had professed the belief that gradual emancipation would end the practice, as it did in northern states with large
slave populations, such as New York. But as time went on and emancipation never reached the Chesapeake or crossed the Ohio, the gradualist
hope became increasingly desperate. By 1819, Jefferson, Madison, and
Monroe were reduced to arguing that if slavery were allowed to spread
over the entire west, it would weaken by being diluted. In their valedic-
tory correspondence, John Adams and Jefferson exchanged a few wary
references to the Missouri question, Adams writing, in a weird and powerful image, that he imagined "armies of Negroes marching and counter-
marching in the air, in shining armour." Jefferson gave a much more
down-to-earth explanation of the reluctance of older southerners to
question slavery. "Are our slaves to be presented with freedom and a
dagger?" [18]

But even the fantasy of dilution, or the argument from fear, did not
assert that slavery was good. That was left to a new generation. In 1820
John Quincy Adams recorded a conversation he had with Calhoun, after
a cabinet meeting on the Missouri question. Could Congress control the
extension of slavery into new territories? Adams thought the power to
do so was granted by the Preamble to the Constitution, which listed "establish[ing] justice" as one of the ends of government. "What can be
more needful for the establishment of justice than the interdiction of
slavery where it does not exist?" [19]

Calhoun agreed that Adams's principles were "just and noble" but
added that in the south, "they were always understood as applying only
to white men." The division of society into white freemen and black
slave laborers, he went on, had "many excellent consequences. . . . [I]t
was the best guarantee to equality among the whites. It produced an un-
varying level among them," and prevented any "one white man" from
"domineer[ing] over another." [20]

Adams did not comment on the notion of Calhoun, Crawford, Clay,
or Jackson (slaveowners all) as mild-mannered egalitarians. That would
have been a clever riposte, but the issue Calhoun had raised was more
profound. Classical republican theory, ancient and modern, had always
accepted—even required—the existence of a class of slaves. Ancient
Athens and the Roman Republic were slave societies. Slaves spared mas-

ters the deadening effects of hard labor and freed them to consider the public good. The founders had modified republican theory in numerous ways, to accommodate common law, Christianity, contracts, and their own political experience. But here was one of its ancient doctrines, reappearing in the slogans of the modern Republican party. Jefferson had written that all men were created equal. John Adams had disputed that, and he had fallen. Now Calhoun was saying that slavery made all free men equal.

The Missouri debate, Adams wrote, had "betrayed" the secret psychology of slaveowners. "[W]hen probed . . . they show at the bottom of their souls pride and vainglory in their condition of masterdom. They fancy themselves more generous and noble-hearted than the plain freemen who labor for subsistence. They look down upon the simplicity of a Yankee's manners, because he has no habits of overbearing like theirs and cannot treat negroes like dogs."[21] There is Adams pride here—the touchiness of a cosmopolitan whose father had been president, yet who was forced to treat dueling frontiersmen as equals. Yet he saw through Calhoun's pretensions to equality: He and his slaveowning peers were not domineering men who had somehow escaped the ameliorating effects of their institutions; their lust for domination flourished under their institutions.

Adams was shaken because of the respect he had for Calhoun's intellect and broadmindedness. If Calhoun thought this way, who in his world could fail to?

Adams did nothing with his insight except write it down. Clay managed the political crisis, cobbling together, by the summer of 1821, an elaborate compromise whereby Maine, which was about to split off from Massachusetts, would match Missouri in the Senate as a free state; no more slave states north of Missouri's southern border would be admitted (leaving, in the original Louisiana Territory, only Arkansas as a future slave state); and Missouri would allow free Negroes to move there. Rufus King, the old Federalist who was a senator from New York, opposed Clay's handiwork as giving slavery too much leeway. Adams, though he found King's speech "dignified, grave [and] earnest," also thought it too timid: Why, he wondered, are "all the most eloquent orators" on the "slavish side"? Yet Adams gave no speeches himself. He had reasons for

ducking: His job did not require him to speak out; it was politic to keep
silent, with the White House looming before him; what could he have
said on a vast and troubling question, which he had not yet fully grasped?
Still, his silence gave him no standing to criticize those who spoke. In
February 1821, while the compromises were still being worked out, he
issued a *Report on Weights and Measures,* responding to a congressional
request that he survey existing systems and advise whether America
should adopt some new one. Adams produced a history of human meas-
urement and pronounced that the man who devised a universal system
would be a "benefactor . . . of the human race."[22] He let a jockeying
politician and an old Federalist deal with Missouri, while he fussed with
rods and liters.

Adams's attention was claimed by matters more serious than weights
and measures. Like any ambitious secretary, he tended to see the Monroe administration as an appendage of his department. In his case, however, the agenda before him was full, and several of the issues he dealt
with were as important as slavery.

When Henry Adams the brewer was scratching out his farm on
Merry Mount, Spain's empire in the New World, which stretched from
California to Patagonia, was already a century old, ruled from imposing
baroque capitals. By the eighteenth century, however, the long decline
was well under way. The later kings of Spain, when they were not imbe-
ciles, tended to be melancholics devoted to the hunt. Complimented on
his marksmanship, Ferdinand VI sadly remarked, "It would be hard if
there were not something I could do."[23]

Americans cast covetous eyes on their territory. John Adams's scape-
grace son-in-law dabbled in a scheme to liberate Venezuela. General
James Wilkinson, acting as Aaron Burr's proxy, sent Zebulon Pike to ex-
plore Mexican invasion routes. Early in 1818, Don Luis de Onis, Spain's
minister in Washington, complained to Secretary Adams that his win-
dows had been broken and a chicken tied to his bell-rope. He called it "a
gross insult to his sovereign and the Spanish monarchy, importing that
they were of no more consequence than a dead old hen." Adams told him
he "hoped it was nothing more than the tricks of some mischievous
boys."[24] Months later, Andrew Jackson invaded Florida.

Once Spain had swallowed the insult of invasion, it was not unwilling to surrender its lawless subtropical wasteland, for a price, so long as it safeguarded Mexico's silver mines. Adams, for his part, wanted to secure American access to the Pacific Ocean. Russia and Britain had claims to the north Pacific coast; America, whose fur traders were already operating there, did not want to be left behind. The boundary line Adams negotiated with Onis made a zigzag turn above Texas, up to the forty-second parallel (the northern border of present-day Nevada and California). A fault-finding Henry Clay noticed that the treaty granted huge tracts of Florida real estate to Spanish noblemen. Once Adams cleared this up, the final version was ratified on Washington's birthday, 1821.

Spain, Adams, and Clay had even larger problems than Florida or the Pacific to deal with. There had been smoldering revolutions in Latin America for years; two Mexican priest-rebels had been executed in the preceding decade. Clay thought Latin America's struggle for independence was a continuation of ours—"an elder brother," he told Congress, ". . . rising, by the power and energy of his fine native genius, to the manly rank which nature, and nature's God, intended for him"—and he wanted the United States to recognize it. Adams was skeptical. He had no doubt that Latin Americans would become free from Spain, but he had little hope that they could sustain free governments. "Arbitrary power, military and ecclesiastical, was stamped upon their education, upon their habits, and upon all their institutions," he told Clay in a private conversation. "Civil dissension was infused into all their seminal principles. . . . Nor was there any appearance of a disposition in them to take any political lesson from us." In a letter to his father, John Quincy compared Clay to the "ardent spirits" of the 1790s who had equated the French and American revolutions.[25]

As sweeping as his own dismissal was, history proved him closer to the truth than Clay. Mexico degenerated into a despotism under Santa Anna, after fifteen years of intrigue for and against Spain. Argentina fell into civil war between Buenos Aires and the provinces. One great liberator, Simon Bolívar, forced another, José San Martín, out of the political arena. There were too many leaders ready to seize power by force, and too few republicans, on the continent. John Adams, interestingly, had agreed with his son's diagnosis: The South American rebels, he wrote in his retirement, "will succeed against Spain. But the dangerous enemy is within their own breasts."[26]

Adams stated his views publicly in a Fourth of July oration in 1821. Like Clay, he looked back to America's independence; he brandished the original of the Declaration of Independence, which, as secretary of state, he had custody of, and recited a long list of Britain's oppressions. But other countries, he insisted, would have to fight their own struggles. The United States "goes not abroad, in search of monsters to destroy. She is the well-wisher to the freedom and independence of all. She is the champion and vindicator only of her own." If America took up every attractive cause, it would become entangled "in all the wars of interest and intrigue . . . which assume the colors and usurp the standard of freedom." "She might become the dictatress of the world. She would be no longer the ruler of her own spirit."[27]

American noninterference in Latin America's revolutions had a corollary: Europe would have to exercise the same restraint. In 1823, the powers of Europe, calling themselves the Holy Alliance at the prompting of Adams's former friend, Czar Alexander, now a reactionary mystic, invaded Spain to restore order. It was feared they might extend their efforts to Latin America; indeed, Russian fur traders were pushing into Spanish territory from Alaska—the Russian River, in northern California, commemorates their activities. In the summer, British foreign minister George Canning proposed an Anglo-American alliance to stop the Holy Alliance.

Canning's offer was approved by Thomas Jefferson. The old Anglophobe wrote President Monroe that this was "the most momentous" question since "Independence. That made us a nation, this sets our compass . . . to steer through the ocean of time." Would the New World become a "hemisphere . . . of freedom," or a "domicile of despotism"? With Britain and America acting together, Europe's despots would be powerless to intervene. As a bonus, we might pick up Cuba ("the most interesting addition which could ever be made to our system of States").[28]

Adams had known, and disliked, George Canning since his days as minister to Britain. Canning, an actress's son, had risen in the world through his skill as a Tory journalist; Adams thought he had "a little too much wit for a Minister of State." Adams wanted Cuba almost as much as Jefferson did (as he delicately put it in a November cabinet meeting, its "inhabitants . . . may exercise their primitive rights, and solicit a union with us"). But he would not take Cuba, or keep the Holy Alliance out of Latin America, by acting in concert with Canning. At the same cabinet meeting, he said the United States should not "come in as a cock-boat in the wake of the British man-of-war."[29] His position was the most consistent, and thoroughgoing, of anyone in the cabinet: The New World should be kept free of both European threats and British help.

President Monroe decided to include an official statement of foreign policy in his annual message to Congress in December. Another issue then commanding public attention was the Greek War of Independence. The Ottoman Empire, which still ruled the Balkans and the Middle East, was the Moslem Spain—autocratic, yet weak. The Greek patriots were often brigands and pirates, who fought each other as much as they fought the Turks. "When I hang up one of these wretches on the plane tree," said a local warlord, "brother robs brother under the very branches." But Britain and America invested the Greeks with the glow of classical civilization. Lord Byron fought on their behalf, and Clay gave speeches in Congress about "a nation of oppressed and struggling patriots in arms."[30] Monroe proposed to recognize Greek independence and condemn the Holy Alliance's invasion of Spain for good measure, even as he warned the allies away from the Western Hemisphere.

Adams did not like Monroe's comments on Greece and Spain. He thought they would put the United States in the position of practicing what it preached against—interfering in the affairs of remote peoples. In the end, the president stopped short of recognizing the Greeks. "In the wars of European powers in matters relating to themselves," Monroe said, "we have never taken any part."[31]

The final form of Monroe's message, known today as the Monroe Doctrine—no American meddling in European affairs; no European meddling in the Americas; and no Anglo-American pact to keep the Europeans out—was Adams's document. There were elements of shadow-boxing in it: apart from Russia's foray into California, it was unlikely that the Holy Alliance could do anything about the Western Hemisphere. Any effort to repel whatever it did would depend on the British fleet, which Britain would deploy whether it had a pact with the

United States or not, since it was in its interest to trade with free Latin American countries. Canning took all the credit for Latin American independence, boasting that he had "called the New World into existence to redress the balance of the old."[32]

The advice of major American politicians was shaped, as Ernest May has argued, by their presidential prospects. Clay pushed an activist policy because its idealism was attractive, and because it wrong-footed his rivals in the Monroe administration. Calhoun, who agreed with Jefferson on a British alliance, and who claimed to fear that ten thousand European soldiers could subdue all of Latin America ("perfectly moonstruck," snorted Adams),[33] had an interest in dire scenarios, since military spending would increase War Department patronage. Adams had to demonstrate independence from Britain, to shake any regional taint of Federalism.

Yet these positions also reflected the political personalities of these men. Clay was an ardent spirit, in the best and worst senses of the word. Calhoun had always had a bellicose streak; that was one reason he became secretary of war. The Adams family could show fifty years of opposition to Britain. Their backstage maneuvers were less important than the outside story of their careers.

Ultimately Adams was following the foreign policy of the first president who employed him as a diplomat. "It is a maxim founded on the universal experience of mankind," George Washington had written when John Quincy was only eleven years old, "that no nation is to be trusted farther than it is bound by its interest."[34] The ideological affinities, real or imagined, of foreign powers or peoples counted for less than sober calculation. The Monroe Doctrine was a commentary on Washington's Farewell Address.

The long race to see who would become the sixth president staggered to its finish. Everyone minded everyone else's business. One senator told Adams that after returning from a trip to Philadelphia, he had been accosted by Senator Martin Van Buren, a smooth little man who was the son of a New York–Dutch tavern keeper, unless (as rumor had it) he was the illegitimate son of Aaron Burr. Van Buren, who had not been told of his fellow senator's trip, seemed to know all about it nonetheless, and gave his colleague a summary of all the political conversations he had had.

Adams felt goaded by the past. The vote would be a judgment on a public career that had begun when he was fourteen; that had begun, really, before he was born. In the run-up to the election, his father wrote Louisa that John Quincy was like "an Indian warriour, suffering under the most cruel torments of his enemies," and chanting: "I go to the place where my father has gone. His soul shall rejoice in the fame of his son."[35] It was striking to compare political life to torture and the presidency to death, but however grim they were, they had been marked as the goals of John Quincy's life.

Calhoun decided to content himself with the vice presidency, which left the field to Adams, Clay, the faded Crawford, and Jackson. In the event, Clay got 37 electoral votes, Crawford 41, Adams 84, and Jackson 99. Since no candidate had a majority, the House would pick the winner from the top three.

In the interval before the House's choice, Adams's diary becomes reticent. It is not hard to figure out what happened. Henry Clay, the disappointed candidate, was Speaker of the House. The victor would have to make an arrangement with him. Despite Clay's clashes with Adams, Jackson was a rival in Clay's own region. It was natural for Adams to seek Clay's support, and natural for Clay to give it. When Clay agreed to serve as Adams's secretary of state, he perhaps gave the bargain excessive emphasis; yet the fact that Clay was a talented diplomat may also have been a factor in Adams's offer and Clay's acceptance. Only Adams, who had been obliged to behave like a normal politician, and Jackson, who had lost, could consider the transaction shameful.

Adams made other arrangements, signaling former Federalists in Maryland and New York that he would not avenge twenty-year-old feuds upon them. When the House voted, the New York delegation, balanced between Adams and Crawford, hung on the choice of Stephen Van Rensselaer, a rich old landowner and a brother-in-law of Alexander Hamilton. Martin Van Buren claimed, in his memoirs, that Van Rensselaer prayed for divine guidance; when he opened his eyes, he saw an Adams ballot on the floor and cast it, giving Adams the state, and a majority of the state delegations. But Adams had been corresponding with his father's enemy's relative, to bring him around.

General Jackson attended Adams's inauguration and shook the new president's hand. Jackson's behavior in the preceding weeks, Adams noted, had been "placid and courteous." [36] They never met again.

John Adams was eighty-nine years old when his son was elected president. In July 1826 John Quincy learned that his father was failing. He hurried home, but the old president had died even before the new one set off. The loss became real to John Quincy when he sat, during a Sunday service, in his father's pew. "The memory of my father and mother, of their tender and affectionate care, of the times of peril in which we [had] lived . . . came over me, till involuntary tears started from my eyes." [37] The death of any parent moves us one step closer to mortality and puts us in his or her place. John Quincy had literally taken his father's office, even as he occupied his seat.

His term was, if possible, even worse than his father's—a long nightmare, oppressed by a succession of alternately terrible and trivial events, which he seemed powerless to control or avoid.

His domestic program was one of ambitious internal improvements. "Liberty," he told Congress in his First Annual Message, "is power," and men enjoyed it "upon condition that it shall be exercised to ends of beneficence, to improve the condition of [their] fellow-men." He proposed a program based on an "enlarged" view of internal improvements: not only roads and canals, but a national university (an old recommendation of George Washington's), astronomical observatories, and geographical and scientific expeditions, like Lewis and Clark's. "Of the cost of these undertakings . . . it would be unworthy of a great and generous nation to take a second thought." [38]

This was the direction in which the Republican party, which had long since stopped fretting about clearing the Potomac, had been tending since the War of 1812, but Adams's defeated rivals, who could not now control the movement themselves, attacked his message as a betrayal of party principle. Adams's interest in astronomy gave them a convenient target. For years he had loved stargazing, which his early rising facilitated; he called the constellations his "celestial acquaintance." In his First Message, he praised national observatories, which he called "lighthouses of the skies." The image was just quaint enough to seem ludicrous, and his enemies delighted in it. A pained Clay called Adams's program "entirely hopeless." [39]

He was equally disappointed in foreign affairs. Simón Bolívar issued invitations to a Pan-American conference in Panama in 1826. Bolívar's career justified Adams's fears for Latin America's future, rather than Clay's hopes (he believed, he confided to an associate, in "democracy on my lips, and aristocracy *here*" [40]—indicating his heart). But he and his fellow revolutionaries were by then undisputed masters of the continent, and Adams and Clay wanted the United States to attend their gathering. Congress balked, and John Randolph, his power long lost to opium, alcohol, and irresponsibility, but his tongue still bright and gleaming, attacked Clay with sparkling malice. "Like a rotten mackerel by moonlight," Randolph said, Clay "shined and stunk." [41] The secretary of state challenged him to a duel. Both men missed twice and shook hands. While Adams's friends and enemies posed and ranted, his foreign policy piddled away.

Day to day Adams, like most nineteenth-century presidents, had little to do. Unlike his father, he stayed in the capital, where his time was mostly wasted. Old women asked him for charity, madmen discussed the Book of Revelation with him, a cashiered army doctor threatened to kill him, and stalked him into the White House. Even his relaxation was vexed. While canoeing on the Potomac, his boat sank, and he had to swim for his life. "I . . . had ample leisure to reflect upon my own indiscretion," he wrote in his diary. [42]

He could not take the most elementary steps to defend himself. Jackson was out for revenge, Vice President Calhoun was out for himself; only Clay was loyal. Three and a half years into his term, Adams agonized in his diary over the treachery of his own postmaster-general, John McLean, who was a tool of Calhoun. McLean "plays his game with so much cunning and duplicity that I can fix upon no positive act that would justify the removal of him." [43] But why did he need a "positive act"? The Post Office was an acknowledged political machine, an agency for doling out patronage in the form of postmasterships. Loyalty was the only qualification of a postmaster-general. Any other politician would have fired McLean in a minute; perhaps Adams was inhibited by guilt over the politicking that had brought him so far. It was the tragicomedy of his father's cabinet, sapped by Pickering and Wolcott, repeated as farce.

The election of 1828 was one of the dirtiest in American history, all the more so because there were as yet no substantive differences between Adams and Jackson, the main candidates (Calhoun ran once again for vice president). Jackson's supporters accused Adams of having pimped an American woman to Czar Alexander when he was minister to Russia. Adams's supporters accused Jackson and his wife, Rachel, of being adulterers and bigamists (unbeknownst to them, her divorce to a first husband had not gone through when she and Jackson married); when Mrs. Jackson died after the election, Jackson blamed the rumors for killing her. Adams let the filth flow beneath his notice.

Adams got the virtually solid support of New England, losing only one electoral vote in Maine (in the four presidential elections in which Adamses ran, it was the only New England electoral vote they did not get). Jackson swamped him in every other part of the country, for a final tally of 178 electoral votes to 83. Adams called the end of his term the "close . . . of my public life." Ten days before he left office, Red Jacket, an old Seneca Indian chief who had sided with the British in the Revolution, called on Adams and told him they "were of the past age, and should soon be called for by the Great Spirit."[44] Adams agreed. Like his father before him, he did not attend his successor's inauguration.

*J*OHN ADAMS HAD been the first loser in American presidential politics; John Quincy Adams was now the second. Of the first six presidents, four had been re-elected, three by immense margins. The only presidents to be rebuffed after one term were both named Adams.

John Quincy's postpresidential career would last more than nineteen years, almost as long as his father's. Unlike his father, John Quincy could not redeem any of that time by corresponding with a once-loved and worthy rival, because he did not believe any of his rivals were worthy, nor had he ever loved them. They were scoundrels, every one. He collected Washington gossip about their pratfalls with a miser's avidity, and his diary glitters with malicious pen portraits and Homeric catalogues of enemies. In one entry he reckoned up thirteen public figures who "from the day that I quitted the walls of Harvard . . . used up their faculties in base and dirty tricks to thwart my progress in life and destroy my character." Among the tricksters he listed Henry Clay, who had served him loyally as secretary of state. In another entry, Adams noted the resemblance of Martin Van Buren, the only member of the Jackson administration to be courteous to him, to James Madison—except that Madison lacked Van Buren's "obsequiousness," "sycophancy," and "duplicity. In the last of these" defects, Adams went on, Van Buren "much more resembles Jefferson, though with very little of his genius. The most disgusting part of his character, his fawning servility, belonged neither to Jefferson nor to Madison."[1]

He cast a baleful eye on the career of his successor, Andrew Jackson. Once again an Adams had been put in the shade by a military hero, whose career an Adams had encouraged. But Jackson had not sailed to the presidency on the unanimous wishes of his countrymen, he had reached it after two sharp-elbowed fights with John Quincy. In time,

Jackson expressed willingness to forgive him for slandering his wife; Adams never forgave him for winning. When Harvard announced that it would award President Jackson an honorary degree, Adams announced that he would skip the ceremony: As "an affectionate child of our Alma Mater," he could not "witness her disgrace in conferring her highest literary honors upon a barbarian who could . . . hardly spell his own name."[2] He was the only good son of Harvard, almost the only good son of America; he had become a connoisseur of his political brothers' warts and sins.

Not all of his bitterness was self-generated. Within six years of leaving the White House, his two oldest sons, George Washington and John II, and his last surviving brother, Thomas, all died. All three were drunkards; George Washington, who fell or jumped at night from a boat in Long Island Sound, left a servant-girl mistress and an illegitimate child. The spectacle of blood brothers falling by the wayside was repeated in a second generation of Adamses. John Adams had written about families inheriting respect and political power; John Quincy's youngest son, Charles Francis, now observed that "vices are hereditary in families."[3] So too, it seemed, was suffering.

One project urged on Adams by his youngest son and his wife was to write a biography of his father. Adams had unique qualifications for the job. He had known his father for over fifty years, lived with him at home and abroad, and served in his administration. All the family papers sat in the house in Quincy; John Quincy Adams was an industrious researcher and an able writer. He had known many of his father's great peers, and he shared many of his enemies, from diehard Federalists to supple Republicans.

He made several starts, but (like his father's memoir) the project languished. The reason, surely, was that John Quincy Adams had already done enough for the old man. He had reproduced his father's career. John Adams had been an important diplomat; so had he. John Adams had helped found the country; he had witnessed the founding, having heard the gunfire on Bunker Hill, and having known Washington, Lafayette, and Jefferson personally. Most important, John Adams had been president, and so had he. He had risen to the head of his country, as his father had challenged him to do. Like the Indian warrior, he had gone to the place his father had gone. Now he was free to make the end of his life his own.

He chose to devote it to the talent that he, unlike his father, possessed, however ambivalent possessing it made him feel: the talent for electoral politics. From 1831 until his death, he represented his Massachusetts district in the House of Representatives.

His willingness to hold lower office was a measure of his ardor for politics. In the last wrathful days of his administration, John Adams bitterly said he might serve in Congress if he was turned out of the White House, though he never did. Only two other presidents (John Tyler and Andrew Johnson) would be willing to re-enter the arena at a lower level; John Quincy Adams set a precedent that has hardly ever been followed.

Another measure of his zest for public life was his willingness to cultivate the Anti-Masonic movement. Federalist clergymen in New England had denounced Masonry in the 1790s as an agent of French atheism. They had a difficult case to make, since Jefferson, their enemy, was not a Mason, while Washington, their idol, was. In 1826, Anti-Masonic anxieties were rekindled by a crime in western New York, then the California of America—a hotbed of strong passions and strange beliefs. William Morgan, a renegade who planned to reveal Masonry's secrets, was kidnapped by his former fellows and vanished. Local officials who casually, and vainly, investigated the matter turned out to be Masons themselves. After a decomposed body washed up on the shore of Lake Ontario in 1828, three separate inquests gave different verdicts as to whether it was Morgan's. Thurlow Weed, an upstate newspaper editor and politico—he boasted, at the end of his life, that he had handed out eighty thousand cigars—supposedly said the corpse would make a "good enough Morgan" until election day,[4] and ran with the story.

Anti-Masonry spoke to democratic sentiment; Masonic titles and secrecy affronted republican mores. It also offered to fill the political void that had opened in the 1820s. Once Federalism died as a national force, all leading politicians were Republicans, and their struggles were matters of personality and regional differences. But after Jackson became president, he and his supporters discovered they had an ideology: They were Democratic-Republicans, or Democrats for short. The people were Jackson's "blood relations," Van Buren declaimed "—the only blood relations he had."[5] The Adams-Clay wing of the once-omnipotent party called itself National Republicans, claiming to represent the national interest across class lines, but if such a lofty ideal could not attract popular support, then Anti-Masonry offered madder music. Conveniently, Jackson was an active Mason. Calhoun intrigued for Anti-Masonic support; so did Clay, though he too was a Mason and would not attack the order to win votes.

Adams intrigued as hard as any of them. He wrote of Masonry's "execrable mysteries" and offered to reveal the secrets of Phi Beta Kappa, the scholastic society to which he belonged. He had a three-hour meeting with William Seward, an associate of Weed's, in which he indicated that he would accept an Anti-Masonic presidential nomination in 1832. Seward reported to Weed that saddling the new party with a loser would be "disastrous."[6] The Anti-Masons settled on former attorney general William Wirt, Clay ran as a National Republican, and both candidates were buried by Andrew Jackson. In 1833, Adams ran for governor of Massachusetts as an Anti-Mason, finishing second in a field of three.

The Anti-Masonic party did not seem as crazy in the early 1830s as it now does. But for a man who had dealt with war and peace, and rising and falling empires, it was a slender and desperate basis for a second political career. Still Adams tried it.

It can be tempting to read the biographies of the Adams family as a condensed history of the United States. Yet some great controversies passed them by. John Quincy's congressional career coincided with battles over tariffs, nullification, and the second Bank of the United States; Andrew Jackson's imperiousness and his popularity so enraged his rivals during his second term that they named themselves Whigs, to suggest that opposing him was akin to opposing the House of Stuart and George III. Adams took positions on all these disputes. But the main actors in them were Jackson, Clay, Calhoun, and Daniel Webster, who had moved to Massachusetts, which he represented in the Senate as a Whig (he too made Adams's enemies list).

There were two issues that Adams made especially his own. One, small but important, concerned a bequest by James Smithson, an English chemist and the illegitimate son of a duke, of half a million dollars to the United States government for "the increase and diffusion of knowledge."[7] Here, it seemed, was a way to make real some of the hopes of Adams's first message to Congress. For years, he fought almost single-handed to prevent Smithson's bequest from being frittered away on patronage and pork, insisting that the money be devoted to one enterprise, not many, and that only the interest be spent, not the principal. In 1846, thanks to his efforts, the Smithsonian Institution was chartered.

The motor of Adams's congressional career, which made him famous, feared, and (in some parts of the country at least) loved, was his contest with the political power of the slave states.

Adams came face to face with slavery only occasionally. In 1840, Joseph Cartwright, a "dark-colored mulatto man," and a Methodist preacher, came to Adams's office trying to raise money to buy the freedom of his grandchildren. In twenty years he had managed to buy the freedom of himself and his sons; liberating a daughter-in-law had cost him another $575. Now he was looking for $450 to buy the freedom of her three children (two girls and a boy, all below the age of four). To establish his bona fides, he showed Adams "certificates of two white Methodist ministers . . . to the respectability of this man—a preacher of the gospel! What a horrible exemplification of slavery!"[8] But such encounters were rare. Adams concerned himself not with slaves, but with the power of their masters.

The Missouri Compromise seemed to confine slavery's new outposts to Missouri and Arkansas. But it marched on, in different directions and forms, supported by the representatives of the states where it already flourished, and by their allies in the north. The struggle against the political power of slavery joined all Adams's enemies in one attackable mass. There were slaveowners, like Calhoun, his nationalist days now over, challenging the federal government in the name of states' rights and the south. There were slave-owning nationalists, like Jackson and Clay, who opposed the slave states only incidentally, in the course of other disputes. There were northern leaders, like Van Buren and Webster, who hesitated to offend the southern wings of their parties: the political success of the Democrats, going back to their Republican incarnation, had depended on a union of New York and Pennsylvania with the south, while the Whigs made ad hoc alliances with Calhoun, and with old southern Republicans of unblemished states' rights principles, such as John Tyler of Virginia. In fighting the power of the slave states Adams could fight them all.

His newfound role borrowed from the political creed of one enemy, Timothy Pickering (who had died in 1829). It was Pickering who had taught New England Federalists to rail against "Negro presidents and Negro congresses," by which he meant presidents and congresses elected, thanks to the 3/5 rule, with the disproportionately weighted votes of the owners of Negroes. In this sense, Adams now set himself to combat Negro politics, with echoes of Pickering's arguments and his caustic, dogmatic style.

Failed ambition—failed, after first being satisfied—liberated him for the fight. In 1820, when he silently committed his shock at Calhoun's opinions to his diary, he was still in pursuit of the White House. The White House had come and gone; so, soon enough, had his flirtation with Anti-Masonry. He would never again consider an office outside his own state, nor run for one outside the safe seat of his district. His only responsibility was to do the right thing, and to smite his enemies.

The blow for which (thanks to Hollywood) he is now best known—his struggle on behalf of the Africans aboard the *Amistad*—was in fact not, on his part at least, notably effectual. The *Amistad* was sailing between Cuban ports in 1839 when its cargo of slaves rebelled, killing most of the crew and ordering the survivors to take them to Africa. The sailors, tricking the Africans, took them instead to Long Island, and Spain demanded custody of them as murderers and escaped slaves.

Martin Van Buren, who had succeeded his idol and patron, Andrew Jackson, in the White House in 1836, owed his election to the union of northern and southern Democrats, and any hope of re-election depended on maintaining it. His administration now took Spain's side in the *Amistad* case, which went to the Supreme Court. Lewis Tappan, a rich New York silk merchant who subsidized religious revivals and assorted good works, urged Adams to help defend the Africans.

When Adams appeared before the justices in February 1841, he was "distressed and agitated." The last time he had appeared before the Supreme Court had been over thirty years earlier, in the interval between resigning from the Senate and being sent to Russia. He spoke for four and a half hours, relying on "aid from above." That night, one of the justices died in his sleep. When the Court reconvened, Adams spoke for another four hours. Associate Justice Joseph Story wrote that Adams's presentation had been extraordinary for "power," "sarcasm," and "dealing with topics far beyond the record and points of discussion."[9]

The majority opinion, delivered by Story, followed not Adams's oration, but the more pertinent arguments laid out by his co-counsel: that the federal government had no standing in the case, because slavery was a state matter, and that the blacks were not in fact slaves at all, their youth and their ignorance of Spanish proving that they had recently been taken from Africa, in defiance of international agreements banning the slave trade (the United States had prohibited the slave trade in 1808). The Africans were sent to Sierra Leone, a British colony for free Negroes on the West African coast.

Adams's argument was noteworthy in one respect: his invocation of the Declaration of Independence. "The moment you come" to the idea "that every man has a right to life and liberty, as an inalienable right, this case is decided. I ask nothing more on behalf of these unfortunate men, than this Declaration."[10] He would refer to it again.

The *Amistad* case was symbolism. The question of Texas statehood was a matter of major importance, affecting not only the borders, but (it seemed to Adams) the spirit of the nation. Adams opposed it vigorously.

Americans had been launching illegal private invasions of Texas since the 1790s. In 1821, a party of southerners settled there with the permission of the Mexican government (Stephen Austin, the leader of the project, was born in Virginia; Sam Houston, another settler, had been governor of Tennessee). By the mid-1830s, the population of Texas had quintupled, largely from American immigration. Chafing under the vagaries of Mexican politics, the American-Mexicans revolted in 1836 and applied for statehood.

Adams objected on several grounds. Annexing Texas would involve the United States in war with Mexico; the only gainers would be "land-jobbers" and their "insatiate rapacity." The most important factor was slavery: The Texans were presented as "struggling for their liberty," while in fact, they were slaveowners, fighting to expand their institution (Mexico had abolished slavery in 1829).[11]

These were new arguments for Adams, who had supported war and expansion—the Louisiana Purchase, the War of 1812, Jackson's invasion of Florida—throughout his career. He had done so, moreover, regardless of the fact that New Orleans was a slave city, or that Florida was coveted by slaveowners. But now he had defined slaveowners as his enemies; therefore he was the enemy of any expansion they favored.

Northern reluctance to annex Texas kept it out of the union for nine years. When annexation finally came in 1845, Adams saw it as an unmitigated disaster, the "first step" toward the conquest of Mexico and the West Indies, by a "maritime, colonizing, slave-tainted monarchy." Some of this was rant, but not all of it, for the United States soon went to war with Mexico. Adams opposed the war too, a minority view, though not unique. Ulysses Grant, who fought in it as a lieutenant, called it "the most unjust war ever waged by a stronger against a weaker nation." [12]

A related, long struggle, at its core against slavery, which Adams did win, was against gag rules restraining antislavery petitions to Congress. The right of citizens or subjects to solicit the attention of their rulers is a minimal political right, sometimes granted by societies that grant few others. The Declaration of Independence mentions it in passing ("In every stage of these oppressions we have petitioned for redress in the most humble terms: our repeated petitions have been answered only by repeated injuries"); the First Amendment guarantees "the right of the people peaceably to assemble, and to petition the Government for a redress of grievances." When Adams entered the House, an hour a day for the first thirty days of a session, and then an hour every other Monday, was set aside for members to present petitions that had been submitted to them. Petitions might come to a particular member from anywhere in the country; they might even come from nonvoters—such as women. The roll of members was called geographically, starting with Maine in the north, and moving south; as a rule, petitions were not read, but referred to the relevant committee. Adams found it a "tedious operation," but "to a reflecting mind a very striking exemplification . . . of the sublime principles upon which our government is founded." [13]

Some of the first petitions Adams submitted at the start of his congressional career in 1831 asked Congress to abolish slavery and the slave trade in the District of Columbia. Petitions on slavery had been coming to Congress since its first session, when Pennsylvania Quakers, joined by

Benjamin Franklin, petitioned to discourage the importation of slaves. Their appeal was referred to a committee, which reported that the Constitution gave Congress no power to prohibit importation until 1808. In the case of Adams's petitions, four decades later, Congress could arguably act: Article I, Section 8 gave it "exclusive" legislative power over the District "in all cases whatsoever." But, given the makeup of the House, Adams expected the committee on the District of Columbia to propose no action on slavery; indeed, he claimed not to support any.

Four years later, a South Carolina congressman, possibly inspired by Calhoun (then a senator), asked the House to "put a more decided seal of reprobation" on antislavery petitions by refusing even to receive them. In 1836, the House voted to table all petitions relating to slavery, without printing them or referring them to committees. In the ensuing discussion, Adams was cut off by a procedural motion and asked the Speaker "if he was gagged or not."[14] The Speaker ruled that he was, and an eight-year debate began.

The gag rule came in the 1830s rather than the 1790s because of an exponential increase in the volume of antislavery petitions. A small but active minority of abolitionists, from rich idealists like Lewis Tappan to upstate New Yorkers who brooded on a potpourri of radical subjects including anti-Masonry, Mormonism, and women's suffrage, had been deluging Congress with their pleas. There was a simultaneous hardening of southern attitudes: The cause of southern emancipation died in 1832 when Virginia narrowly voted not to pursue it; Nat Turner's rebellion the year before, in which sixty whites were murdered, roused ever-latent fears; South Carolina politicians, feuding with Jackson and Van Buren, needed a polarizing issue. Finally, southern pride was offended: The constant flow of petitions, said Calhoun, would make slaveowners "degraded on our own estimation."[15]

Their pride had not reckoned with Adams's pride. Southerners might own men; he owned the American Revolution, it was his family legacy. Adams was not going to be instructed in national principles by protégés of John Calhoun, who was himself Adams's junior.

Every year, at the start of a new session, the House had to renew the gag rule, or let it lapse; every year Adams tried to block it, or evade it once instituted. The struggle harnessed both his virtues and his vices. He employed intelligence, fervor, sophistry, and denial. He needed the strength to ignore his colleagues' hatred, and the ability to make himself hateful. He showed enormous tenacity. Sometimes he flouted the rules of the House, shouting out, when a simple yea or nay was called for, such minispeeches as "I hold the resolution to be a direct violation of the Constitution of the United States, the rules of this House, and the rights of my constituents." Most times he followed procedure with a parliamentarian's skill. "Boon [a hapless opponent] asked if my motion was debatable. I said I hoped it was, and that the House would allow me to debate it. Boon moved to lay my motion on the table." He was as resourceful as he was tenacious. In 1837, he asked the Speaker to rule on the genuineness of a petition that had supposedly been submitted by slaves. The minutes noted "Loud cries of 'he ought to be expelled.' Cries of 'no!' 'no!' " Southern members debated what rebuke would be fit for a colleague who would bring such a thing before them. Then Adams revealed that the slaves had written that they were better off under slavery, and were petitioning that Adams be expelled from the House if he persisted. (Now Adams was accused—quite rightly—of "trifl[ing]" with the House.)[16] Always his goal was to show the slaveowners and their allies in stances more unattractive than his, which was not difficult.

All the while, he claimed to be debating procedure rather than substance: the right of petitioners to be heard, not the good or ill of slavery. In 1832 he had told a Quaker abolitionist that, though he "abhorred" slavery, he did not want it discussed in the House lest discussion cause "ill will" and "heart-burnings."[17] But from 1836 on, he did not care how much ill-will and heart-burning his war on the gag rule caused.

His sudden new prominence, after years of merely customary prominence; the explosiveness of the underlying issue; and the delicacy of his strategy all forced restraint on him. He had need of "perpetual control over passion," he reminded himself in his diary; more, he wrote on another day, "than belongs to my nature." Some of the passions he had to control were bad. Hatred of wrong is hatred still, and twists and corrodes. His private reflections on his contemporaries—he would never had said peers—became if possible even more acrid. When the Bunker Hill Monument was dedicated in 1843, he had spent the day where he spent the day of the battle sixty-eight years earlier, in Quincy. He would not take

part in a ceremony conducted by Massachusetts politicians less pure than
he, and by President John Tyler, a slaveowner. "What have these to do
with a dinner in Faneuil Hall, but to swill like swine, and grunt about the
rights of man?" He saw himself as struggling to banish slavery and war
"from the face of the earth"—heady words from a man who had rebuked
Henry Clay's comparatively modest hopes for Latin America—though
he seemed strangely insensible to possible wars closer to home. In
Springfield, Massachusetts, he toured the armory. "[W]e saw the various
processes of making the gun-barrels and the black walnut gun-stocks. I
had seen these processes in 1828, but they are constantly making improvements."[18] There was no imaginative apprehension of what all these
guns going off might be like.

Yet the passions of slaveowning congressmen, their allies, and their
followers were worse. The ranting violence of their rhetoric was matched
by the actual violence of their behavior. Southern congressmen threatened abolitionists with lynching, and Adams with lynching if he went to
the wrong parts of the country. Nor were the "right" parts of the country
safe: A mob broke into Lewis Tappan's house in New York and burned
his furniture; an abolitionist editor was lynched in Illinois.

Violence could be presented by slaveowners as pre-emptive self-
defense: defense of their lives, against the possibility of insurrection; defense certainly of their way of life. But what had their way of life become
in their own minds, and words? The changing attitude toward slaves,
foreshadowed by Calhoun in 1820, had borne fruit. Slavery was no
longer talked of as a regrettable wrong, or even a necessary one, but as a
good; slaves were talked of as an inferior subspecies of men. A coinci-
dental metaphor made the change plain. In the last public letter of his
life, Thomas Jefferson, who had balked and despaired on the politics of
slavery, still offered as a general proposition the belief that "the mass of
mankind has not been born with saddles on their backs, nor a favored
few booted and spurred, ready to ride them." Eleven years and a moral
revolution later, one of Adams's colleagues, responding to the supposed
petition from slaves, declared that Adams might just as well have offered
a petition "from a cow or horse—for he might as well be the organ of one
species of property as another."[19] Slaveowners now shamelessly claimed
their boots, spurs, and saddles.

Adams, who was nothing if not acute, well understood the psychological forces at work. "In the South, [there] is a perpetual agony of conscious guilt and terror attempting to disguise itself under sophistical argumentation and braggart menaces. In the North, the people favor the whites and fear the blacks of the South." The "zeal" of the abolitionists "kindle[s] the opposition against themselves into a flame."[20] But he would not spare his enemies' guilt, terror, or fear, or abate his own zeal.

In 1842, the sixth year of the controversy, Adams seemed to go too far. He presented a petition from Haverhill, Massachusetts, in the Merrimack Valley near the New Hampshire border, complaining that one section of the union was being "drained to sustain the views and course of another,"[21] and asking that the union be peaceably dissolved. The petitioners did not mention slavery, and Adams said he disagreed with their arguments, but the oppressive section they had in mind was clearly the south, and Adams's true opinion of their argument was at least open to question. Did he not protest too much?

Thomas Marshall, a Whig of Kentucky, moved to censure Adams for preaching disunion. Marshall acknowledged that he and Adams were linked: His uncle, John Marshall, had been appointed Chief Justice by John Adams. But now the link was severed: By introducing the Haverhill petition, Adams was inviting the members of the House to commit treason. Marshall ended by regretting that Massachusetts, "through a man bearing the name which the gentleman did," should be the source of such a proposal.

Adams replied by asking the clerk of the House to read the Declaration of Independence—not to recall, as he had in the *Amistad* case, the rights to life and liberty, but the right "of the people to alter or to abolish" oppressive government. The Haverhill petitioners were claiming nothing more than what the thirteen colonies had claimed.

Adams also answered Marshall's lament for Massachusetts. Adams recalled Virginia's presidents—Washington, Jefferson, Madison, and Monroe. He had known all four, and served three. "[T]hey all abhorred slavery, and he could prove it, if it was denied now, from [their own] testimony." Now, because he would not submerge every consideration to the self-esteem of slaveowners, he was attacked by Virginia congressmen, and by a great Virginian's nephew. "He should have hoped better things of Virginians." [22]

These proceedings were entangled in Adams family politics, even as they went beyond it. In 1825, John Adams had written Jefferson about the "golden days" when Virginia and Massachusetts had acted "like a band of brothers." [23] Now the brothers were falling out, and John Quincy Adams was claiming to be the good one. He knew about good and bad brothers from his siblings and his children, but this fraternal conflict was symbolic and national. In repeatedly citing the Declaration, he was correcting his father's problems with that document. But he was also putting it to his own uses. John Adams and the other founders had been creating a country. John Quincy Adams was now at least willing to entertain the notion that an unjust country should be broken up. In his seventy-fifth year, the son was going to a place his father had not gone.

Adams's self-defense provoked a flood of petitions—the very thing the gag rule was supposed to stop. Adams had become a popular figure, at least in the north. The boy who had been ashamed to ask his parents about *Paradise Lost* was given an epithet—"Old man eloquent"—from one of Milton's sonnets. Milton's "Old man" was the Greek orator Isocrates, who supposedly committed suicide after Athens lost its freedom to Philip of Macedon. Adams lived on. The House declined to censure him, by a vote of 106 to 93. He took a triumphal tour of upstate New York and Ohio, greeted by William Seward, the man who had warned the Anti-Masons to steer clear of him. "Among the women, a very pretty one . . . kissed me on the cheek. I returned the salute on the lip, and kissed every woman that followed, at which some made faces, but none refused." In Utica, New York, a speaker at one meeting read two published letters, almost seventy years old, by Abigail Adams, one to his father, one to him. "I actually sobbed as he read, utterly unable to suppress my emotion. . . . I answered I know not what." [24]

He was a celebrity. A daguerreotype (then a brand-new process) taken of him in 1843 shows surprisingly mild, even sweet eyes, set in a face like a pulpit. The margins sustaining the gag rule narrowed until, in December 1844, the gag went down, 108 to 80.

An admirer had given Adams an ivory cane, inscribed with a line from

Horace (*Justum et tenacem propositi virum*—"the just and steady-purposed man") and the motto, "Right of Petition Triumphant." Adams was asked to add the date when he prevailed, which he did in the spring of 1845. "I crave pardon," he wrote in his diary, "for the vanity of this memorial." [25]

Charles Francis Adams

CHARLES FRANCIS ADAMS had a childhood unusual even for an Adams, fantastic for any other American. One of the first adults to pay him a compliment was the emperor of Russia. The boy was accompanying his father on one of his daily walks in St. Petersburg when they ran into the monarch. Emperor Alexander and his wife had played with Charles Francis on the palace floor when he was an infant; now he was four years old, and the emperor asked him if he could speak English (polite society in St. Petersburg, such as the Adamses and the Romanovs frequented, spoke French). Charles Francis was "too intimidated" to answer;[1] when his father explained that he could speak a little English, French, German, and Russian, Alexander observed that he was a very bright young man.

Charles Francis Adams, his father's third and youngest son, was not marked for greatness by his christening. The oldest boy had been named for the father of his country, and the next for John Adams. Charles Francis's names commemorated his dead drunken uncle and the young diplomat whom John Quincy Adams had assisted in his first assignment. But by being taken to Russia in 1809, when he was not quite two, Charles Francis got something his older brothers missed by staying home: six years of his father's attention.

Not that this was always a blessing. John Quincy was a conscientious parent, teaching his young son how to read. But he taught him the rigors of being an Adams. "[W]hen I am pointing to one letter, he insists upon looking at another, upon turning over the leaf, upon hunting for a picture, upon anything but naming the letter to which I point." The same quality of divided attention, John Quincy fretted, was the reason his own life was "in the shallows." Surely it was absurd to compare the concentration of a young boy with that of a middle-aged man, or to criticize either, especially when the man was as accomplished as John Quincy was, but that was the family way. In 1816, when Charles Francis was nine, John Quincy wrote Abigail Adams that he was resigned to the prospect that his children would be "like other men," the goal of "ideal excellence" being beyond their reach. After the family returned to America, John Quincy decided to send Charles Francis to Harvard at the age of fourteen (not an uncommon age to matriculate in earlier centuries, but young for the nineteenth). The professor who examined him for admission, however, found that the boy bungled a Latin translation and would have to be tested again. John Quincy, forgetting—or perhaps remembering—his own troubles with Harvard, was enraged, and rode from Quincy to Cambridge to tell the president in person that his son had been "unfairly treated." The secretary of state was allowed to sit in on Charles Francis's second examination in Latin, which he passed with only one mistake, giving the English for *vindicatum* as "vindicated," rather than "punished."[2] The Latin word can mean either, depending on the context; the young scholar was understandably anxious about his own context.

After being thrust into Harvard with such effort, Charles Francis sank almost to the bottom of his class and decided to drop out. John Quincy wrote him a letter of reproof, disguised as sympathy. "Morals," his father admitted, were after all the most important thing. "[L]et your scholarship be as it pleases heaven. If I must give up all expectation of success or distinction for you in this life," at least "preserve me from the harrowing thought of your perdition in the next."[3] This was stronger even than the harangues that John had sent John Quincy: John Adams only taxed his son with laziness, slovenliness, and obstinacy; John Quincy threatened his with damnation. Charles Francis finished Harvard.

The youth who emerged from this upbringing was remarkably self-contained. Adulthood came early to him, and with it middle age; as Charles Francis himself put it, he was "grave, sober, formal, precise and reserved." Perhaps this was his protection against the anxiety of performance: His brothers drank; he was calm. He could be censorious: During his father's presidency, he went to a party at Henry Clay's and found it filled with "vulgar people" (no doubt it was). But the explosions and onslaughts of his father and grandfather were foreign to his nature. This was a matter partly of choice, partly of sensibility. He did not wish to be as angry as they habitually were, and he was too self-possessed to register as provocations many of the slights and disappointments that set them off. His sangfroid, which he maintained his whole life, would bring him a certain amount of derision: He was called a "cold, wet blanket"; "the greatest iceberg in the Northern hemisphere." His style as a speaker, wrote one acquaintance, was to utter "commonplaces slowly and deliberately, as if they were something he thought his audience was listening to for the first time." When he was long dead and his sons were older men, they argued about him: Charles Francis Adams, Jr., nourished a lifelong grudge against his father's coldness. Henry Adams was more charitable. "Had there been a little more, or a little less of him, he would have been less perfect." Charles Francis frequently doubted the value of his perfection, especially compared to his father; reading John Quincy's youthful diplomatic correspondence made him reflect that "at my age" his father had been "infinitely superior."[4]

In 1827, at age nineteen, this quiet young man proposed to Abigail Brooks, the daughter of Peter Brooks, a Boston banker and marine underwriter, who was worth $2.5 million. Mr. Brooks asked Charles Francis to postpone the marriage until he was twenty-one, and he equably agreed. John Adams had raised the family's station from the yeoman level, but financial disasters like bank failures or soured investments gave him and John Quincy real anxiety, and neither man was rich. Abigail Brooks Adams's share of her father's fortune (she had six siblings) would make Charles Francis so. As an adult, he would help his father manage his money and help him out of several financial jams. Abigail was a nervous woman, prey to "perpetual feeble worry."[5] Yet she and her husband must have done something right: None of their six children who lived to adulthood (four sons, two daughters) were self-destructive. Finally, the family cycle of hard-driving fathers producing only a single successful son amidst failed siblings was broken.

Charles Francis studied law at the Boston office of Daniel Webster, who seldom appeared, and had only one short talk with him. He also considered politics. The Anti-Masonic movement, which tempted his father with visions of a return to the White House, briefly engaged his attention. He wrote some Anti-Masonic articles, which he was not satisfied with, and attended the state party's convention in 1833 (he didn't like that either). The fact is, the son and grandson of presidents did not like politics. Charles Francis particularly did not like John Quincy's decision to go back into politics after leaving the White House. When his father was losing his bid for re-election in 1828, Charles Francis hoped that the family would finally stop being "the eternal subjects of contention and abuse." He wanted his father to devote his retirement to writing the biography of *his* father, and was distressed when John Quincy was elected to the House instead. His "temperament . . . very much unfit[s] him for that body"; it was not "beneficial to be always struggling before the public."[6]

John and John Quincy had both professed to be above the scrum of partisanship; to desire office only when it came to them; to disdain the fever of ambition. They were sincere enough in these professions to hobble themselves in their practice of politics; not nearly sincere enough to stay home. Charles Francis was the first Adams to really mean the family line on politics. He thought the techniques of electioneering and deal-making were sordid; he thought office-holding itself, even purged of these arts, was desirable only as a means to a higher end.

One of his skeptical comments on his father suggested a still more radical transvaluation of family values: The former president, he wrote sadly, is "not proof against the temporary seductions of popular distinction, to resist which is the most solid evidence of greatness."[7] An evidence, surely: A great man cannot be the slave of transitory acclaim. But "the most solid evidence"? John would have derived greatness from founding a state; John Quincy, from purging an unjust one. Charles Francis came close to saying that greatness was a matter of spiritual poise.

One cause tempted him into the arena—the politics of slavery. On this issue he agreed with his father. In 1836, Martin Van Buren became only the third northerner (and the first northerner not named Adams) to be elected president. As slavery once again became a contentious question, Van Buren's response was to give slaveowners whatever they wanted. His administration supported the gag rule; he announced that he would veto the abolition of slavery in the District of Columbia (gratuitously, since there was no prospect of Congress enacting it); at the end of his term, his attorney general intervened in the *Amistad* case. Charles Francis had supported Van Buren the first time he ran, but four years of Van Buren in office convinced him that the Democrats should be thrown out of office, for "truckling to Slaveholders."[8] In 1840 he ran for the Massachusetts House of Representatives as a Whig.

Few Whigs shared Charles Francis's goals. The Whig party had coalesced to oppose Andrew Jackson and all his works. Their opposition was often ad hoc and opportunistic. The Democrats said they stood for the common man. But so did the Whigs. They called William Henry Harrison, a hero of the War of 1812 whom they ran for president in 1840, the Log Cabin and Hard Cider candidate, after his supposed abode and favorite drink. Harrison was in fact the son of a Virginia grandee, Benjamin Harrison, "the indolent, heavy luxurious gentleman" John Adams had described at the Continental Congress. Both Whigs and Democrats were, in the words of historian David Hackett Fischer, "omnibus" parties,[9] trying to maintain broad national coalitions, which proved to be highly unstable (the White House would change hands in every election between 1840 and 1852). Symbol of the broadness of the Whigs was Harrison's running mate, John Tyler, a strict states' rights Republican of the old school who agreed with his new colleagues on nothing except the desire to win office. When the victorious Harrison died thirty days after his inauguration, Vice President Tyler unexpectedly won the highest office in the land.

Adams served five years in the state legislature, three in the state House, two in the state Senate. He disliked being a "mere party hack"; loyalty to party, as biographer Martin Duberman put it, meant disloyalty to his self-image as an Adams.[10] But whenever slavery came to the fore as an issue, so did he. In 1843, he presented to the state House a huge petition, with almost sixty-three thousand signatures, asking that Massachusetts be excused from assisting in the return of fugitive slaves (unlike his father in Congress, he was allowed to be heard). The Constitution provided that escaped persons "held to service or labour" in one state should be "delivered up" to their masters if found in another. Charles Francis supported this provision of the Constitution, but wanted the federal government to do the dirty work of enforcing it. Asked by the legislature to prepare a report on the petition he had delivered, he revived an old Federalist nostrum: Massachusetts should ask Congress to amend the 3/5 rule. The legislature asked; Congress declined.

In February 1844, "Peacemaker," a gun on the USS *Princeton,* blew up during a presidential excursion, killing the secretary of state. Tyler picked Calhoun to fill the gap, and the two pushed ahead with the annexation of Texas. Charles Francis was the main author of resolutions, adopted by the state legislature, condemning annexation as a plot to expand slavery, and announcing that Massachusetts would not acknowledge annexation after it happened. Charles Francis was not opposed to all expansion—he wanted the United States to assert its claim to the entire Oregon Territory, a tract stretching from California to Alaska, which had been jointly ruled by American settlers and the Hudson Bay Company. Charles Francis wanted it entirely ruled "by settlers from the states, who would carry with them our habits and feelings."[11] But these were settlers from New England, who carried nonslaveholding feelings.

When South Carolina began arresting free black sailors on Massachusetts ships that called at South Carolinian ports (free Negroes were not welcome in the state), Massachusetts sent a Boston judge to investigate, with a view to preparing a Supreme Court test case. The South Carolina legislature expelled him from the state as a "conspirator . . . against the public peace" and asserted that free Negroes were not citizens "within the meaning of the Constitution." Charles Francis prepared another legislative report calling these "acts of war."[12]

He retired from the legislature in 1845, but became even more active outside it, taking over the *Boston Daily Whig,* a limping party newspaper with only 212 subscribers. He paid for two-fifths of it, made himself editor, and had all the complaints that editors always have. At the start of his tenure, he found he had to write all the editorial copy himself. "How," he wondered in his diary, "could I ever have supposed this undertaking could prosper?" The *Daily Whig* prospered in the only way in which it was essential that it should: by catalyzing and mobilizing a faction in the Massachusetts Whig party that saw things as Adams did. By 1846, the party had divided into two wings: majority regulars, called "Cotton Whigs," and a hard-line antislavery minority, called "Conscience Whigs." *Cotton* referred to the economic tie between southern growers and the Yankee millowners who spun their crop into cloth. The Cotton

John Trumbull's famous painting of the signing of the Declaration of Independence. John Adams stands beneath the drum. *Yale University Art Gallery.*

John and Abigail Adams, as depicted in 1766 by Benjamin Blyth. *Courtesy of the Massachusetts Historical Society.*

John Adams in 1823 by Gilbert Stuart. *Adams National Historical Park.*

John Quincy Adams by John
Singleton Copley in 1797.
Adams National Historical Park.

A bust of John Quincy
Adams by Cardelli in 1818.
Adams National Historical Park.

Louisa Catherine Johnson Adams in 1816 by Robert Charles Leslie. *Adams National Historical Park.*

Charles Francis Adams. *Adams National Historical Park.*

Charles Francis and Abigail Brooks Adams in 1829 by Charles Bird King. *Adams National Historical Park.*

Charles and Abigail in old age at Quincy. *Courtesy of the Massachusetts Historical Society.*

Henry Adams as a young man. *Courtesy of the Massachusetts Historical Society.*

Henry at 1607 H Street. *Courtesy of the Massachusetts Historical Society.*

Marian Hooper in 1869. *Courtesy of the Massachusetts Historical Society.*

Henry Adams as an old man, in 1914. *Courtesy of the Massachusetts Historical Society.*

Two of Henry Adams's acquaintances: Mary, Queen of Heaven, South Portal, Chartres Cathedral; nameless figure by Augustus Saint-Gaudens, Rock Creek Cemetery, Washington, D.C. *Chartres courtesy Mary Ann Sullivan; statue courtesy Jeffery Howe.*

The house at Quincy. The graves in Quincy today. *House courtesy Adams National Historical Park; graves courtesy of the Massachusetts Historical Society.*

Whigs were accused by their enemies of not wanting to offend the upper class at home, or its business partners nationally. *Conscience* was what the antislavery Whigs believed they were guided by; it was also what the regulars accused them of being obsessed with. The Conscience Whigs, wrote one Cotton opponent, "expect to work faster than the Almighty."[13] At the Whig state convention in 1846, the Conscience wing proposed an antislavery litmus test for all candidates. The move failed, but Adams believed the Conscience Whigs had dented "the supremacy of the cotton power."

All these activities were important, but only at the state level. Massachusetts was an important state, because of its prosperity, its intellectual power, and its past. But Massachusetts was no longer as prominent as it had been. Maine had become a separate state in 1820; more important, Massachusetts had been losing population to emigration. As soon as the Revolutionary War ended and the Indians beyond the Alleghenies began to be subdued, the state shed waves of its children to western New York, the midwest, and finally Oregon. The exodus spread Massachusetts ideals across a continent, but it left the home state shrunken, and its politicians diminished accordingly. The Adams family's representative in the third generation was lowering his sights. In 1846 Charles Francis was, it is true, still not yet forty. But at that age his father had been a U.S. senator, and his grandfather had been a delegate to the First Continental Congress. Like them, Charles Francis had his eyes on issues of the highest national importance, but his range of action was contracted. Unconsciously, he was emulating the most unlikely family model: his distant cousin, Samuel Adams. Nothing could be less like Charles Francis's propriety than Samuel's hail-fellow-well-met disarray. But both of them were newspaper editors, stirring a local pot. He had more political influence as a journalist; he was also released from the duties and distractions of being a partisan hack.

Even within his state, Charles Francis stood in a minority position. "The wealthy classes," he wrote, "care very little for an abstract principle."[14] More exactly, they cared for a different one than he did. The Cotton Whigs were not merely defending their investments; they could claim to be defending the union against sectional agitation, and none claimed it more eloquently than the leader of their faction, Daniel Webster. John Quincy Adams had battled with Massachusetts's wealthy classes when he deserted Federalism for the Republican party, although he had then been the champion of union (and of working with southerners), while the wealthy classes had supported secession. The issues had changed, but business was feuding once again with an Adams.

But now Massachusetts was home to still other interests and tendencies, which Charles Francis found unsympathetic. Beyond him in the antislavery spectrum lay the abolitionists, who favored immediate manumission. William Lloyd Garrison, a journalist from Newburyport who had been a youthful admirer of Timothy Pickering, revived Pickering's spirit in his crusade for abolitionist views. Garrison revered the Declaration of Independence, but called the Constitution, which offered guarantees to slaveholders, "a covenant with death and an agreement with hell." Charles Francis's attitude toward death and hell was to keep them strictly within their constitutional limits. Although a mob hustled Garrison through the streets of Boston, he appealed to the wilder shores of New England Protestantism, what Ralph Waldo Emerson half-seriously called "Madmen, madwomen, men with beards, Dunkards, Muggletonians, Come-outers, Groaners."[15] Charles Francis would have none of that.

Emerson himself was another figure apart. The future poet and seer had been a Harvard classmate of Charles Francis's oldest brother, who had beaten Emerson out of the Boylston Prize for oratory in their junior year. Ordained as a Unitarian minister, Emerson found even that church's doctrines too confining and left his pulpit to preach, in clear and flawless prose, the identity of the soul and the universe. John Quincy called Emerson's ideas "crazy"; Charles Francis thought they would "degrade the morals . . . of the public." To Emerson, meanwhile, and to the writers and beautiful souls who gathered round his home in Concord, the Adamses, as Charles Francis's son Henry wrote, "were minds of dust and emptiness, devoid of feeling, poetry or imagination . . . natures of narrow scope."[16]

Even as its native sons moved west, Massachusetts was the destination for Irishmen moving in the same direction. The influx began decades before the potato famine; those who could not afford to cross the Atlantic in one trip stopped in Nova Scotia to earn further passage and were called "two-boaters." The Irish startled what had always been one of America's most homogeneous colonies and states. The people who had taken Louisburg from Catholic France now found a colony of Irish Catholics in their midst. Native-born Americans quickly organized against them. In the mid-1840s the newfound Native American party sounded out Charles Francis (no one was more indisputably American than he) as a possible standard-bearer. He dismissed them as "the worst principled of all the third parties which have risen in late years." Nativism, he believed, "perpetuate[s] instead of expunging . . . traces of distinction between men equally anxious to become the supports of their common country."[17] This was remarkably evenhanded, but it was a statement of principle, not based on any contact or even sympathy with its objects.

Charles Francis was an essentially conservative man, whose tradition was becoming less representative, even as his family had become more venerable. "For myself," he explained in 1840, "I am content to go on in the path marked by my fathers before me."[18]

Charles Francis's path unexpectedly took him onto the national stage in the late 1840s. But first, he had a political quarrel with John Quincy. In the fall of 1847 the Whigs had a narrow majority in the U.S. House of Representatives. Their candidate for Speaker was Robert Winthrop of Massachusetts, descendant of John Winthrop, founder of the Massachusetts Bay Colony ("[I]n any village of New England," John Adams had written, "is not gratitude the sentiment that attends" the name of Winthrop?). But Robert Winthrop was a Cotton Whig. Hard-line antislavery Whigs refused to vote for him unless he promised to appoint antislavery men to committee chairmanships, which he would not do. Winthrop was not elected until the third ballot, and then by a margin of only one vote.

One of the votes in Winthrop's majority had been cast by eighty-year-old John Quincy Adams. The elder Adams not only supported Winthrop, but lobbied one of the hardliners, a fellow representative from Massachusetts, to do so as well. "If I can vote for Mr. Winthrop with a clear conscience," John Quincy said, "I should suppose" the Conscience Whig could. Charles Francis feared that his father's support for Winthrop would be used against the Conscience Whigs—even the Old

Man Eloquent, their enemies would say, was not as extreme as they were—and he feared that his father would continue to cooperate with Winthrop, whom the old man liked. Charles Francis wrote his mother in despair. "*Don't let my father play into their hands.* I don't ask him to help us—All I want is to have him stand aside and see fair play." John Quincy explained that he had voted out of ancestral esteem, not for John Winthrop, but for Robert's father, Thomas Lindall Winthrop, longtime lieutenant governor of Massachusetts, who had stood by him during the lonely days when local Federalists had shunned him for his political apostasy. Louisa wrote her son that John Quincy "intended no wrong to you . . ." but "that desire which has ever possessed him, of striking out a new path for *himself,* led him to this." She also suggested that John Quincy's health—he had had a stroke in 1846—"renders him at times the creature of impulse." [19] At all times, John Quincy Adams had been the creature of a handful of impulses, among them rewarding friends and punishing enemies. The son of an old ally took precedence, in this case, over his own son.

Eighteen forty-eight was a presidential election year, and the Conscience Whigs, who had been willing to block the party's choice for Speaker, prepared to sabotage its presidential candidate, if he were faint-hearted on slavery.

There already existed a small party of abolitionists, called the Liberty party. Twice they had run James Birney, a Kentuckian who had freed all his own slaves. Birney's first tally in 1840 was tiny, but in 1844 he had capitalized on the issue of Texas by opposing annexation, and on the political finesse of Henry Clay, making his third and final run. Clay had said he would support annexation only if the whole country did: Practically, this meant that he opposed it, but Clay cast his position in this form to give the appearance of flexibility to southerners. The maneuver did not fool hard-core slaveowners. "Da nigger vote am quite surprising," wrote one southern wit of Clay and his running mate. "We's all for Clay, and Frelinghuysen." But it was enough to damn him in the eyes of the Liberty party, and Birney took enough votes in New York to deprive Clay of the state, and the election, won by James K. Polk. Charles Francis had regretted Clay's loss, as did the rising Illinois Whig Abraham Lincoln: "As I always understood, the Liberty-men deprecated the annexation of Texas extremely; and, this being so, why they should refuse to so cast their votes as to prevent it . . . seemed wonderful." Polk justified Charles Francis's and Lincoln's worst fears, annexing Texas and declaring war on Mexico in 1846. Radicals were enraged; Henry David Thoreau, a friend of Emerson's, declared he would "do justice . . . to Mexico, *cost what may*;" justice cost him a night in jail for nonpayment of taxes.[20] Polk pressed ahead, and by war's end in February 1848 had acquired, not only Texas, but the northern two-fifths of Mexico, from Santa Fe to San Francisco—an area larger than the Louisiana Purchase, or the original United States.

In 1848 the national Whig party nominated Zachary Taylor, one of the Mexican War's victorious generals, who had no known political opinions, and who refused to give any antislavery pledges. That galvanized the Conscience Whigs of Massachusetts, who gathered, five thousand strong, in Worcester in June. They held off nominating a presidential ticket of their own until a national convention of all antislavery groups later in the summer, but they inspired themselves with speeches. The most striking was given by Charles Francis Adams. It was a triumph of situation over natural ability. John Quincy had died of a stroke earlier in the year; the squall over Winthrop ("a tempest in a Boston teapot," the poet Longfellow called it) was forgotten; Charles Francis Adams had now become, in the minds of his audience, the stand-in for John Quincy—and for John. "His marvellous resemblance to his father and grandfather," wrote one delegate, "made a great impression. . . . It seemed as if old John Adams had stepped down from Trumbull's picture of the Signing . . . to give his benediction." [21]

When the Liberty party and the Conscience Whigs met together in Buffalo, New York, in August, they were joined by a third group: a faction of the New York State Democratic party, led by none other than former president Van Buren. New York Democrats had split into a regular wing, the Hunkers, and a minority wing, the Barnburners, with which Van Buren was allied. The Barnburners declared themselves to be against the expansion of slavery. Latter-day Jacksonian Democrats, like Arthur Schlesinger, Jr., have draped the mantle of conviction over Van Buren's shoulders. Van Buren himself explained that the Mexican War had changed everything: So long as the country had been fixed in its pre-

1845 boundaries, he had been willing to truckle to slaveholders. But the acquisition of so much new territory made it necessary to set limits. Perhaps he was telling the truth. The Liberty party and the Conscience Whigs believed him; the men who had balked at Henry Clay and Robert Winthrop made Van Buren their presidential candidate in Buffalo.

When it came time to pick a running mate, the convention's managers, seeking geographical balance, asked the delegates of the midwestern states to give the nod, expecting them to name one of their own. But they wanted Charles Francis Adams. The New England diaspora was asserting itself: Men who lived in Ohio or Illinois had been born in Massachusetts and Connecticut. The weakening effect of emigration became, in this situation, a strength. But Charles Francis Adams's attraction in Buffalo, as in Worcester, was his name, and the recent passing of his father. A delegate from the brand-new state of Wisconsin, "with sun-burnt face, hook nose, deep voice, and a noble, ardent countenance," told the writer Richard Henry Dana, "Yes, sir, we want him. He's the man for this day and time—There he is *with the crape on his hat now.*"[22]

The invocation of the Revolution and the Founding showed how radical the new group, which named itself the Free Soil party, was. The Free Soilers were not only declaring independence from the contemporary major parties, they were suggesting that the country was in danger of becoming as corrupt as the British Empire had been when the Founders broke from it. John Adams would appreciate the irony of the Free Soil delegate linking him to the Declaration of Independence, with which he disagreed. He would also appreciate the irony that one of his reasons for disagreeing with it—his belief in the persistence of prominent families—was being ratified by his grandson's nomination.

The election was disappointing. The Free Soilers got only 10 percent of the popular vote (29 percent in Massachusetts), and carried no states. Van Buren's strength in New York, where the Democrats finished third, probably helped tip the state to Taylor and the Whigs, who won the election, beating the northern proslavery Democrat Lewis Cass.

Yet the effort had been a serious one. Van Buren's presence at the top of the Free Soil ticket gave it more gravitas than poor William Wirt had been able to lend the Anti-Masons. The two-party system was still somewhat new. Over the last sixty years, one major party, the Federalists, had died, and its rival, the Republicans, had been transformed into the Democrats. Both Whigs and Democrats now seemed shaky. "The time cannot be very far off," Adams had written, "when the present organization of parties must be shaken to its center." He was prophetic, not because he was a keen analyst, but because he and others willed that it should be shaken. At age forty-one, he had helped give the first serious shock. The effort, he reflected, "places me somewhat near the level of my fathers." [23]

---

*A*DAMS WAS AHEAD of his time. The country reacted to the prospective collapse of its political arrangements by making one more effort to prop them up. It was the last hurrah of the freshman class of 1811. Adams went to Washington in 1849, as the new administration and Congress were getting under way, to scout the situation for the Free Soil party. He concluded that the seventy-two-year-old Henry Clay did not know "at which end to begin," and that the "only *systematic* statesman remaining" was the dying sixty-seven-year-old John Calhoun. "His system . . . is 'a dissolution of the Union' and its consequence, 'a slaveholding confederacy.' " But Clay trumped Calhoun. Clay's last negotiation, known as the Compromise of 1850, extended the line of the Missouri Compromise to the border of California, which was admitted as a free state; sixty-eight-year-old Daniel Webster, of the class of 1813, gave his last great speech in support of it. The boundaries of bondage and freedom in North America seemed settled, and both the establishment and the public hoped not to discuss the question again. The mood, Adams realized, left the Free Soil movement "afloat on a wide sea of uncertainty."[1]

But at the same time new politicians were emerging who disliked the new mood. Two of the most prominent, on the antislavery side, already well-known to Adams, would be colleagues and rivals for the next twenty years.

In 1851, Democrats and Free Soilers in Massachusetts made a deal dividing the important offices among themselves, and freezing out the Whigs. The Free Soil party gave its spoil, a Senate seat, to its most eloquent orator, Charles Sumner. Sumner had grown up in Boston, on the wrong side of Beacon Hill: His mother was a seamstress, his father the illegitimate son of a lawyer. As a boy Charles persuaded his father to send him to a good school by teaching himself elementary Latin in secret. He claimed Demosthenes and Pericles as models; though the law was his profession, the podium was his home. He had a strong bass voice, and a face that managed simultaneously to be striking, brutal, and sensual. He quickly made a reputation for high and uncompromising idealism, and for venomous attacks on those who did not share it. Sumner was one of the small group of friends who advised Adams when he bought the *Daily Whig* (he was not rich enough to help Adams pay for it). When Sumner entered the Senate, southern orators were finally confronted with a northerner as talented and as unrestrained as they were.

Already in the Senate when Sumner arrived was William Seward, the man who had vetted John Quincy Adams for the cause of Anti-Masonry. Seward was the son of an upstate New York land speculator. He met his lifelong political counselor on a trip to Niagara Falls with his fiancée: In Rochester, New York, Seward's carriage lost a wheel, and one of the crowd of helpful strangers who gathered was journalist Thurlow Weed. Seward, who ultimately became governor, was a loyal Whig, but he always stood in the liberal wing of the party, favoring Irish immigrants and slaves. Seward was small and slight, with a big nose and pitcher-handle ears. Adams's sons variously described him as "a wiry old scarecrow," "a wise macaw," "dressed in a coat and trousers made apparently twenty years ago and by a bad tailor at that." But while lacking Sumner's presence or eloquence, he had a knack for powerful phrases. Sent to the Senate in 1849, he opposed Clay's great compromise on the grounds that it allowed slavery in New Mexico, declaring there was "a higher law than the Constitution,"[2] which governed America's government of its territories.

Photographs of Adams taken at about this time show the high family forehead, and a face that is mild, even sweet. There is something, however, in the eyes and the set of the mouth that might be implacability. When Seward first met Adams, he noted that he was "a little taller than his father, and looks very like him."[3]

Adams spent the bulk of the decade in political limbo, reading the classics and tending to his gentleman's hobbies. "My impression," wrote his son Henry forty years later, "is that he thought he wanted to be in Mt. Vernon Street [his Boston address], polishing his coins."[4] In 1852 the Whigs nominated another Mexican war hero, General Winfield

Scott, for president, but carried only four states, a showing reminiscent of the Federalist Party on its deathbed. In 1856 a new party, the Republicans—composed of Free Soilers, as well as antislavery Whigs, nativists, and Democrats—held a convention in Philadelphia, which Adams attended. He would have liked a Republican congressional nomination, and he stumped for the party nationally, but the Republicans in his district passed him over, and their presidential ticket, though it made a respectable showing, carried only greater New England, the homeland, plus New York and four midwestern states. Two years later, the Republicans gave Adams the nod he wanted, and he won a Massachusetts congressional seat.

But for all the years of practicing politics, from the state legislature through the Free Soil campaign, Adams was still not, at heart, a politician. In 1856 he had insisted that a congressional nomination come to him, and it hadn't; in 1858, when it came, he did no campaigning for himself. The energy and deal-making that propelled Seward, Weed, and Sumner (to say nothing of his father) were not for him.

He had re-entered the arena at a moment of maximum rancor. The spirit of the Compromise of 1850 had lasted only a few years, destroyed by yet another territorial question, this time involving the northern remainder of the Louisiana Purchase. When Jefferson bought this land, Alexander Hamilton complained that it was desert that would not be settled for centuries. Half a century later, Americans were moving in, and Congress proposed to allow Kansas and Nebraska, which had been reserved by the Missouri Compromise for freedom, to be free or slave as their inhabitants should decide. The Kansas-Nebraska Act seemed like a populist measure that would be universally appealing. In fact it set off a competitive land rush of southern and northern settlers, inflamed by marauding guerrilla bands. The proxy war irritated and excited the nation; noncombatants cheered as at some bloody sport. Snug in Concord, Henry David Thoreau hailed the later career of John Brown, the greatest of the antislavery killers: "we are lifted out of the trivialness and dust of politics into the region of truth and manhood."[5]

Politicians could have resented Thoreau's insult, for they were not notably pacific. Sumner said his southern colleagues behaved as if Congress were "a plantation well stocked with slaves, over which the lash of the overseer had full sway." After one of Sumner's rougher speeches, a representative from South Carolina beat him on the head as he sat at his desk, with a gold-tipped hard rubber cane that finally snapped. "I did not intend to kill him," the attacker remarked, "but I did intend to whip him."[6] Sumner was out of commission for three years.

In this sulfurous atmosphere Adams was as calm and composed as his portraits. He waited until May 1860 to give his maiden speech. Like his father, he recurred to the Declaration of Independence, which, he said, was now being interpreted as if it applied only to white men. He invited the south to secede if it wished, but warned that the experiment of independence would fail. The remaining United States, for one thing, would no longer return fugitive slaves. Seward called the speech "strong as iron, clear as crystal, genial as dew."[7] A century earlier, Adams's cousin Samuel had been a radical firebrand with a conservative religious core. Adams in 1860 was an unassuming conservative gentleman, fond of his books and coins, who was as determined as any radical to be pushed only so far.

That same month the Republican convention in Chicago, judging Seward to have too much baggage, nominated Abraham Lincoln. In his single term in Congress, the Illinois Whig had voted with Adams's father in the hard-core antislavery minority. Adams now thought him "honest and tolerably capable." This tepid estimate was quite common in the east. George Templeton Strong, the New York diarist, wrote that Lincoln was being "commend[ed] to popular favor . . . because he cut a great many rails, and worked on a flatboat in early youth; all which is somehow presumptive evidence of his statesmanship."[8] Lincoln swept the north, and the electoral college. The 3/5 rule, though still in place, had finally collapsed as an effective bulwark of the slave states. Adams was re-elected handily.

Presidents were then inaugurated in March, which left four months of dead time between the election and Lincoln's swearing-in. South Carolina seceded almost immediately, followed by the rest of the Deep South. The lame-duck interval was spent in what Adams called a "queer struggle" of congressional maneuvering. In piety toward the Revolution, the Senate picked a Committee of Thirteen to try to adjust sectional differences; the House chose a Committee of Thirty-three, with one

member from each state. Adams represented Massachusetts, and soon
became the dominant member—"a very Jove," wrote his son Henry, a little absurdly.[9] Adams was no thunderer; he stood out because of his tact
and skill, and because of his closeness to Seward, the leading Republican
in Washington until the president-elect arrived.

Forty years of compromises, going back to Missouri—eighty-three
years, if one went back to the Constitutional Convention—had culmi-
nated in this point. Adams did not expect southern hardliners to make
any deals now. He and Seward had three goals: to let hard-line sentiment
burn off, so that unionists might take control in the Deep South; to de-
tach the upper south from its fellow slave states; to keep the government
together until Lincoln could take the oath of office.

All this took place in an atmosphere of giddy depression. "The un-
heroic," remembered Adams's most caustic son, Charles Francis, Jr.,
"was much in evidence." The lame-duck president, James Buchanan,
was a gracious, gutless homosexual whose lame-duck cabinet was filled
with traitors. Rumors of reconciliation alternated with rumors of southern coups. Asked about a financial panic, Seward said airily, "You can't
run a financial and a political panic together; the first will regulate itself."
At the close of one trading day in New York, "a report was circulated that
President Buchanan had gone insane, and stocks rose." Hard-line Republicans, led by Sumner, denounced Seward and Adams as temporiz-
ers; at the same time, Sumner was given to nervous tale-bearing. "He
was plainly off his balance," Charles Francis, Jr., remembered, and his
eyes "gleam[ed] with something distinctly suggestive of insanity."[10]

Adams was willing to accept a constitutional amendment explicitly
guaranteeing slavery where it existed, and to admit New Mexico as a
slave state. He drew the line at a proposal by Thomas Nelson of Tennessee, that slavery be guaranteed below the old Missouri Compromise
line, in all present states and any "hereafter acquired." The south had lost
the political game within the current boundaries of the United States; it
could only regain parity by expanding the country, and slavery, into the
West Indies and Central America. This was a real threat. In the 1850s,
William Walker, a Tennessee-born adventurer, had invaded Baja California and Honduras, and actually made himself president of Nicaragua,
until he double-crossed Cornelius Vanderbilt over a steamship line and

was deposed. Three American diplomats, including James Buchanan in his prepresidential career, had plotted to buy Cuba from Spain. Adams and some Republicans were willing to let the south have New Mexico; they were not willing to underwrite its efforts to carve up Mexico and the Caribbean. Calhoun had told Adams's father that slavery was republican; Nelson and other southerners now wanted the republic to become a conquering slave empire. If that was the south's price for peace, said Adams in a speech to the House at the end of January 1861, "let the heavens fall." [11]

In the end, Adams and Seward (who was to be the new secretary of state) were partly successful. Unionist sentiment did not revive in the Deep South or Virginia. But Missouri, Kentucky, Maryland, Delaware, and one Tennessee senator, Andrew Johnson, remained loyal, and Lincoln was inaugurated early in March 1861.

His progress from Illinois to the capital had not impressed Adams, who found his speeches along the way "uncertain"; they "put to flight all notions of greatness." At the ceremony, Charles Francis, Jr., compared Buchanan's "tall, large figure, and white head" to Lincoln's "lank, angular form and hirsute face": "the outgoing President was undeniably the more presentable man of the two." Down a side street, the younger Adams saw seventy-four-year-old Winfield Scott, commanding general of the army, sitting in a carriage in full uniform, "surrounded by mounted staff officers . . . holding himself ready for any emergency." [12]

Republican victory set off a scramble for office. Sumner had wanted to be minister to England, but Seward lobbied successfully for Adams instead. When Adams went to the White House to accept the appointment formally, Lincoln gave him a few quick words, then turned to the secretary of state and said, "Well Seward, I have settled the Chicago Post Office." [13] The encounter did not raise Adams's opinion of Lincoln's statesmanship, but it did show who was the better politician. The country had just fallen apart; now was precisely the time to cement the remainder with patronage.

Adams took with him his wife and three youngest children (Henry would be his private secretary). On the boat he read Macaulay's new *History of England.* Soon after he settled in, he made a change in diplomatic dress: Recent American ministers had worn plain republican black to call on Queen Victoria, but when Adams was told that it made him look like a butler, he resumed the conventional gold lace and silk stockings.

Adams, the third member of his family to serve as minister to England, had by far the most important assignment. John and John Quincy Adams had gone to London as postwar placeholders; Charles Francis Adams was representing the United States at the most important crisis (but for the Revolution) in its history. As in the Revolution, diplomacy was a key factor. If Britain, and other European powers, treated the war as a rebellion, then they would not give the South help or diplomatic recognition. If they considered it a war between two nations, then they might offer to arbitrate, or even take the South's side (which would force Washington to declare war in return). The United States could have won independence without French help, and the South could win it without foreign help. But foreign interference now would all but guarantee rebel victory, just as it had in 1778.

Adams was taking on this assignment alone. There would be no Franklin or Clay to help or frustrate him. Transatlantic communication was quicker than it had been in his ancestors' time, when diplomats were as out of touch as voyageurs (Adams and his family had come over on a steamship in twelve days). But though he was on a shorter leash, he was by himself.

England held natural reserves of sympathy for the North. English Liberals (the name was coming to mean both a party and a worldview) considered themselves both enlightened and progressive: They believed in liberty, and they believed that History did too. The British Empire had abolished slavery in 1833; at last the United States seemed to be catching up. So strong were these sentiments that some Englishmen favored the North despite their own economic interests. Millowners who needed American cotton resented the North's blockade of Southern ports, but their workers—often belonging to the same Protestant sects that had peopled New England—rallied in favor of the cause that kept them unemployed.

Many Tories, meanwhile, preferred the South because they imagined that it was upholding a hierarchical society like their own (so much for Calhoun). But the great motive for wishing the North ill was realpolitik.

If the United States split in two, there would be one less rival in the world. When John and John Quincy Adams had dealt with England, they represented a minor power. The United States was not yet a great power, but it was clearly becoming one. Southern secession would be the last chance to contain it. As an incidental benefit, American divisions would open new opportunities in the Western Hemisphere. Southerners would seek to expand into Central America and the Caribbean. But, as a smaller country, they would need allies and patrons, if only to fend off other predatory European powers (in 1864, Napoleon III would take advantage of American distraction by making a Hapsburg prince emperor of Mexico). A successful secession would repeal the Monroe Doctrine.

The balance wheel between these forces was the prime minister, Lord Palmerston. Palmerston had a lively interest in foreign policy; in previous governments, in which he had been foreign secretary, he had dragged Britain into arcane international disputes, without consulting his colleagues, or even the queen. He "could no more resist scoring a point in diplomacy," wrote Henry Adams, "than in whist."[14] Moderation was not to be expected of him. But Palmerston was seventy-six years old when Adams arrived in England, having sat in Parliament since 1807. Time and experience had mitigated his natural temperament.

Inertia favored the North. If England were to interfere, it would have to act outside the established course of things. Adams's course was to give no offense, take no offense, and warn England of the risks of doing anything new. It was a strategy easy to conceptualize, hard to execute.

Adams suffered a setback before he even landed. England had recognized the South as a belligerent while he was crossing the Atlantic. Belligerent status was not the same as acknowledged nationhood, but it did allow the South certain benefits, such as the freedom to supply (though not arm) its warships in English ports. If England went so far so early in the war, why would it not go all the way to diplomatic recognition (which, among other things, would force Adams to go home)?

Adams was so unsure of his tenure that he rented a house by the month only. From the moment he arrived in London, he was serving on borrowed time. He filled it by discharging his duties and attending the dinners thrown by the North's friends, and by such of its enemies as would receive him. Going out was showing the flag. "Minister Adams," his son Henry wrote years later, "was better received than most nullities because he made no noise."[15]

Sometimes he had to deal with American provocations. In May 1861, Seward wrote a bumptious message to the British government, warning them against getting involved in American affairs. Seward, every bit as aggressive as Palmerston, was an expansionist and an Anglophobe who, before Lincoln's inauguration, had toyed with the idea of picking a fight with England as a way of uniting America and averting a civil war. Seward's message was toned down twice—by Lincoln, before it was sent, and by Adams as he delivered it. Later that year, an American sloop stopped a British mail packet, the *Trent*, in the Caribbean and removed two Confederate diplomats who were passengers. England's anger at that bit of high-handedness was only smoothed over at the urging of the queen's dying husband, Prince Albert.

In June 1862 Palmerston chose to be provoked, when the military governor of New Orleans (which the North had just captured) ordered any women who were disrespectful to Northern soldiers to be arrested as if they were prostitutes. Palmerston himself wrote Adams a letter expressing his "disgust";[16] Adams defused this missile by asking whether the prime minister's note was official or personal, and then insisting that they communicate only through the foreign secretary, Lord Russell. Palmerston let the matter drop.

British provocations were the most delicate matter Adams had to deal with. In October 1862, William Gladstone, then chancellor of the exchequer, gave a speech that seemed to signal a shift in policy. Gladstone was a man who exceeded the Adamses at their stiffest in rectitude and self-importance. (Bertrand Russell, the foreign secretary's grandson, would write that though he had faced angry judges and hostile mobs, the only man who had ever made him afraid was Gladstone, demanding to know why his port had been served in a sherry glass.) Gladstone now declared that the Southerners "have made an army; they are making, it appears, a navy; and they have made, what is more than either . . . a nation." Though this looked like a trial balloon for diplomatic recognition, Russell told Adams that Gladstone had been speaking only for himself. Russell did not tell Adams that the government had indeed considered recognizing the South, and that Gladstone had simply jumped the gun. The chancellor of the exchequer, wrote Palmerston (no stranger to imprudent statements), should "steer clear of the Future unless authorized by his colleagues."[17]

Gladstone's reference to the Southern navy was doubly indelicate because whatever navy the South had was being built in English shipyards. The South had little manufacturing capacity, and its ports were either blockaded or occupied by the North. But Southern agents had paid for a splendid gunboat, the *Alabama*, which sailed from Liverpool in 1862, and wreaked havoc on Northern shipping. In 1863 Adams learned that two new vessels—ironclad, with ramming prows, perfect for attacking blockading ships—had been laid down in the same yards, supposedly for the khedive of Egypt. They were finished in the summer, and in early September he wrote Russell complaining that the ships were in fact meant to "carry . . . on war against the United States."[18] Adams's note crossed one from Russell, denying that there was sufficient evidence to prove where the ships were bound.

This was a particularly blatant evasion—everyone knew they were not bound for Egypt—and Adams answered it with a note containing the most famous words he ever wrote: "It would be superfluous in me to point out to your lordship that this is war."[19] Adams's father and grandfather were masters of short, sharp phrases, mostly amusing or bitter. But Adams's sentence was as cool as it was compact. It did not bluster; it did not even threaten. Russell and Palmerston had made the threat, by allowing a belligerent to build warships in a supposedly neutral port. Then they had lied about what they had done. Adams laid the threat and the lie before the aggressors. His only role was to call things by their right names. He even denied that his role was necessary ("It would be superfluous in me to point out . . ."). Russell and Palmerston should know what they were doing; they already knew it. If, as Henry would write, Adams succeeded in English society by making no noise, he was playing high-stakes diplomacy almost as quietly.

Adams's letter was literally superfluous, since Russell decided to stop the ships from leaving Liverpool even before he received it. This followed the pattern of alternating menaces and hesitations that had characterized English policy since the war began. But the possibility of intervention remained on the government's agenda through the fall, and in the minds of certain ministers for months thereafter.

In the end, however, England did what Adams hoped, which was nothing. Years after Adams had died, when memoirs appeared and archives opened, it became clear that the decisive voice for inertia was Palmerston. He thought Gladstone's analysis of Southern nation-building was "not far wrong," and he fretted about "Yankee bullying."[20] But when it came to action, he always chose the additional delay, until accumulated delays made their own choice. Palmerston was following the war news: The North had an army too, and Vicksburg and Gettysburg had happened in July 1863. But the soldiers were thousands of miles away. The American on the spot was Adams. His demeanor, his formulations, and the consequences they implied were also part of the picture that made Palmerston cautious.

At the end of the year, England had to consider a new problem—Prussia's claim to Schleswig and Holstein, two small duchies in northern Germany. Palmerston complained that he was one of only three men in Europe who had ever understood the issue, and he had forgotten. England turned its attention to the rising great power of the Old World, leaving the New World to settle its own claims, with its own blood.

When he had accepted the Free Soil vice presidential nomination in 1848, Adams had felt "near the level" of his ancestors. But he had gotten there as a symbolic substitute. Fifteen years later, he had done something great for his country on his own.

CHAPTER 10

ADAMS STAYED ON as minister to England for four and a half more years, a tenure he rightly saw as unprofitable. The turning point of the war left him little to do; peace, even less. Adams's judgment of Lincoln after his murder in 1865 was mixed: Though granting Lincoln "a clear sense of right," he felt he was "deficient in almost all the ordinary requirements of a statesman." Weirdly, Adams found Lincoln "kind without sentiment or imagination."[1] He always believed that his friend Seward had been the prime mover in the administration, and the posthumous deification of Lincoln proceeded so fast that when Adams said as much in a tribute to Seward in the early 1870s, he was widely condemned. Like his ancestors, he had trouble judging his peers.

When Adams came home (he had two, one in Quincy, one in Boston) he was sixty, and he settled into the well-regulated routine of an even older man. He returned to the classics and his coins. He joined two dinner clubs: One included Emerson, Longfellow, and William Dean Howells as members; he preferred the other, as being more low-key. His taciturnity, he admitted, began to cover him "like an outer shell to a turtle." Writing of him as "the Chief," his son Henry was "pain[ed] to see him so separate from the human race. I crave for what is new. I hanker after a new idea, in hopes that it may solve some old difficulty. He cares nothing for it."[2]

Serving abroad, Adams had missed some extraordinarily acrid postwar politics. Lincoln's successor, Andrew Johnson, the loyal Tennessee Democrat who had been put on the Republican ticket in 1864 for balance, was impeached and almost removed from office because of his conciliatory postwar policy toward the South. Adams agreed with the president. He suspected that Negroes were inferior—reading an explorer's book on the headwaters of the Nile in 1864, he wrote in his diary

that "it is almost impossible to resist the conviction that there is a decided natural inferiority of race"—and did not think they should soon be
given "absolute political equalisation."[3] He had risked war not to help
blacks, but to resist their overweening masters. Once they were masters
no longer, he had no further quarrel with them. The year Adams returned to America, the Republican party and the nation turned with relief from these disputes to the victorious Northern general, Ulysses S.
Grant.

Adams would have little more contact with Grant than he had had
with Lincoln, but Lincoln had at least been a type—the politician—
which he had long known. Grant was outside Adams's ken. Son of a
prosperous Ohio farmer, he had led an undistinguished life—mediocre
West Point cadet, Mexican War officer, failed farmer and business-
man—until the Civil War proved him to be a genius. Moving from theater to theater solving every problem he was presented, he was given
command of all the Northern armies when he was not yet forty-one
years old. Grant could see both the big picture and the task at hand. His
overview is exemplified by the moment in his *Memoirs* when he drops,
into an account of the battle of the Wilderness, a two-page description
of how teams of men with mules laid down telegraph wires every night
when the army dug itself in. This was not a housekeeping detail; it was
how he kept a million men in multiple fronts at his fingertips. His refusal
to be distracted was illustrated during the same battle when a distraught
officer burst in on him with a prediction of what Robert E. Lee was
about to do next. "Go back to your command," Grant told him, "and try
to think what we are going to do ourselves."[4]

Grant followed Washington and Jackson as a hero/president, but unlike them, he was a political innocent. Jackson had held elective office,
and engaged in rough frontier diplomacy before he became chief executive; the prepresidential Washington had done all that, and picked the
brightest brains of the political class. Grant had scarcely ever voted. To
him politicians were alien beings who supplied soldiers and got, or didn't
get, in his way. To inexperience he added a mild and trusting nature. His
campaign slogan was, "Let us have peace."

Adams had an odd interview with him in the fall of 1871. The Southern privateer *Alabama* had caused huge losses to American merchant

shipping, from outright captures to high insurance rates. The United States demanded that Britain, which had allowed it to be built, make amends. (Seward had suggested the Bahamas as appropriate compensation.) Adams, given his experience with the issue, was chosen to represent the United States at an international arbitration in Geneva, and before leaving he went to the White House to meet with Grant and the new secretary of state, Hamilton Fish. Ten years earlier Lincoln had struck him as crass; now Grant seemed uncomprehending. The president suggested that the arbitrators keep meeting even if Britain pulled out. Adams and Fish stared in embarrassment at the fire. Arbitration, like dancing, requires two parties, and Grant didn't know such a basic fact. On the other hand, he understood an even more basic fact, which was that the British didn't want a quarrel—they were afraid that the United States might take Canada in a fit of pique, which, in the aftermath of the Civil War, it could easily have done—and that however much they balked, they would see the arbitration through. Adams went to Switzerland for three months.

When he came back in February 1872, during a break in the discussions, he found that he was being run for president himself. Even with Johnson out of the way, the Republican party was split into warring factions. The majority regulars ran a machine, and justified it with the moral credit accumulated by winning the Civil War. The dissidents, called Liberal Republicans, had the same tone of fighting purists that had characterized the Conscience Whigs, without the focus of a single issue like slavery. They were outraged by scandals that had touched the unsuspecting Grant's friends. They condemned Republican efforts to enforce black suffrage in the south, as a naked partisan maneuver (which it was); also because, like Adams, they did not particularly care whether southern blacks voted. They were for clean government, a higher tone, and a dozen unclassifiable things that made them (in their view) better people than the regulars. On the sidelines, the Democrats, whose party was tainted by treason, hoped to cut a deal with the Liberals. Carl Schurz, a German exile who had become senator from Missouri, called a Liberal Convention in Cincinnati in May.

Adams was a natural choice for the Liberals. He favored reconciliation with southern whites. He disliked Grant. Most important, he dis-

liked politics. Though they were all politicians, the Liberals professed to
be above politics as usual. What better candidate for them than a man
who held himself above politics of any kind? Charles Francis, Jr.,
thought his father's nomination was a "pretty sure thing."[5]

Adams proved too astringent even for the purists, however. He was
due to return to Geneva in May (where he would win a fine settlement—
$15.5 million, though no Bahamas). Before he left, he wrote a letter to a
Liberal supporter explaining that he would reject any nomination that
had "to be negotiated for."[6] The Liberals were not supposed to ask
Adams what he would do in the White House; they should put him
there because he was a man of honor. This lofty tone damped his
prospects. After six ballots, the Cincinnati convention chose Horace
Greeley, longtime editor of the *New York Tribune,* who had supported
every crackpot enthusiasm from communism to table-rapping to phre-
nological tests for train conductors. Grant crushed him.

Adams would surely have suffered the same fate, and his cold precon-
vention letter may have been an unconsciously prudent way of protect-
ing himself from it. His admirers nevertheless kept proposing him for a
variety of offices, leading Hamilton Fish to write sarcastically of the "an-
nually returning periodical demand" that Adams be "Governor, President—Town Clerk or something." In 1876 Schurz called a meeting of
prominent men in New York to nominate Adams as a Republican, Liberal, or Independent presidential candidate. The meeting was by invita-
tion only—an unpromising base for a national campaign—and nothing
came of it. James G. Blaine offered a regular Republican congressman's
view of the family's political track record: "No Adams ever headed a
party without taking the life out of it." Blaine cited the evidence for this
harsh judgment: John had destroyed the Federalists, John Quincy had
split the first Republicans. The current Republican party "can be beaten
in 1876 and still have a future; but with Charles Francis Adams for a
candidate, it would never have breathed again."[7]

But Adams had something more important to do in his retirement
years than run for president, and that was edit his father's diaries. Instead
of making history, he wanted to publish it.

He had been concerned with the family's history for a long time.
When he was a teenager, he had sat with his aged grandfather while

Gilbert Stuart, himself an old man, painted the president's portrait. Stuart's hands shook so that he feared the paint would be slapped on anyhow, but the brush always touched the right spot. Each decade of his adult life had its own attendant ancestor, whom he wished to capture in words. In his early twenties, he had vainly urged John Quincy to write John's biography; in his early thirties, he had brought out a small selection of Abigail Adams's letters; in his forties, he himself wrote the project his father had abandoned, the biography of John Adams, and brought out a ten-volume edition of his papers. Henry Adams remembered, when he was a boy, reading the proofs of the John Adams papers in the library of the family's Boston house, while Charles Francis sat at another table, planning editorials for the *Daily Whig* (Adams told his son he was careless with punctuation; the son thought his ancestor's prose was dull). Charles Francis began his magnum opus, an edition of his father's diary, after he returned from England in 1868. The work must have been rewarding, because John Quincy's diary is a masterpiece, a lode of glittering observations and judgments, all of them intelligent, some even fair-minded. But it was also taxing: Paul Nagel estimates that the twelve published volumes contain only half of the whole diary. Adams also took a step better to preserve the family papers he was not publishing, adding a stone library to the Quincy house.

The systematic writing of history was a new thing in the family. John and John Quincy were obsessed with history, but they pursued it to satisfy their nervous and promiscuous curiosity, or to lay their hands on some immediately useful point. John wrote long justifications of his career, to little effect, since he was so easily distracted by side issues or temper tantrums. John Quincy could not seriously embark on John's biography because he was too interested in reviving his own public career. Charles Francis stayed the course.

His writing and editing could serve a public purpose. On the eve of the Civil War, Sumner wanted an edition of John Quincy Adams's speeches, to provide ammunition for the coming clash. John Quincy had made some pregnant statements: His references to the Declaration anticipated the Gettysburg Address (1863 minus fourscore and seven years equals 1776), while another of his arguments—that in a civil war or a slave uprising, the government could free slaves under its war powers—

anticipated the Emancipation Proclamation. Adams, who did not want to bring out his father's works piecemeal, did not take the suggestion up. Sometimes Adams's work benefited his political enemies: Blaine, in his assault on the family, said that John Quincy Adams would be remembered chiefly "as the author of a diary conspicuous for its malignity, and father of a son unwise enough to publish it."[8]

But Adams also had a personal purpose in being a historian: He wanted to protect his privacy. Bringing out twenty-plus volumes of family history may seem like a strange way to do it, but it was the way available to him. He had not wanted his father to go back into politics after losing the White House, and he hated being in the public eye "without rest or intermission."[9] He might have blamed himself if he had avoided public life only to polish coins or read ancient history. His family's history was the unchallengeable alternative to public activity. When Adams came back from England, he was offered the presidency of Harvard. He was flattered; a more spiteful man (his father? his grandfather?) might have been pleased at the thought of lording it over a place that had made him take his Latin test twice. But Adams turned the offer down; even such a Brahmin job as that would keep him away from his father's diaries. He would rather write than be president.

Charles Francis Adams should have been the end of his family's dealings with greatness. He had participated in one great moment, the secession Congress of 1860–61, and he had himself done one great deed, helping to keep England out of the war from 1861 to 1863. But the rest of his political career, from 1840 to 1876, was minor or futile. His project in life was to act as a conscientious caretaker. Doing so required the modesty of unarticulated self-knowledge. His soul was not spacious enough to make a greater impact on his country; he served himself and his family instead.

The twelfth and final volume of his father's diaries came off the presses in 1877, not two weeks after his seventieth birthday. He wept as he held it. "I am now perfectly willing to go myself," he wrote in his own diary. "My mission is ended."[10]

Henry Adams

CHAPTER 11

HARLES FRANCIS ADAMS looked like the end of his family's greatness; three of his four sons were children of the aftermath.

John Quincy Adams II, the eldest, told his father, "I want to be left alone" when it came to public life.[1] He accomplished this by being a perennial Democratic candidate for governor in Republican Massachusetts, and by farming that part of the family estate that was most remote from John Adams's house, now called the Old House.

Charles Francis, Jr., the second son, opinionated and strong-willed, joined a Massachusetts cavalry regiment early in the Civil War, thinking it would be a "disgrace" if the Adamses, "of all possible families American, [had] been wholly unrepresented in the field." His unit spent the battle of Antietam on the bank of Antietam Creek, in the eye of a thunderous artillery duel. But it was never ordered into action, and the noise and the strain made him fall asleep. At war's end, when he had risen to the rank of colonel, he did capture and burn Richmond. After the war, railroads struck him as "the most developing force . . . of the day." He moved smoothly from writing exposés of corruption and mismanagement, to being a state railroad regulator, to being a railroad executive, until he was forced to sell his stake in the Union Pacific to a Wall Street operator sharper than he was. "Money-getting," he wrote in his memoirs, a little sourly, "comes from a rather low instinct."[2]

Brooks, the fourth son, clamorous and intense, had the personality of an exploding soda bottle. His wife told him she would call him Brook, since "Brooks" was plural, while he was singular. He became a historian, distinguishing himself, not by searching for laws and patterns—historians have done that since Herodotus—but by searching for laws that would be scientific. He wrote an account of the laws of social decay, which he held to be inevitable, though he thought America might rule the world before it smashed. In his late sixties, he was elected to a convention to revise the Massachusetts state constitution. John Adams had helped write the existing constitution in 1779; his great-grandson now harangued his fellow delegates on the need for a militarized authoritarian state.

All of them were successful and, given the peculiarities of their temperaments, happy. Unlike their uncles and great-uncles, none of them destroyed himself. "By some happy chance," as their brother Henry put it, "they grew up to be decent citizens."[3] They add their particular glints and twists to the texture of American life; their stories could fill a novel, or several paragraphs of a reference work. But a gentleman farmer, a gentleman railroad executive, and a crackpot historian have nothing to do with greatness.

The fourth generation of Adamses is of more than narrative or sociological interest because of the third son, who came between Charles Francis, Jr., and Brooks.

When Henry Adams was born in 1838, it was only seventy-some years since anyone outside Massachusetts had first heard of an Adams. Henry was relatively close in time to his first famous forebears; the iteration of their deeds by his family and his country made them seem closer still. In a letter written in his thirties, Henry would refer to "my uncle Sam."[4] Samuel Adams was his second cousin, three times removed—an awkward distance on a family tree, but the perspective of history foreshortened it.

His grandfather, John Quincy Adams, was present to him in the flesh. Henry remembered that his first "serious contact" with the old man, whom everyone in the family simply called "The President," came one summer day in Quincy when the boy, age five, flew into a "passionate outburst of rebellion" against going to summer school. The door to the president's upstairs library opened, and John Quincy left whatever he had been thinking about—southern wickedness? northern weakness?—to take his grandson's hand and walk him out the door. "After the first moments of consternation," Henry "reflected that an old gentleman close on eighty would never trouble himself to walk near a mile on a hot summer morning over a shadeless road to take a boy to school." But that is what the old gentleman did. Not until Henry was seated at his desk "did the President release his hand and depart."[5] Recalling the incident decades later, Henry was most struck by his grandfather's silence. He neither chided him, nor tried to instruct him. If Henry was remembering accurately, it is one of the few recorded instances of John Quincy Adams refraining from either.

Henry was impressed by his grandfather's eminence, but he also felt at home with it. In another early memory, he recalled that "[t]he Irish gardener once said" to him, "You'll be thinkin' you'll be President too!"[6] What is missing from this line is the setup. Gardeners, even Irish gardeners, do not typically offer such opinions to a child of wealthy employers, unless the child has somehow prompted it. Young Henry may have been putting on innocent airs, or unconsciously anticipating what was due him.

When he was older, his father took him on a trip to Washington, and together they called on President Zachary Taylor at the White House. (Though Taylor's nomination had caused the Conscience Whigs to bolt their party, in office he proved to be more firm on the issue of slavery than they had expected.) The White House was then a relatively simple place. "Outside," Henry remembered, "in a paddock in front, 'Old Whitey,' the President's charger, was grazing . . . and inside the President was receiving callers as simply as if he were in the paddock too." Henry felt no awe. Taylor was only the twelfth president; Adamses still accounted for one-sixth of all who had held the office. Three generations of his family had lived in the White House, and Henry "half thought he owned it, and took for granted that he should some day live in it" too.[7]

Before that day arrived, he would have to think of a career. He made no impression at Harvard, and Harvard made almost no impression on him. After graduating in 1858, he came up with the idea of going to Germany to study the history of European civil law. This scheme foundered when it turned out that he had no interest in law, and a hard time learning German. He passed his time making a grand tour of *Weinstuben*, until his older brother Charles Francis suggested in a letter that he try writing professionally. Henry had been bookish, dreamy, and curious as a boy; the suggestion was inspired. He worried at first that journalism represented a falling off from the family standard: "if it has come to that," he wrote his brother, then "verily . . . mediocrity has fallen on

the name of Adams." Their father cautioned Henry that magazine articles were "ephemeral." These were strange scruples for Adamses to have:
John had written numerous polemics; John Quincy's polemics had
brought him to the attention of George Washington; Samuel and
Charles Francis himself had been editors. On a jaunt to Italy in the
spring of 1860, Henry sent a series of letters to the *Boston Daily Courier*,
which were slight enough, except that he did get to meet Garibaldi
in Palermo shortly after the patriot had conquered Sicily. Garibaldi's
European admirers, wrote Henry, called him "the Washington of Italy,
principally because they know nothing about Washington. Catch Washington invading a foreign kingdom on his own hook, in a fireman's
shirt."[8] The rebel leader was energetic, genial, and opaque. Years later,
Henry decided that Garibaldi was the first man of action he had ever
met, and that he could not understand the type.

On his way south, in Rome, Henry had another important encounter,
with a book: Edward Gibbon's *Memoirs*. He read the grave and melancholy passage describing the moment Gibbon decided to write the *Decline and Fall of the Roman Empire:* "It was at Rome, on the fifteenth of
October 1764, as I sat musing amidst the ruins of the Capitol, while the
barefoot friars were singing vespers in the Temple of Jupiter, that the
idea of writing the decline and fall of the city first started to my mind."
Gibbon was inspired by Rome; Henry was inspired by Gibbon. "Our
house," he wrote his brother, "needs a historian in this generation."[9]

After Henry returned from Europe, he went to Washington to serve
as his father's private secretary during the lame-duck session of Congress, between the 1860 elections and the presidential inauguration in
March 1861. Here were events more pressing than the conquest of Sicily
or the fall of Rome, and he wrote about them for the *Boston Daily Adver-
tizer*, and, more frankly, in letters to his brother Charles Francis. "I want
to have a record of this winter on file . . . a century or two hence when
everything else about us is forgotten, my letters might still be read and
quoted as a memorial of manners and habits at the time of the great secession."[10]

The letters are still readable, a quantum above his Italian notes. "President [Buchanan] divides his time between crying and praying; the Cabinet has resigned or else is occupied in committing treason. Some of

them have done both." "Seward sprawls about . . . and snorts and belches and does all sorts of outrageous things." "Ultra as [Sumner] is, he is the most frightened man round." At times Henry can be as scathing as his grandfather's diary. Senator Stephen Douglas of Illinois "is a brute . . . gross, vulgar, demagogic; a drunkard; ruined as a politician; ruined as a private man; over head and ears . . . in debt; with no mental or literary resources; without a future; with a past worse than none at all." Then, the climax, as surprising as it is sharp: "[O]n the whole I'd rather not be Mrs. Douglas."[11]

His thoughts went back to the past, for encouragement and contrast: Was he living through times as trying as his ancestors had? Was his father performing as well as they did? "Pennsylvania is rotten to the core just as she was in the revolution when John Adams had such a battle with [John] Dickinson." But the present was every bit as exciting. "No man is fit to take hold now, who is not cool as death," he declaimed. "I feel in a continual intoxication in this life. It is magnificent to feel strong and quiet in all this row, and see one's own path clear through all the chaos." So absorbed was Henry in his path that he gave little thought to the paths of others. The South, he wrote, must be "put . . . in the wrong." If the garrison at Fort Sumter "were all murdered in cold blood, it would be an excellent thing for the country, much as I should regret it on the part of those individuals."[12] In the end, the garrison surrendered before the Southern bombardment killed any of them. But no one in Washington, loyal or rebel, sensed how many thousands were about to die.

In May 1861, Henry accompanied his father to England, once again acting as a private secretary, and as a scribe, supplying *The New York Times* with anonymous articles (even though it was against State Department regulations for diplomats to write for the press).

The intimacy of the American minister and his son irked the official assistant secretary of the London legation: The two Adamses, he wrote, "sit upstairs . . . exchanging views on all subjects, and as each considers the other very wise, and both think all they do is right they manage . . . to do some very stupid things." The stupid thing Henry managed to do, seven months after arriving, was to send an anonymous piece to his old outlet the *Courier,* poking mild fun at the after-dinner fare in London houses ("thimblefuls of ice cream and hard seed cakes"). The *Courier,* however, identified Henry as the author, and the London papers, picking up the story, needled the American minister's son as a censorious rube ("this should be a caution to all persons giving parties").[13] Henry writhed, partly from sensitivity, partly from the unnecessary distraction his escapade had caused his hard-pressed father, mainly because he feared his more serious—and more compromising—contributions to the *Times* might be discovered next. He abandoned journalism for the duration.

Henry was forced to emulate his father, saying and doing nothing that might be needlessly provocative. The discovery, the moment they landed, that London had recognized Southern belligerency, was a shock to both of them. "The Ambassador," Henry wrote his brother Charles Francis, "is more snappish and sulky than I have known him to be for a long time." In public, however, his father maintained the necessary façade. "His manner was the same as ever," Henry wrote years later; ". . . not a word escaped; not a nerve twitched."[14] By sharing in his father's performance, he came to admire him greatly.

Henry was observing the war at a double remove. Charles Francis Adams took his cue from external events: instructions from Washington, challenges from the ministry, news from the field, and the reactions of English society to such news. Henry took his cue from his father. The hard seedcakes and thimblefuls of ice cream among which he spent his time were the scrim through which he followed the agonies of armies and the working of the Lincoln administration's mind. Rebel victories heartened the United States' enemies; rebel defeats cast them down. When the North captured New Orleans in May 1862, the news fell on English rebel-lovers like a "blow in the face on a drunken man."[15] Spending the Civil War in London was like a watching a disaster in a dream.

Henry found occasional diversion in the social scene itself (London society was so compact that even someone as minor and unpopular as the private secretary of the American ambassador could get around). He even got a second look at Garibaldi, when he made a visit to London and was lionized. "I discovered poor Garry in a blue military poncho with a red lining, in the middle of a big room," with one duchess "gloating on him . . . in front," while another "hovered heavily, like a bloated and benevolent harpy, on his shoulder," and a third "blandly protected his rear."[16]

Henry hoped that something new and better would arise from the Civil War. Like many other Americans he entertained fantasies of purgation. Europe was full of movements like Garibaldi's, calling themselves Young Italy, Young Germany, and so on, with similar aspirations. Prewar American politics had seemed mired and old: The generation of Clay and Calhoun had gotten its start in the War of 1812; Henry's grandfather had gotten his almost at the Founding. After the war there might be a chance for a fresh start. When the North, after three and a half years of conflict, held a presidential election, pitting Lincoln against George McClellan, a disaffected former general, and Lincoln was peacefully re-elected, it seemed like a downpayment on future triumphs for America and its political system, and Henry's letter to Charles Francis, Jr., glowed with confidence. "I never yet have felt so proud . . . of the great qualities of our race, or so confident of the capacity of men to develop their faculties in the mass. I believe that a new era of the movement of the world will date from that [election], which will drag nations up still another step, and carry us out of a quantity of old fogs."[17]

A month after his second inauguration, and a week after the South surrendered, Lincoln was murdered. Henry got the news in Rome, where he had gone with his mother. Everything conspired to magnify the impact of the killing: the timing; the assassin's theatricality (Booth, the actor, struck in a theater); the fact that assassination was not yet a recurrent episode in American history. Thirty years earlier, when a lunatic had shot harmlessly at President Jackson, John Quincy Adams thought America was becoming like some turbulent Italian republic of the Renaissance. Lincoln's death at the hands of a band of political plotters (who nearly killed Secretary of State Seward the same night) reminded Henry of the deaths that attended Rome's rise to power. "I have . . . buried Mr. Lincoln under the ruins of the Capitol, along with Caesar," he wrote his brother bleakly. "We must have our wars, it appears, and our crimes, as well as other countries."[18]

H ENRY ADAMS MOVED to Washington in October 1868, three months after returning from England. That winter, someone calling at the home of the attorney general "found a strange young man there who was monopolizing the conversation . . . and laying down the law with a certain assumption."[1] As Adams aged, Washingtonians would call on him, and he would sometimes affect taciturnity. But he stayed in Washington most of the rest of his life, and always laid down the law.

Adams belonged to the first generation of his family obliged by fashion to wear unflattering facial hair. As a young man, he sported a drooping mustache; as he aged, he added a short pointed beard. For the rest, he had what one friend called the characteristic look of the family, a broad forehead with "abundant room behind it."[2]

Moving to Washington as he did was an innovation. Adamses had been living there for years, but chiefly to hold office. By going there without an office—and except for a "very high" one, as he wrote his brother Charles Francis, "I would take none"—Henry was professing his interest in politics as such. He cared for the game as well as the ends, and he wanted to be at the center of it. "I gravitate to a capital by a primary law of nature."[3] Unlike his ancestors, he professed his interest in politics; but unlike them he wanted to participate as a commentator and a wirepuller.

Adams's attraction to Washington was also sensual. In the early nineteenth century, the city had been a meager and squalid place, with lawmakers cooped up in boardinghouses and a few declamatory buildings. As the century passed, it filled out, without losing easy access to streams, gullies, and flowering trees. Some of Adams's best writing describes its springs. "The Potomac and its tributaries squandered beauty. Rock Creek was as wild as the Rocky Mountains. Here and there a negro log cabin alone disturbed the dogwood and the judas-tree, the azalea and the laurel. The tulip and the chestnut gave no sense of struggle against a stingy nature. . . . No European spring had . . . the same intermixture of delicate grace and passionate depravity that marked the Maryland May."[4]

Adams briefly pinned his political hopes on the newly elected president Grant. The outgoing administration of Andrew Johnson had marked an apogee of congressional power. Adams's opinion of congressional arrogance was heightened by the fact that Senator Charles Sumner, who had been a family enemy since Adams's father sided with Seward, denied his eldest brother, John Quincy II, a post in the Boston Customs House. Grant the hero might be the force who could bring Sumner and other barons of Congress to heel.

These hopes were unrealistic. The dominant Republican party had its established powers, and as a political novice, Grant let them be. His failure to do what was expected of him turned Adams permanently against him. For the next forty years, the subject of Grant would call forth all of Adams's resources of wit and condescension. In 1869 Adams made his first call on President and Mrs. Grant. He found the General "smoking as usual." Their conversation was "rather dull . . . I chattered, however . . . and I flatter myself it was I who showed them how they ought to behave. One feels such an irresistible desire, as you know, to tell this kind of individual to put themselves at their ease and talk just as though they were at home." The Grants were at home; they were in the White House. But could the mere fact of the election of 1868 give them better title to it than he had? Eight years earlier, Adams's father had written of President and Mrs. Lincoln, after calling on them, that they were not "at home in this sphere of civilization."[5] Grant and Lincoln were very different from each other, but both were beyond the Adamses' understanding or sympathy.

In the wake of the war, the country was awash in economic energies that were arguably more important than who occupied the White House. Railroad mileage doubled; capital investment in railroads tripled. Much of this expansion was vital and productive; the North's superior railroad network had helped it win the Civil War; in peacetime railroads brought midwestern wheat to the world market. But both the

federal and state governments subsidized needless construction—
"railroads from nowhere to nowhere," as Cornelius Vanderbilt put it[6]—
and allowed railroad companies to manipulate their own stock for the
benefit of their directors. The grease in both transactions was supplied
by bribery. Henry's brother Charles Francis was right to see that railroads were the country's most developing force, but Henry was equally
right to have gravitated to politics as a vantage point for observing them.

The postwar economy cast up strange types. Jay Gould, son of a New
York farmer, was a quiet, austere little man. "Perhaps," one journalist
wrote, "you could not put a napkin ring over his foot and push it up to his
knees; I am not certain." Gould's partner in many a venture, Jim Fisk,
was his opposite, a strapping peddler's son with a brash and brassy manner and a gift for a phrase. Together they controlled the Erie Railroad,
one of the nation's three main arteries to the east coast. In an effort to
fight off one hostile takeover, Gould and Fisk spent hundreds of thousands of dollars bribing New York legislators. In another such struggle,
they hired hundreds of New York City gang members to battle for physical control of a strategic upstate railroad station. When their bruisers
were beaten, Fisk remarked that "nothing is lost save honor."[7]

Charles Francis, Jr., wrote about the various Erie wars; Henry picked
up the trail of Gould and Fisk when their next scheme encompassed
Washington. During the war the country had gone on a double monetary
standard: gold, plus paper money—or greenbacks—printed at will by
Congress. Greenbacks had stabilized since the high inflation of the war,
but there was still enough differential in price to encourage speculation. In
the summer of 1869, Gould and Fisk decided to corner the gold market.

The success of their efforts depended on the federal government not
selling any of its gold reserves, which were many times larger than all the
available gold on the open market. Gould sought to guarantee the government's inactivity by establishing a relationship with President
Grant's brother-in-law, one Abel Rathbone Corbin. Gould opened a
gold account for Corbin with no margin (that is, he gave it to him). In
return, Corbin acted as a listening post in the White House and enabled
Gould and Fisk to socialize with the president on vacations.

In New York, where gold was traded, Gould and Fisk drove the price
steadily higher. The White House finally understood that something

was afoot about the same time New York merchants holding gold contracts tired of the speculative frenzy. In September Grant told a servant
he no longer wanted to see Gould, because he "was always trying to get
something out of him."[8] The bubble broke in New York, just as the federal government was about to begin selling off its gold. Telegraph wires
carrying the news of plunging prices melted with the sudden volume of
sales. A few small fry were ruined, though Gould and Fisk seem to have
emerged unscathed. Fisk's career ended some years later when he was
murdered by his mistress's lover; Gould ultimately drove Charles Francis
Adams, Jr., from the Union Pacific Railroad.

Henry Adams described the spectacle in a lively article called "The
New York Gold Conspiracy." Gould's "nature," he wrote gleefully, "suggested survival from the family of spiders; he spun webs, in corners and
in the dark." Fisk was "large, florid, gross, talkative and obstreporous . . .
a young butcher in appearance and mind."[9] He offered the piece to an
English quarterly, seeking the snob value of foreign publications, but the
journal refused it on the grounds that it was libelous; the *Westminster Review,* another quarterly, published it in 1870.

The article satisfied Adams's standards for both journalism and personal advancement. "[T]he easiest way" to make a mark, he said, "is to do
something obnoxious and to do it well." Economic polemic was a new
field of interest in his family. His ancestors had opposed champions of
the business class for political or moral reasons having little to do with
economic theory. John Adams had supported Alexander Hamilton's financial program when it was being enacted, and only turned on Hamilton when he suspected the former treasury secretary of scheming with
his disloyal cabinet. John Quincy Adams and Henry's father opposed
Cotton Whigs for doing the south's bidding, but supported most of the
economic policies—a national bank, protective tariffs—they endorsed.
Henry's opinions at this point were a mixture of conservative and critical. He thought speculation in gold could be ended by a single gold standard. At the same time, he wrote that "the corporation" was "in its nature
a threat against . . . popular institutions."[10]

Adams's journalism had a definite political goal in view: to replace the
current set of leading Republican politicians with another, consisting of
his friends and soulmates. "We despise all the people in control," he

wrote an English friend.[11] One of the politicians he approved of was
Carl Schurz, the Missouri German. Another was James Garfield, a poor
Ohio farm boy who had become a professor of ancient languages. As a
congressman, Garfield investigated the gold conspiracy and submitted a
report that damned Gould, Fisk, and the monetary system, and was not
flattering to Grant.

Adams thought himself engaged in an effort to arrest the deteriora-
tion of American political culture. The Grant administration, he
claimed, had brought in a new class of men, displacing the selfless public
servant of yore, who held "his moral rules on the sole authority of his
own conscience, indifferent to opposition whether in or out of his party,
obstinate to excess . . ." This was the Adams family self-description
going back three generations; the age of the lament suggested that the
new class of selfish politician Henry reproved was not that new. Adams
was well aware that most of his allies were not politicians, but journalists,
and that they accomplished, at least initially, nothing more than hubbub.
"I have had a political convention of half the greatest newspaper editors
in the country at my rooms," he wrote one friend tongue-in-cheek,
". . . and the foundations of Hell were shaken." He did hope, however, in
time to found nothing less than "a new party."[12]

In 1870 he took a step away from Washington that was actually less
far than it seemed. Charles Eliot, president of Harvard, asked him to
teach medieval history. Adams told Eliot that he knew nothing about
the subject. "If you will point out to me anyone who knows more, Mr.
Adams," Eliot replied, "I will appoint him."[13] Eliot wanted mental ability, confident that expertise would follow. Adams moved back to Boston
for seven years.

He disliked the city for its dullness and its climate and had mixed
feelings about his alma mater. The main perquisite of his job, however,
pleased him greatly: Harvard hired him in part to relieve the chairman of
his department of the responsibilities of editing the *North American Review,* the country's premier serious journal of ideas. As editor Adams
could make article assignments to the likes of "Harry (or better, if he
would) Willy James,"[14] and use the *Review* as a platform for his own political opinions. Moving to Harvard to edit the *Review* recalled his father leaving the legislature to edit the *Daily Whig.*

He added to his course load History VI, on American history from 1789 to 1840, a subject closer to home. He must have been an excellent teacher. His classroom manner was brusque: When one medieval history student asked him to explain the doctrine of transubstantiation, he snapped, "How should I know? Look it up." "He awakened opposition to his own views," remembered Henry Cabot Lodge, one of his students, "and that is one great secret of success in teaching."[15] When Lodge—who was also a political heir, the great-grandson of a Federalist senator—joined the Harvard faculty himself, Adams proposed to Eliot that two sections of his American history course be offered: one taught by himself, reflecting his (and John Quincy Adams's) Republican views, the other taught by Lodge from the viewpoint of Federalism. Eliot, unhappily, rejected the idea, and Adams and Lodge would carry on their disputes through the medium of books.

He kept up with his political plotting from Boston. During his father's doomed bid for the Liberal Republican nomination in 1872, Henry was out of the country. But he became active again as Grant's second term wound down. "As yet," he wrote early in 1875, "I have only three allies: a broken-down German politician [Schurz]; a newspaper correspondent [Horace White, of the *Chicago Tribune*], and a youth of twenty who is to do all the work [Lodge]. With these instruments I propose to do no less than decide the election of 1876." Adams's first thought was "to force my father on the parties."[16] Eighteen seventy-six was the Centennial Year, and who would be a more fitting president than John Adams's grandson? But that idea never caught fire; what the country got instead was a deadlock in the Electoral College, broken by a process as drawn-out and acrid as the endgames of the elections of 1800 and 1824. Adams foreswore active politicking after this election, though in 1881 he did invest twenty thousand dollars in the *New York Evening Post*, with the understanding that Schurz would become editor.

What did Adams want from his failed third parties? In one letter he defined his agenda as "revenue reform, free trade, and what not." "What not" included a gold standard and replacing patronage appointees with civil servants. These sound suspiciously like what historian Forrest McDonald has called "ideal issue[s] from the politicians' point of view": "an ideal issue . . . had little substance and was ethically neutral but could in-

flame voters as if it were a primal moral cause."[17] Adams's agenda was
not quite as meretricious at that: Trade and currency, badly managed, can
stunt a nation; the evils of patronage, which grew with the size of the
federal government—fifty thousand employees by 1870—were made
lurid in 1881 when Adams's friend, James Garfield, newly elected president, was murdered by a disappointed office-seeker. Missing from
Adams's goals was any plan for the South or its freed slaves. During the
war, he thought the North should establish a system of military colonies,
on the Roman model, of veterans and free blacks, scattered throughout
the South, under direct federal control. As plantation agriculture withered, these would become the pattern for southern development. But
once the war ended he gave the problem no more thought.

Adams suffered, as a would-be politician, from his time spent abroad
during the Civil War. If he had a more immediate experience of the
struggle, he might have realized that it had fixed the political loyalties,
and the two-party system of 1860, for a century. New parties would
arise, but they would never have the success of the Republicans, or the
Whigs.

In 1872, Adams had taken time out from teaching and politics to
marry Marian Hooper, the daughter of a rich Boston eye doctor. Four
years younger than Adams, Marian (known as Clover) was tart and spirited. The novelist Henry James called her "a perfect Voltaire in petti-
coats." "She talks garrulously," Adams wrote, "but on the whole pretty
sensibly."[18] The couple took a year-long honeymoon trip to Europe and
Egypt.

The great call on his time began to be historical writing. He focused
on the period covered by his Harvard course (what might be called the
middle period of his family), particularly the middle of the middle—the
ascendancy of the first Republican party, from Jefferson's first election
through the War of 1812. In five years, from 1877 to 1882, he produced
five books that covered the subject, written with a journalist's speed and
frequently a journalist's dazzle.

The first was an answer to Henry Cabot Lodge, who had written a bi-
ography of his Federalist ancestor, George Cabot. Lodge had painted
Cabot as a moderate, opposed to secessionist extremists like Timothy
Pickering. Adams, drawing on materials collected by his grandfather

John Quincy, sought to show that all New England Federalists had been implicated in schemes of disunion. This was score-settling, refighting the civil war between his family and their neighbors. Next came a biography, and a collection of the papers, of Albert Gallatin, the Republican treasury secretary who had been one of the American commissioners at the Treaty of Ghent. Adams's treatment of Gallatin was earnest and respectful, and a little solemn: He admired Gallatin because he was a statesman/financier, not a political campaigner; because he had been a scholar who had written on American Indian ethnography; and because he had worked with his grandfather. His next two books—written in two months—were in a different spirit. For the American Statesman Series, a collection of biographies by the Boston publisher Houghton Mifflin, Adams offered Aaron Burr and John Randolph. The publisher asked if an amoral plotter like Burr was a suitable figure for memorializing as an American statesman; Adams remarked that Burr resembled many statesmen he had seen in postwar Washington.

With his book on Randolph, Adams created a masterpiece of malice. Randolph was held up for examination like some gaudy and repellent beetle. Every sixty- or seventy-five-year-old insult the Virginian had directed against John or John Quincy Adams was repaid with compound interest. "During [his] last years," Adams wrote, "Randolph was like a jockey, thrown early out of the race, who rides on, with antics and gesticulations, amid the jeers and wonder of the crowd. . . . He despised the gaping clowns who applauded him, even while he enjoyed amusing them. He despised himself, perhaps, more than all the rest."[19]

Yet on one issue, Adams endorsed his family's old enemy. In the 1790s, the Georgia legislature had sold a 35-million-acre tract of frontier called the Yazoo country to northern land speculators (every member of the legislature but one received a kickback). A popular backlash swept in new legislators, who indignantly rescinded the deal. The ensuing claims and counterclaims wound through the courts and appeared before Congress. Alexander Hamilton gave his legal opinion that the contract was valid. James Madison tried to broker a compromise. The case of the speculators, when it appeared before the Supreme Court, was argued by John Quincy Adams (his last appearance before the Court until the *Amistad* case). Randolph sided entirely with the people of

Georgia and made "Yazoo men" an epithet for corruption. Henry Adams, thinking of his journalism, agreed. "Were a state legislature to-day bribed by a great railroad company to confer a grant of exclusive privileges, fatal to the public interests . . . it would be dangerous to the public safety to affirm that the people could never free themselves from this servitude."[20] On the issue of corruption, the old Republican and the Liberal Republican joined hands; journalistic experience trumped even family loyalty.

All these works were tributaries to a great gathering project, a history of the Jefferson and Madison administrations. (Adams's Burr book, which never appeared—evidently Houghton Mifflin was unpersuaded by his joke—was cannibalized for the larger work.) He expected it to take at least ten years: "it will exhaust all that I have to say in this world, I hope."[21] In 1877 he gave up his Harvard post and moved back to Washington, where he would have the time and the resources to work. Adams's political friends gave him a desk at the State Department and access to its files; when he traveled abroad, he got his foreign friends, now foreign ministers and diplomats, to open the archives of Britain, France, and Spain.

Adams's project represented a change of direction. "I am satisfied," he told a friend, "that literature offers higher prizes" than politics. But Adams still valued Washington as a vantage and a stimulus. He could see scenes he wrote about, and rub up against the sharp minds of observant Washingtonians. One of the most observant was a dear friend, John Hay. Adams had met the Indiana-born Hay in Washington in 1861. "Friends," Adams would write, "are born, not made." He and Hay had almost parallel lives. They were the same age; they both spent the Civil War as private secretaries, Hay to the man who taught him law, Abraham Lincoln. They both wrote: In the 1870s Hay was famous for *Pike County Ballads*, a book of light verse in dialect, which is not quite as tedious at it sounds, and he had begun a biography of Lincoln. But Hay was a successful politician; he did not try to hew out new parties, as Adams had, but stuck with the Republican establishment. "I never could understand why," Adams wrote an English friend, "except that I never knew more than two or three men born west of the Alleghenies who knew the difference between a gentleman and a swindler."[22] As a result,

Hay served as assistant secretary and secretary of state. He had the career Adams might have had; by being his friend, Adams experienced it vicariously. Hay and Adams began building new houses on Lafayette Square, opposite the White House, an address that symbolized Adams's political stance—intimately aloof.

Photographs taken at this time, by Marian, who had become an avid amateur photographer, show a dapper little man, whom one can easily believe to be smart and lively. When he is playing with one of their big-eared Skye terriers, master and creature rather resemble each other.

The pictures are winning. The life is not entirely so. There now seeps into Adams's writing the arsenic whiff of unrelieved irony, the by-product of forswearing power. His youthful comments on Stephen Douglas or Garibaldi had been sharp; so had his judgments of Gould and Fisk. He was still sharp, though he increasingly pretended to be flippant. He studied the passing scene, though he pretended to be above it all. There was no pretense in his scorn, but what is the effect of spending so much time among what we scorn? Henry James, who liked Adams and his wife, was alive to this quality. "They are eagerly anxious to hear what I have seen and heard at places which they decline to frequent . . . after I had dined with Blaine [the congressman who had summarized the family so bitingly in 1876], they fairly hung upon my lips." He put them in a short story about Washington, entitled "Pandora," in which he gave them a surname that was probably more mocking than he intended: Bonnycastle. "Let us be vulgar and have some fun," says Mr. Bonnycastle, planning a party—"Let us invite the President." [23] Adams's father had written in his diary that he had met "vulgar" people at Henry Clay's. But he had meant it as a simple judgment. His snobbery had a certain dignity to it. Adams/Bonnycastle meant his put-downs too, but offering them to the public as bon mots drained them of dignity.

Adams's novel of Washington life, *Democracy*, perfectly captured this voice. He published it anonymously in 1880. The hunt for the author became a Washington parlor game; Hay and Marian Adams were among the suspects. *Democracy* has been overpraised since the day it appeared. The greatest nineteenth-century American writers spent much of their time on Indians, whales, and black cats. They barely scratched New York; they did not attempt Washington. *Democracy* stands out by default. Everybody notices the same handful of epigrams and set pieces; yet the book as a whole is creaking and melodramatic. Poor Grant takes another beating: The fictional president and his wife are described at a reception as a pair of "toy dolls." Blaine gets paid off by serving as model for the villain, Senator Ratcliffe (the surnames, when they attempt humor, are not very funny: A rich Liberal Republican is called Schneidekoupon—coupon clipper).

The only vital writing occurs during a trip that the characters take to Mount Vernon. "Why was it," the heroine thinks bitterly, "that everything Washington touched, he purified, even down to the associations of his house? and why is it that everything we touch seems soiled? Why do I feel unclean when I look at Mount Vernon?"[24] The weakness of this passage is its sentimentality, which springs from its cynicism. Washington was noble; but he was not inhuman, nor did he live in a purely golden age. His great colleagues made many mistakes; his not-great colleagues included Benedict Arnold and Aaron Burr. Adams could have used his historical perspective for wisdom. Living in his own and his grandfather's lifetime simultaneously might have given him stereoscopic vision, enriching his image of each. Instead he used Washington as a stick to beat the present. It was as childish as saying that the eighteenth century was inferior to the nineteenth because it lacked steam engines and cameras.

In 1880 Henry and Marian Adams formed a circle within their circle, consisting of themselves, the Hays, and Clarence King, a wealthy geologist with a black common-law wife. They called themselves the Five of Hearts, and wrote little notes to each other on Five of Hearts stationery. The house on Lafayette Square grew, watered by buckets of money. The Brooks inheritance had multiplied over the years, and Adams was a rich man. He already owned a collection of Old Master drawings and Turners; for the new house, he spotted "a small slab" of green onyx "so exquisite as to make my soul yearn."[25] But all the while his history proceeded. The world forgives many antics in return for good work.

Work stopped at the end of 1885 when Adams, coming to his wife's room to ask if she would see a caller, found her on the floor, dead from a dose of potassium cyanide (one of her darkroom chemicals). The *Boston Evening Transcript*, that aegis of the upper class (Boston joke: "There are five reporters to see you, and a gentleman from the *Transcript*"), concealed the fact that she had killed herself, but other papers up and down the east coast soon ran the truth.

When Henry and Marian had gotten engaged, Charles Francis, Jr., blurted out that all her family were "crazy as coots"; Marian's aunt had been a suicide. Marian had had serious bouts of depression before; her father, to whom she was deeply attached, had died earlier in the year. But these were occasions, not causes. Henry James perhaps came closer to an explanation of her suicide when he wrote in a letter of "the sad story" of "poor Mrs. Adams [who] found, the other day, the solution to the knottiness of existence."[26] Solutions are found; they are choices.

After three weeks of shock, Adams, who had refused to see anyone outside his family, at length began answering the letters of his many friends. "I feel," he wrote Hay, "like a volunteer in his first battle. If I don't run ahead at full speed, I shall run away . . . my only chance of saving whatever is left of my life" is to go "straight ahead without looking behind."[27]

CHAPTER 13

JOHN QUINCY ADAMS had a major stroke at the age of seventy-nine, and though he survived it, he considered the remainder of his life to be posthumous. After his wife's death, Henry Adams, age forty-seven, had more than three decades still to live. He treated them as a premature old age. At fifty-five, he called himself a "poor old ghost," who "pretend[ed] to be alive when noticed." At fifty-seven, he said he had "not enough vitality left to be sensual" (at that age, his grandfather had enough vitality left to run for president). When he became actually old, he pretended to be ageless. When he was seventy, he wrote that he was 1.2 trillion years old. *The New York Times* went him one better, referring to him as "the late Henry Adams."[1]

He could not, as his ancestors had done, take pleasure in his successful children, because he was childless.[2] His older brothers both had families. Adamses would go on, but they would not be his Adamses. Henry Adams, defined as a descendant, knew himself to be a terminus. He tried other strategies for living without his wife, and with the knowledge that she had killed herself, in their home, with the chemicals she had used to develop pictures of, among other subjects, him.

The first strategy was silence. *The Education of Henry Adams*, a memoir he wrote almost twenty years after her death, makes a break in his life, from 1871 to 1892—all the years of their marriage, and his most immediate grief. Mrs. Adams's name never appears. There is a description of the statue he commissioned for her grave, in the passionate depravity of Rock Creek Park, from his friend, Augustus St. Gaudens, the greatest American sculptor of the day. Adams wanted a Buddha, inspired by images he had seen in Japan, representing contemplation and nirvana. The statue St. Gaudens produced, though not oriental, was calm—a hooded figure, of ambiguous sex. There was neither name nor inscription. Adams

enjoyed sitting at a distance from it and overhearing the puzzled comments of tourists; he would make none himself.

The second strategy was motion. He was already a habitué of London
and Paris, and in 1871 he had taken a trip to the Rocky Mountains, then
true wilderness (that was where he had met Clarence King). For the rest
of his life his travels spanned the globe. He went to Asia, the Pacific, and
the Arctic Circle. He met the royal family of Tahiti (dispossessed, like
the Adamses) and wrote a history of them. He measured the waists and
hips of girls in Samoa and visited the temple of the Buddha's Tooth in
Ceylon. He poured his impressions into spacious letters to his friends, or
into later writing. "One delights to see splendid men and women," he
wrote from the South Seas, ". . . and no clothes." "Could inertia of race,
on such a scale," he wondered of Russia, "ever be broken up, or take new
form?" Mexican peasants had, he thought, "the peculiar look . . . that the
Roman empire left forever on its slave-provinces." When the automobile was invented, he became a devotee. "My idea of paradise," he once
wrote, "is a perfect automobile going thirty miles an hour on a smooth
road to a twelfth-century cathedral." [3] There were many times when his
idea of paradise was to be going thirty miles an hour, anywhere.

A third strategy was hatred. Anger—with his wife, with himself—on
the scale that he felt it would be intolerable. Suppose, instead, that it was
the property of malignant others, and that whatever residue still remained with him could be safely directed at them? His journalism suggested an outlet. The finaglers of Wall Street were now joined by the
finaglers of international finance. Prompted by the economic theories of
his brother Brooks, he changed his mind about the gold standard. What,
in his days as a Liberal Republican, he had thought of as sound money,
now struck him as a deflationary trap, putting all the world, from farmers to Adamses, at the mercy of European financiers.

Many of them, as Adams saw it, were Jews. His rancorous opinions
about Jews break out in his books only in pustules, though they riot
through his correspondence. Two late references, in his memoirs, are
more interesting than the run-of-the-mill pornography of aversion.
After describing his birth, Adams adds that if he had been born "in
Jerusalem under the shadow of the Temple . . . under the name of Israel
Cohen," he would have been "not much more heavily handicapped in the

races of the coming century . . ." Later on, describing his return from England after the Civil War, he introduces two more hypothetical Jews, arriving, like him, on the boat. "[N]ot a furtive Yacoob or Ysaac . . . snarling a weird yiddish to the officers of the customs—but had a keener instinct, an intenser energy, and a freer hand than he."[4] Isaac Cohen and Henry Adams start out equally unprepared for modern American life. Yacoob and Ysaac, it seems, are better prepared. But in both cases the comparison is notably personal. Being a Jew and being an Adams have in fact certain similarities. Both are hereditary distinctions. Both are serious matters—Judaism is a religion, Adamshood is close to it. Adams picked an enemy who was somewhat like him.

The final strategy was work. The long end of his life was his period of achievement. Almost by chance, he had more political effect than in all his partisan scheming. More important, he published three major books, one of which is great.

Adams's *History of the United States in the Administrations of Thomas Jefferson and James Madison* came out from 1889 to 1891. It contains delightful things. The portrait of Jefferson is critical, even harsh, without losing sympathy. Using well-chosen quotations, Adams makes a grave comedy out of his White House etiquette. A "tall, high-boned man came into the room. He was dressed, or rather undressed, in an old brown coat, red waistcoat, old corduroy small-clothes much soiled, woollen hose, and slippers without heels. I thought him a servant, when General Varnum surprised me by announcing that it was the President."[5] Aaron Burr winds through the story of the Jefferson administration like a snake.

But the vast bulk of the *History*'s many, many pages are written with a studied flatness of tone. Adams seems determined not to let himself go. He does not want any writerly flourishes or picturesque events to distract from his lesson, which is that no leaders are great men.

No one knows what he is doing; every judgment is wrong; all plans go awry. Worse, every leader betrays his principles: Republicans, libertarian and pacific, once in power impose an embargo and wage war; Federalists, proud nationalists, once out of power plot treason and secession. Americans, Adams declared, could not face the intellectual and moral vacuum at the seat of power, then or later: "they adorned with imaginary qualities scores of supposed leaders, whose only merit was their faculty of reflecting a popular trait."[6]

Some reviewers saw this relentless debunking as a paying off of old family scores, like his book on New England Federalism: The *History*, wrote one, offered the "prejudices and hatreds of the elder Adams [John] and his son." But that is not fair. John Quincy Adams is not spared; when he appears onstage to lead the negotiations in Ghent, he must be saved from disaster by Gallatin and Bayard. "I am at times almost sorry that I ever undertook to write" the *History*, Adams complained in midwork, for its main actors "appear to me like mere grass-hoppers, kicking and gesticulating, in the middle of the Mississippi river." In the *History* itself, this image was transformed into a lurid description of the aftermath of Napoleon's 1808 invasion of Spain, which Adams saw as the turning point of the world war. "Spain, France, Germany, England, were swept into a vast and bloody torrent which dragged America, from Montreal to Valparaiso, slowly into its movement; while the familiar figures of famous men . . . emperors, generals, presidents, conspirators, patriots, tyrants, and martyrs by the thousand,—were borne away by the stream, struggling, gesticulating"—echo of the grasshoppers—"praying, murdering, robbing."[7]

However caustic, the *History* was not hopeless—for there could still be a great people. The first six chapters, describing the condition of the United States in 1800, was a tough-minded love letter to ordinary Americans. In the backcountry beyond the Appalachians "pioneers were at work, cutting into the forests with the energy of so many beavers, and with no more express moral purpose than the beavers they drove away." Europeans, and skeptical Americans, saw this activity as mere greed: Dollars were the average American's god, "and a sordid avarice his demon." But accompanying and ennobling the greed was hope: What "any inventor or discoverer must [see] in order to give him the energy of success." America invited men to partake of a national wealth that was as yet mostly uncreated; the openness of the offer tapped reservoirs of energy and devotion. "The poor came, and from them were seldom heard complaints of deception or delusion. Within a moment, by the mere contact of a moral atmosphere, they saw . . . the summer cornfields and the glowing continent."[8] America's natural resources were not gold or coal, but opportunity and the people the opportunity attracted.

From time to time Adams brought forward enterprising individuals as symbols of this frame of mind. Sometimes they were fighting men. The *Chesapeake,* the frigate whose capture by the *Leopard* was the great humiliation of the prewar years, fired one shot before its colors were struck because W. H. Allen, a third lieutenant, carried a burning coal in his fingers to a gun. Sometimes they were inventors, such as Robert Fulton and John Fitch, designers of steam engines and steam boats. There lurked a danger in Adams's admiration for Fulton and Fitch, for their work was scientific, which prompted Adams to think scientifically in turn: "knowing the rate of increase of population and of wealth," he wrote in his summary, Americans "could read in advance their economical history for at least a hundred years."[9] In this passage formulae have taken the place of hope as an explanatory principle; things happen because they have to. But Adams did not cancel his introduction, which still shaped all that followed. The men who do great things are sailors and boat makers, and they stand for millions of their fellows. Adams can't be one of them, but he can describe them.

In the 1890s, Adams fortuitously returned to active war and politics. His friend Clarence King, recovering from a nervous breakdown, suggested a trip to Cuba. The two men spent a month in the British consul's country house outside the southern city of Santiago early in 1894. Exploring the countryside, King fell in with Cubans who chafed at Spanish rule, and he interested Adams in their cause.

American southerners had coveted Cuba as a slave state in the 1850s. Northern veterans had helped in a failed revolution after the Civil War. Adams and King now lobbied for the United States to drive Spain out of the Caribbean. Their coconspirators included Henry Cabot Lodge, who had abandoned third parties for regular Republican politics—"Make yourself as useful and as busy as you can,"[10] Adams had said encouragingly when he first ran for office—and was now a senator from Massachusetts; James Cameron, senator from Pennsylvania and, equally important in the Washington status system, husband of the lovely and intelligent Elizabeth Cameron (Adams was one of many men smitten with her); and John Sherman, senator from Ohio, who happened to be Mrs. Cameron's uncle. All three senators served on the Foreign Relations Committee, which Sherman chaired. Adams's scruples about con-

gressional power subsided when congressmen and their wives agreed
with him.

Another plotter was a friend of Lodge's, Theodore Roosevelt. Twenty
years younger than Adams, Roosevelt was also a seventh-generation
American, of a family of Dutch New York merchants. Sickly and excitable
as a child, he had turned himself into a robust and excitable young man
through boxing and weight lifting. His brief career—he was not yet
forty—had already been a blizzard of heterogeneous activity. He wrote a
history of the naval war of 1812 and two biographies for the same series for
which Adams had done John Randolph (Roosevelt's were more fair, and
less interesting). He hunted and ranched in the west, and led a posse after
cattle thieves (he read Matthew Arnold during the dull parts of the chase).

He got into politics as a Republican reformer in Tammany New York.
"He was a young Harvard man," as H. L. Mencken would put it, "scan-
dalized by the discovery that his town was run by men with such names
as Michael O'Shaunessy and Terence Googan." Elected to the New
York state assembly, the freshman legislator appeared in Albany wearing
a monocle and a cutaway coat. "He carried a gold-headed cane in one
hand [and] a silk hat in the other. . . . His trousers were as tight as a tailor could make them, and had a bell-shaped bottom to cover his shoes."
A colleague asked, "Who's the dude?" Over time, Roosevelt would become known by his flashing spectacles and teeth. Edith Wharton con-
flated the two field markings, when she described him "gnashing his
eyeglasses."[11] Roosevelt served as New York City police commissioner,
enraging Republican German-Americans by enforcing Sunday saloon
closings, and finished last in a three-way race for mayor. It was hard to
say whether he was rising politically or exploding, but he was full of energy and committed to the Cuban cause.

Adams ghosted a Foreign Relations Committee report for Senator
Cameron that called for Cuban independence, and Lodge pushed the
Republican convention of 1896 to adopt an independence plank. After
William McKinley, the Republican nominee, won the election, he made
Roosevelt assistant secretary of the navy. "Better a[n] over-readiness to
fight," Roosevelt declared in his maiden address to the Naval War Col-
lege, than "tame submission to injury, or cold-blooded indifference to
the misery of the oppressed."[12]

Adams was traveling with Hay in Egypt when he learned of the explosion of the American battleship *Maine* in Havana harbor. Though the disaster is now known to have been accidental, it was then attributed to Spanish skulduggery. The details of the ensuing war did not interest Adams—he assumed that the stronger power would prevail, through the simple application of its force—though he would take personal, and family, pride in Spain's expulsion from the hemisphere. It seemed a fulfillment of the Monroe Doctrine. He had, he wrote, "won all my stakes"—which included his grandfather's as well.[13]

Roosevelt, meanwhile, was pursuing the stakes of Washington, Jackson, and Grant—victory and reputation. He quit his Navy post and went to Cuba as lieutenant-colonel of a volunteer cavalry regiment of cowboys and swells. In the run-up to the siege of Santiago, Roosevelt's unit captured two key hills, and instant glory. A friend described him "reveling in victory and gore." Roosevelt's adventure made him in quick succession governor of New York, McKinley's running mate in 1900, and, after McKinley was shot by an anarchist six months into his new term, president of the United States, at the age of forty-two. "So Teddy is President!" Adams exclaimed in Stockholm when he learned the news. "Is not that stupendous!"[14]

In the event, Adams's newfound proximity to power—closer than at any point in his life—depressed and irritated him. He sent Mrs. Cameron accounts of dining at the White House that were simultaneously childish, spiteful, and hilarious. "[W]hat annoys me is [Roosevelt's] infantile superficiality with his boyish dogmatism of assertion. He lectures me on history as though he were a high-school pedagogue. Of course I fall back instantly on my favorite protective pose of ignorance, which aggravates his assertions." "We were overwhelmed in a torrent of oratory, and at last I heard only the repetition of I-I-I . . . it is mortifying beyond even drunkenness. The worst of it is that it is mere cerebral excitement. . . . We are a boys' school run wild."[15]

Adams and Roosevelt could never have gotten along for any extended period of time. Although both men had fundamentally sensitive natures, Roosevelt's was hedged with muscle and bluster, Adams's with irony. Their defenses were at odds. Roosevelt could not be patronized like Zachary Taylor or Ulysses Grant. He and Adams came from the same

social class, give or take a few presidents; if Roosevelt was not as intelligent as Adams, he was quite intelligent enough (if he had been smarter,
Adams probably would have liked him even less). Roosevelt was a rebuke to Adams's chosen course in life: He had entered the political fray,
as Adams had in his thirties, but he had stayed in it and come out on top.
Perhaps he cast a garish light on the family's earlier achievements: Was it
the loss of such dinners that had embittered John's last years, or the pursuit of them that had consumed John Quincy's middle ones? However
irksome Adams found his host, he still relished the dinners: "one wants
to listen," he wrote Elizabeth Cameron, "at the key-hole. I think this
place is now the political center of the world."[16]

Adams was more comfortable viewing the world through the
medium of his friend Hay, whom McKinley had made secretary of state
as the Spanish-American War ended, and whom Roosevelt continued in
the post. Adams rather romantically saw Hay as an American Metter-
nich, forging with treaties a modern pax Americana in Europe, the
Western Hemisphere, and the Far East. Thinking so gratified an old
family habit of seeing advisors—the Gallatins and the Sewards—as
more important than the Jeffersons and Lincolns they served.

He found the flower of his life, not in Cuba or the White House, but
in France. In the summer of 1895, just after the beginning of his Cuban
adventure, he and the Lodges took a tour of Gothic cathedrals, mostly in
Normandy. Before he left, he had been oppressed with a sense of his own
"moral death." Seeing these buildings made him feel reborn. They
seemed to make all later art "vulgar."[17] As he did with every thought, he
studied this one, then wrote it up. The result was a book, published privately in 1904, publicly in 1913, *Mont Saint Michel and Chartres*.

The book announces its stylistic and mental departure almost from
the beginning. In a two-page preface Adams invites the reader to consider himself one of the author's nieces; an avuncular Adams will then
act as guide on an artistic lecture tour. This is an amiable version of
Adams's late manner: a little self-conscious, a little fussy, a little too
whimsical. But when Chapter 1 alights at the Abbey of Mont Saint
Michel on the French coast, it is like bursting open a door: "The
Archangel loved heights. Standing on the summit of the tower that
crowned his church, wings upspread, sword uplifted, the devil crawling

beneath." Adams had never used such phrases before: clean, clear, direct. He describes the archangel, the sea, and the age: "The man who wanders into the twelfth century is lost, unless he can grow prematurely young."[18] Other tones of voice will follow, including fussiness; including, alas, from time to time, rancor. But this opening, alert as its subject, hooks the reader and carries him through the next sixteen chapters.

Adams shows how deeply drawn in he himself is when he imagines, in the next few pages, that he must have Norman ancestors. Before the Normans built Mont Saint Michel, they had conquered England in 1066; since then there have been twenty-eight or thirty generations "from father to son" (of which Henry Adams to Henry Adams covered only seven); over that time the spread of descent would be so wide that "if you have any English blood at all, you also have Norman."[19] Mathematics was never Adams's strong point; his ancestors are as hypothetical as his nieces. But the reader forgives his calculations because they stand for his awakened imagination, which has awakened ours. Sympathy is more important than the chain of generation.

The structure of the book is simple. The first ten chapters give a tour of specific buildings, chiefly Mont Saint Michel and the Cathedral of Our Lady at Chartres, fifty miles southwest of Paris; the last six discuss different aspects of the Middle Ages that interest Adams. The effect is elegant and economical. In the *History* he covered sixteen years in 2,700 pages; in *Mont Saint Michel and Chartres* he covers several centuries in 350 pages. He manages it by jettisoning all the grasshopper gesticulations of public life, in order to focus on what the people of the time felt and thought.

He discerns this in a few exemplary lives (Francis of Assisi) and a few thinkers (Abelard, Aquinas), but primarily in the period's architecture, sculpture, and stained glass. Lives, thoughts, and art, however, were all shaped by the age's religious beliefs. So is Adams's account of them; throughout most of his book, he is himself a Roman Catholic of the period. Religious art works frequently show, in some corner, the kneeling figure of the donor, who is praying, or presenting a miniature model of a church, to some divine being. *Mont Saint Michel and Chartres* is Adams's miniature cathedral.

He presents it to the Virgin Mary. Around her, he argues, the hearts and minds of the Middle Ages revolved. Occasionally he casts this belief as anthropology or psychology, making the Virgin Mary a facet of the eternal feminine, along with Isis and Aphrodite (*The Golden Bough*, by Sir James Frazer, which does the same thing, had appeared in 1890). Occasionally Adams treats her as a sociological construct, a way of taming the impulses of men. Women in the Middle Ages, he writes in one place, knew "what a brute the emancipated man could be." The emancipated father, too: The story of Abraham and Isaac is a "compound horror of masculine stupidity and brutality," which must be "revolting . . . to a woman who typifies the Mother."[20]

But mostly Adams writes of the Virgin as a real person. Chartres is her house; she visits it; she created it, inspiring its makers. She is necessary to the scheme of the universe, for she represents the principle of love and mercy. Without her, the justice of God, and even of Christ, would be too severely regular (Adams recounts numerous tales of favors done by Mary to her worshipers, even to—especially to—underserving ones). Without her, the chaos of life as men experience it would be too harrowingly irregular. One of the most eloquent passages in the book—very brief: Its heart is only three words long—is a catalogue of horrors that the students at the University of Paris (the skeptical intellectuals of the day) expected a philosophical system like Aquinas's to account for if it hoped to justify God and His creation. Adams ticks them off: "suffering, sorrow, and death; plague, pestilence, and famine" Then, he comes to this pair: "catastrophes worldwide and *accidents in corners* [emphasis added]."[21] Those little words are as bitter as Swift, as sad as Samuel Johnson. From the perspective of the universe, that is what every death or suicide looks like: a smashed atom. In the corner, it looks bigger.

Here perhaps Adams and his wife reconcile: He has found a woman he can accept, and who accepts him. His love could not help Marian, but Mary's redeems him. More important for us, he has addressed the topic he raised in the *History*: Who are the great men? Once again, there are none. This time, their substitute is not a great people, but a great Woman, who rules kings, subjects, saints, philosophers, and artists.

Adams offers his greatest hymn to the Virgin at the structural midpoint of the book, the end of his tour of the cathedral of Chartres. He has shown us the building, the ornaments, and the glass, and he finishes with a window of the Virgin in Majesty, visible from the floor above the high altar. "There is heaven! And Mary looks down from it, into her church, where she sees us on our knees, and knows each one of us by name. There she actually is,—not in symbol or in fancy, but in person." Why such immediacy? Because "[p]eople who suffer beyond the formulas of expression,—who are crushed into silence, and beyond pain,—want no display of emotion,—no bleeding heart,—no weeping at the foot of the Cross,—no hysterics,—no phrases! They want to see God, and to know that he is watching over his own." Adams thinks next of the women, among the worshipers in the thirteenth century, who have lost children: given the health standards of the day, a large number. "[P]robably every one of them has looked up to Mary in her great window, and has felt actual certainty, as though she saw with her own eyes,—there, in heaven, while she looked,—her own lost baby playing with the Christ-child at the Virgin's knee. . . . Saints and prophets and martyrs are all very well, and Christ is very sublime and just, but Mary *knows!*"

He is building so rapidly and so well at this point that he can afford to relax; he must, for mere relief. The next paragraph, which is the last of the chapter, bumbles a bit at first, then announces that it is time to go. On the way out, he gives a parting look at the Virgin, not from the thirteenth century, but from the twentieth: "looking down from a deserted heaven, into an empty church, on a dead faith."[22] This crash landing must be like the compression of time at the moment of death, when our days shrink to one, then to an hour, then to the end.

This is the problem with Adams's medieval Catholic answer: He can't believe it. He can't even believe it all the time he is writing. But he did the best he could, and left a great book.

The first private edition of *Mont Saint Michel and Chartres* was followed, three years later, by a private edition of another work, *The Education of Henry Adams.* (Wealth allowed Adams in his old age to avoid publishers, and the possibility of poor sales.) He sent copies to several hundred people mentioned in the text, asking them to cross out anything they objected to; in his note to Henry James, he called the book a pre-emptive shield against biographers. Most of his readers approved: Augustus Saint-Gaudens happily read aloud all the passages about himself to dinner guests. A few deeply disliked it: Clara Hay, John's widow (he had died in 1904), wrote Adams that he should read the Bible. Charles Eliot, who had hired him to teach at Harvard, wrote (not to Adams) that he would be "very sorry to wind up" like him; "I shall not unless I lose my mind." [23]

The book is in the form of a memoir, although it is really about its era. It is not a life and times, but a times, told through a life. Henry Adams is the Virgin Mary; even as the Middle Ages revolved around her, so he is the mirror of the nineteenth century. In his preface, Adams cites the *Autobiography* of Benjamin Franklin—the book that so dismayed his great-grandfather—as a model. Bizarre as the comparison is—nothing could be less like Franklin's helpful straight talk than Adams's dark archness— it is true in one sense: The selves in both books are devices. Franklin's "I" shows us how to get ahead in the world; Adams's "Adams" shows us the impossibility of doing so.

The *Education* is a flea market of quotations. The journalist's gifts have not deserted Adams; he still knows how to frame a judgment memorably, or hang a story on a scene. At age five he has his indelible encounter with John Quincy Adams; at age fifty-five he has another with an electrical generator: a "huge wheel, revolving within arm's-length at some vertiginous speed . . . while it would not wake the baby lying close against its frame." From southern congressmen in the winter of 1860–61, "one could learn nothing but bad temper, bad manners, poker, and treason." No politicians (apart from his father and Hay) come off well, nor do many writers: One of Adams's friends meets Victor Hugo, who announces to a conclave of admirers, "As for me, I believe in God!" After a pause, a woman responds: "Awesome! [*Chose sublime!*] A God who believes in God!" [24]

The book fails because of its design. It is supposed to illustrate a theory of human development, from Unity to Multiplicity. The argument over whether the world consists of one thing or many is older than Socrates; Adams surveyed the medieval phase of it in *Mont Saint Michel and Chartres.* In the *Education,* he arbitrarily transposes this debate to history, asserting that the Middle Ages were unified by art, Aquinas, and love of the Virgin. But after six hundred years, the energy of that age divided and accelerated until, during the lifetime covered by the *Education,* the world became disorganized and inconceivable: a "multiverse." In politics the symbol of disintegration is Adams's old bugbear Grant. In a famous crack, he writes that "[t]he progress of evolution, from President Washington to President Grant, was alone evidence enough to upset Darwin." Uncontrollable material progress was epitomized by generators and coal. "No one [in Adams's youth], except Karl Marx, foresaw radical change. What produced it? The world was producing sixty or seventy million tons of coal."[25] Fulton and Fitch, according to Adams, have taken over the world; they certainly take over his book.

If Grant, coal, and electricity represented trends, not mere events, then their direction might be measured. The final chapters of the *Education* contain fitful attempts to do so, along with predictions. By 2000, Adams writes, "every American . . . would know how to control unlimited power." By 1950, mathematicians "should be able to plot . . . the future orbit of the human race" as accurately as meteor showers. Weirdest of all, by 1938, "perhaps" the world would be one "that sensitive and timid natures could regard without a shudder."[26]

The *Education* wrecks on Adams's grandiosity, which is disguised as humility. Not content to tell the story of his life, he must devise a theory of everything, a universal law. Perhaps the law will state that all is chaos, but even that is still a law. If he can't produce such a law, then he can do nothing. The controlling image of the book, especially of its last third where recollections diminish and idle mutterings take over, is of a tightrope walker encumbered by a dwarf (perhaps borrowed from Nietzsche). If he can explain everything, then he is a dazzling acrobat; if he fails, as he does, then he must be less than life-size. This is Adams's third answer to the riddle of great men: for the last time, there aren't any, and he certainly isn't one.

In the *Education* Adams loses the middle ground of action. A visit to Mount Vernon, like that paid by the characters of *Democracy*, illustrates the dilemma. It happens during the same trip on which his father takes him to the White House to meet Zachary Taylor. That is a comic moment, but the journey to Mount Vernon, if not tragic, is disturbing. Father and son ride from the capital out past Alexandria, Virginia, in a carriage over a rutted road. "To the New England mind, roads, schools, clothes, and a clean face were connected. . . . Bad roads meant bad morals. The moral of this Virginia road was clear. . . . Slavery was wicked, and slavery was the cause of this road's badness." Yet at the end of the trip was Mount Vernon.

The mockery in this passage is directed at Adams, not his subject. In 1907, as in 1850, George Washington was a fixed point of selflessness and purpose for him. "All the other points shifted their bearings; John Adams, Jefferson, Madison, Franklin, even John Marshall, took varied lights and assumed new relations, but Mount Vernon always remained where it was"—but here comes the let-down—"with no practicable road to reach it."[27] This is not a crash as devastating as the one before the Virgin in Majesty in Chartres, but Adams still presents it as conclusive.

Yet Washington navigated the roads and lived among slaves all his life. He never fixed those problems, but he fixed others. Perhaps his actions made it easier for his successors to improve roads and free slaves. There can be achievements in corners as well as accidents.

However bleak Adams's answers to the problem of greatness, he at least solved the problem for himself. The burden that had driven his forefathers to greatness and bitterness and their brothers to drink was lifted. There was no point to being an Adams; the family business could, with good conscience, be wound up.

He continued to send wonderful letters to his friends; he continued to be curious. In one note, he tossed off a small essay on Anglo-Saxon poetry, about the same time that the young Ezra Pound was discovering it. When the paintings of cave men were found in southern France, he paid to have them excavated. In 1911, he wrote wistfully to Charles Francis, Jr.—the two brothers were seventy-six and seventy-three—that America had produced no great men in their generation. "If they had existed I should have attached myself to them, for I needed them bad."[28]

A year later, he booked passage on the *Titanic,* then switched, before sailing, to another ship. Coal and electricity had their problems too, it seemed. After the disaster, he suffered a stroke, recovered, then began learning to read music so that he and actual nieces could sing pieces of the twelfth century. When he consulted scholars about performance practice, they told him such questions might be resolved in thirty years. "[W]e're singing for pleasure," Adams retorted. "Besides, I can't wait thirty years!"[29]

Writing and History

CHAPTER 14

A T THE CLOSE OF Henry Adams's life, he could look back on a century and a half of family writing. No American political dynasty has been so prolific. Franklin Roosevelt did not follow his cousin Theodore as a historian. John Kennedy signed a few books, and his son edited a magazine, but none of their relatives has done likewise. The Harrisons and the Rockefellers have been mutes. Not all politicians, even in the lifetimes of the Adamses, wrote all their own material: Washington turned to Hamilton, Madison, and Jefferson for help with important official statements. The Adamses asked for no assistance (although some of them could have used editing). Over four generations they produced an ocean of state papers, polemics, history, letters, and diaries.

They ventured into remote genres. John Quincy's report on weights and measures could be called scientific; *Democracy* could be called literature. John Quincy and Henry each turned his hand to poetry. Henry's best line describes his beloved Washington springs:

In depraved May, dogwood and chestnut, flowering judas

This is from "Gerontion" by T. S. Eliot, who carved the phrases from Henry's description of Rock Creek in the *Education*. By distilling and sharpening, Eliot turned lovely prose into great poetry. The poems that Henry wrote on his own are less happy. "Buddha and Brahma," a clumping comparison of the way of the mystic and the way of the ruler, was done ten times better in Rudyard Kipling's short story "The Miracle of Purun Bhagat" (Adams met Kipling crossing the Atlantic in 1892). Admirers of *Mont Saint Michel and Chartres* can persuade themselves that "The Prayer to the Virgin of Chartres" is a good poem, but they would be wrong. John Quincy's large body of verse is correct, skillful, and forgettable, with a few exceptions. He translated Horace's ode (Book I.22) beginning "*Integer vitae scelerisque purus*" ("The pure in life and free from sin"), which, despite its lofty opening line, is a whimsical love lyric to a sweet chattering girlfriend, Lalage. Adams's version, addressed to a fictional Sally, captures this quality perfectly, with feminine rhymes and far-fetched place names, now prefiguring Cole Porter, now Edward Lear.

> *In bog or quagmire deep and dank,*
> *His [the lover's] foot shall never settle;*
> *He mounts the summit of Mont Blanc,*
> *Or Popocatapetl.*

During the Jefferson administration, John Quincy mocked the discoveries of Lewis and Clark in a poem using the same techniques and mentioning another Sally, Sally Hemings.

> *Let dusky Sally henceforth bear*
> *The name of Isabella,*
> *And let the mountain, all of salt,*
> *Be christen'd Monticella.*

John Quincy's authorship of these lines remained anonymous until 1827, when his enemies identified him on the floor of the House.[1]

Each Adams has distinctive prose voices. John at his brightest can be shrewd and raucous as a geezer in a tavern; at his worst he is discursive, digressive, repetitious, long-winded, and arcane, crowding and distending his argument with illustrations from Bolingbroke, the Abbé de Mably, Etienne de la Boetie, Marchamont Nedham, Enrico Davila, and dozens if not hundreds of others equally obscure. John Quincy brings learning and observation to a fine point, clear as a daguerreotype, sharp as a surgeon lancing a cyst. Charles Francis strikes an earnest pitch, censuring without undue harshness and praising without excessive warmth. Henry has both the greatest resources and the greatest powers of deploying them economically; when the two join hands, he contrives to amuse; when they do not, his prose is scabbed with mere disdain; at his immortal best, he can catch a moment indelibly, or (almost) draw peace from pain.

Historians and biographers take most of their quotations from John Adams from his letters or his diaries; few from his published works of political theory. That is because his published works are hardly ever quotable; in large patches, they are barely readable. His unit of composition is the phrase, the sentence, or the short paragraph. At the length of even a letter, he can become careless and disorganized. In longer works he often loses his way entirely, in thickets of pedantry and aimless point-scoring. His *Defence of the Constitutions* of the United States is typical. After deciding to contrast American governments with those of European countries, he turns to the city-states of Italy. For each city he quotes, usually without attribution, large chunks from Machiavelli and other historians, breaking off when he becomes bored. Evidently he bored his proofreaders: Charles Francis, editing the work, noted that several pages had been transposed, though in two generations no one had caught the error. After Italy Adams takes up *The Excellencie of a Free State,* a tract by Marchamont Nedham, an English journalist of the seventeenth century. Adams spins out a critical running commentary on the early part of Nedham's argument, without reckoning on the qualifications that are to come. He finds himself surprised by Nedham's destination, because he hadn't bothered to read ahead to see what it would be. His accounts of his own career, whether in the newspapers or in his still-born autobiography, are equally jumbled. As he wrote them, he told Benjamin Rush, he "rummage[d] trunks, letter books, bits of journals, and great heaps and bundles of old papers";[2] the chaos of his files passes into the chaos of his work.

These dismal and argumentative productions can yield scattered gems. His "Discourses," the work that almost destroyed him, begins with translated passages from Enrico Davila, an Italian historian who had fought in the French civil wars of the late sixteenth century. Tiring of Davila, Adams begins a series of moral reflections, stimulated by another work, Adam Smith's *Theory of Moral Sentiments,* which the future economist had delivered as lectures at the University of Glasgow. Adams follows Smith closely, incorporating (unattributed) near-quotations. But he expands on them, like a musician making variations on a theme.

SMITH

The poor man . . . is ashamed of his poverty. He feels that it either
places him out of the sight of mankind, or, that if they take any notice
of him, they have, however, scarce any fellow-feeling with the misery
and distress which he suffers. . . . The poor man goes out and comes
in unheeded, and when in the midst of a crowd is in the same obscurity as if shut up in his own hovel.

ADAMS

The poor man's conscience is clear; yet he is ashamed. . . . He feels
himself out of the sight of others, groping in the dark. Mankind take
no notice of him. He rambles and wanders unheeded. In the midst of
a crowd, at church, in the market, at a play, at an execution or coronation, he is in as much obscurity as he would be in a garret or a cellar.
He is not disapproved, censured, or reproached; *he is only not seen.*[3]

Adams loses Smith's rhetorical balance, but he adds pungent specifics—
the groping, the execution, the coronation—and the creepy dread of in-
visibility (emphasized in the original). Here, there is passion in Adams's
clutter, because of his own fears of Washington, Franklin, and the other
glamor boys of the Founding taking all the credit. He is by nature a
counterpuncher—Zoltan Haraszti based a whole book on the comments he jotted in the margins of his own books—and sometimes his
blows hit home.

Adams excused his writing by saying that he had no time to make it
better. Neither did Hamilton, Madison, Jay, Jefferson, or Gouverneur
Morris when they were writing the *Federalist Papers,* the Declaration, or
the Constitution. But no one has ever found those documents impene-
trable or chaotic. One hesitates to suggest conditions that, in a century,
will seem as poorly defined as brain fever or a bilious humor. But if John
were a child in a modern-day school, he would probably be diagnosed
with attention deficit disorder.

One of the functions of writing for the Adamses was to keep watch on
themselves. Hence the family habit of keeping diaries. Diaries were
common among the literate of their day, and many have become famous.
The secret diary of William Byrd of Westover captures the midnight

rambling of a colonial aristocrat; Philip Hone and George Templeton Strong left multimillion-word chronicles of early-nineteenth-century New York. Some politicians kept important journals: Senator William Maclay's diary of the First Congress depicts all the founders, including John Adams, in an unflattering light ("I began now to think of what Mr. Morris told me: that it was necessary to make Mr. Adams Vice President, to keep him quiet");[4] Senator William Plumer's diary contains the description of Jefferson in deshabille quoted by Henry Adams. Jefferson himself kept a Nixonian collection of gossip about Federalists and other evildoers.

The diaries of the Adamses stand out because of the quality of the events in which they were involved; the completeness of the record; and the knowledge, established very soon in the family's history, that succeeding generations would be reading them. They were family, as well as personal, documents.

"Have you kept a regular journal?" John wrote John Quincy in 1783. ". . . We think, and improve our judgments, by committing our thoughts to paper." "Without a minute diary," John wrote his grandsons in 1815, "your travels will be no better than the flight of birds through the air; they will have no time behind them." Whenever John Quincy skipped days in his diary, he lamented them; the loss of the record meant the loss of the experience. "[M]y diary now runs again in arrear day after day, till I shall lose irretrievably the chain of events, and then comes another chasm in the record of my life" (1826). "[M]y stern chase after Time is, to borrow a simile from Tom Paine, like the race of a man with a wooden leg after a horse" (1844). Charles Francis rarely faltered: From 1826 to 1880, his diary never missed a day. The family project continued into the fourth generation, although by then the family grew sick of it. Charles Francis, Jr., thought introspection had been "morbidly developed by the journalizing habit." When he reread his own youthful diary, he was embarrassed by "its conceit, its weakness and its cant"[5] (a morbid reaction?). He burned it all, saving only a few descriptions for his memoir. Henry also burned his diaries after his wife's suicide. So many recollections, so little tranquility. There had been too much time, too much talk about time. The last Adamses, looking back on the family's memories, must have felt like Tithonus, who was granted eternal life without eternal youth. By erasing their own records, they vainly tried to recapture some saving unconsciousness.

More important for the Adamses was keeping watch on public events. They were obsessed with histories, and with history: How should the stream of human events be recorded? Did it flow in any particular direction?

John Adams was skeptical of the work of historians. As he knew from his own files, records could be lost; if preserved, they might be ignored. Even if they were read, they did little good. One of the books Adams studied in his retirement was the *Study and Use of History*, written by Viscount Bolingbroke in his own retirement in France. Bolingbroke, by all accounts an amoral political operator, depicted the historian's work as a moral enterprise. Adams decorated his platitudes with caustic marginal doodles. "The citizens of Rome place the images of their ancestors in the vestibules of their houses," wrote Bolingbroke, to recall "the glorious actions of the dead." "But images of fools and knaves are as easily made as those of patriots and heroes," commented Adams. "The virtue of one generation was transfused, by the magic of example, into several" (Bolingbroke). "The vice too of one generation was transfused into several" (Adams). Leaders have "fewer blemishes," Bolingbroke argued, if their minds are "enlarged" by the reading of history. "His Lordship [that is, Bolingbroke himself] make[s] this a little doubtful" (Adams). History shows us, Bolingbroke claims, that villains are "unmasked at length" ("Not always"—Adams), while honest men are "justified before [the] story ends" ("Not always"—Adams). Or, if justice doesn't come in a man's lifetime, history sets everything to rights for "succeeding ages." "Tradition and history are radically corrupted," wrote Adams.[6] Bad historians were as influential as good ones, and none of them could tell people what they didn't want to hear.

Human stubbornness and perversity made history itself cyclical, a series of rises and falls. Every glory is followed by a decadence. This was not just the conclusion of Adams's retirement, but his conviction at the peak of his career. In the fall of 1787, Adams and Jefferson, fellow diplomats, wrote each other from London and Paris about the chaos then overwhelming Holland. Both men had dealt officially with Dutch bankers; Adams had lived there; the foundering of one of Europe's lone republics was a bad omen for the United States, just recovering from Shays's Rebellion, and waiting to see what the Constitutional Convention would produce. Jefferson, as usual, was "not without hopes"; Adams was possessed by fears. The war that seemed likely to arise from European meddling in the Dutch disaster—a mild overture, as it turned out, to the wars of the French Revolution—"will render our country, whether she is forced into it, or not, rich, great and powerful." Good news? No: "riches, grandeur and power will have the same effect upon American[s]" as they had always had on Europeans; on men everywhere. The "vanity and foppery" of the "next generation" would sap the republic, and make all of Adams's and Jefferson's labors in the cause of liberty vain. Adams nailed down his argument with a metaphor that could not have been sharpened by John Quincy. "A Covent Garden rake will never be wise enough to take warning from the claps caught by his companions."[7]

John Quincy was willing to expect the worst of his country's future, especially when he was in the minority, and the slave power was triumphant. But he was also prey to powerful hopes. In 1843, he wondered seriously whether an approaching comet portended the end of the world: Throughout greater New England, followers of evangelist William Miller were expecting to be taken up into Heaven that year, or the next (Miller had picked several dates). The world went on after the Great Disappointment, but a few years later, John Quincy complained that, if only he had been more talented, he might have banished slavery and war from the earth, and left a book—his diary—second only to the Bible in value. This was insane: Family self-flagellation and grandiosity spinning finally without check. But it was not singular. Many of his contemporaries expected great things from the near future.

They took their impetus from the revolutions that John and John Quincy had lived through—the American, and even more so, the French. In the 1790s, Vice President Adams met with Joseph Priestley, a chemist and Unitarian clergyman, recently driven from England for his liberal views, who told him that the French Revolution was a fulfillment of the Book of Revelation. The Beast with ten horns stood for the monarchies of Europe; by executing Louis XVI, the French had lopped off one horn; the others were sure to go. (Adams kept a straight face; "I listened," he remembered, "with great attention and perfect sang froid.") In France, the marquis de Condorcet, a mathematician who was an acquaintance of both Adams and Jefferson's, wrote *Outlines . . . of the Progress of the Human Mind,* describing nine ages of history and expressing millennial hopes for the tenth, which was just dawning. The Book of Revelation was not fulfilled, and Condorcet, condemned to the guillotine, committed suicide. "The philosophers of France," wrote Adams on the flyleaf of his copy of the *Outlines,* "were too rash and hasty"; they wanted to "arrive at perfection per saltum [in one jump]."[8] But they were the wave of the future of thought, at least in the nineteenth century. Many people, who were neither cultists nor revolutionaries, believed that history had put mankind on an inexorable upward spiral.

Faith in progress was encouraged by exponential material and scientific developments. These can be tracked in the Adams family's experience of travel. Four generations of them went back and forth to Europe. John's trips could be of almost Homeric difficulty; Henry's were the routine pleasure cruises of the idle rich. The sinking of the *Titanic* made such an impression because, by 1912, transatlantic travel was so routine. Henry had a much easier time getting from the United States to France than John had had getting from Braintree to Philadelphia.

The theory of evolution seemed to make progress a law of nature. One of Henry's few interesting experiences at Harvard was a course on glaciers and fossils, and when he lived in England he studied the Darwinian geologist Sir Charles Lyell. In the *Education* Henry joked about seeing fossils "as complete as Adams himself—in some respects more so."[9] Henry's attitude toward evolution was both niggling and credulous—he professed to reject all hypotheses about how it worked, but he completely accepted its view of sweeping, relentless change.

The doctrines of progress came to bizarre fruit in Henry after he stopped writing traditional history. In 1894, he sent a paper entitled "The Tendency of History" to the American Historical Association, which had elected him president without his knowledge (once he learned of the honor, he avoided ever addressing them in person). The paper called for a science of history, which should be "absolute," and "fix with mathematical certainty the path which human society has got to follow."[10] He added that the conclusions of such a science would be so displeasing to the powers-that-would-be that they would suppress historians. This was late Henry at his worst—portentous and coy.

Not quite his worst, though, because in 1908, he wrote another paper, "The Rule of Phase Applied to History," which was not published until after his death. This was an outline of the scientific history for which he had called. He posited seven phases of matter or energy: solids, fluid, vapor, electricity, ether, space, and "hyper-space," or thought. These corresponded to successive eras of history, which shortened as human activity grew more intense and rarefied (he compared their acceleration to the changes in the orbit of the comet of 1843, John Quincy's portent, as it swung around the sun). "Supposing the Mechanical Phase"—characterized at its end by the vaporous power of steam—"to have lasted three hundred years, from 1600 to 1900, the next or Electric Phase would have a life equal to $\sqrt{300}$, or about seventeen years and a half, when—that is, in 1917—it would pass into another or Ethereal Phase . . . which would last only $\sqrt{17.5}$, or about four years, and bring Thought to the limit of its possibilities in the year 1921." He did concede that if his endpoint of the mechanical phase was off by a hundred years, then "the Ethereal Phase would last till about 2025."[11]

This is worse than Condorcet; worse than William Miller. This is at the level of the unsolicited manuscript, handwritten, in colored ink, with multiple underlinings, whose text spills over onto the envelope. How did he come to write such drivel?

Alexis de Tocqueville provides a clue. Tocqueville had interviewed John Quincy when he made his American trip: Would white men labor without slaves in the climate of the American south, Tocqueville asked; they labor in Greece and Sicily, John Quincy answered. Charles Francis and Henry both read the Frenchman's memoirs, which appeared during their time together in London. Young Henry considered Tocqueville a "model" of how to apply learning to the problems of the day.[12]

One application to his own problems and issues as a writer was a chapter in the second volume of *Democracy in America,* on "Some Characteristics of Historians in Democratic Times." Historians of aristocratic ages, Tocqueville argued, focus on individuals, and their plans and quirks. They are right to do so, since in those ages a handful of individuals direct whole societies. In democracies, "on the contrary, all the citizens are independent of one another, and each of them is individually weak." Historians of such societies seek for general causes "which operate . . . upon so many men's faculties at once and turn . . . them simultaneously in the same direction."

That is also the right thing for democratic historians to do. This is what Henry did in the Introduction of his *History*, when he wrote of America's "moral atmosphere" and its effect on ordinary citizens. But Tocqueville thought democratic historians face a related temptation: Staring into the welter of motivation, they come to believe that all "movement is involuntary and that societies unconsciously obey some superior force ruling over them." If historians can identify that force— race, the dialectic, the phases of energy—"they forge a close and enormous chain, which girds and binds the human race. To their minds, it is not enough to show what events have occurred: they wish to show that events could not have occurred otherwise." [13]

Henry must have read this chapter of Tocqueville, as an argument at the conclusion of his *History* shows. To European historians, Henry wrote, "the hero seemed all, society nothing." But in democratic America, "[w]ar counted for little, the hero for less; on the people alone the eye could permanently rest." [14] Henry, writing fifty-five years after the Frenchman, tracked his argument closely—except for his warning. Once Henry's eye drifted from the people, to involuntary movements, he took to predicting what events must occur.

John Adams would have been puzzled, and probably amused, by the turn his great-grandson's thinking took. He was always mindful of human motivation (often, in his view, irrational and self-deceptive). No member of the family had a very clear view of his own heart, and John as often as not used his understanding of men as a shortcut to dismissive and self-justifying judgments. But as a historian and historical actor, he always looked in the right places, not at equations, or comets.

Republic and Empire

A T THE START OF his vice presidency—the very time when his commitment to republicanism was first doubted —John Adams, never one to leave ill enough alone, was explaining to correspondents that England could properly be called a "monarchical republic"—and so could America. Any government with an admixture of popular power was a republic, and any strong executive was a monarch, even if he was elected. "The duration of our president," he told Roger Sherman, ". . . is only for four years; but his power during those four years is much greater than that of an avoyer, a consul, a podesta, a doge, a stadtholder; nay, than a king of Poland; nay, than a king of Sparta."[1]

According to traditional systems of classifying governments, Adams's talk of monarchical republics was not as paradoxical as it now seems. But Americans who liked to think that they had created a government that was new and unique found Adams's recycling of old terms disturbing. Later writers who wish to disturb have an easy time of it, simply by advancing kindred arguments. The novels and essays of Gore Vidal form a long ghost story, telling Americans that their republic is gone, replaced by an empire.

John Adams was unlucky in picking the particular terms "monarch" and "monarchical." A well-read theorist could apply these to doges or stadtholders, but in 1789 the monarch in the forefront of American minds was still the king of England, against whom they had fought for eight and a half years. But the term "empire" did not carry exclusively negative connotations. Most Americans, even in the first Republican party, which came to power by abusing the theories and practice of John Adams, wanted the United States to conquer the continent. George Washington frequently spoke of the new country as a "rising empire"; his first battles, in his early twenties, were fought to drive Frenchmen out of the Ohio Valley, so Virginians could move in unhindered.

When John Adams was born, the geographical center of population in the thirteen colonies was east of Baltimore; all Americans, except for a handful of fur traders, lived in a relatively narrow coastal strip. Even this was not safe; within living memory, the town of Deerfield in central Massachusetts had been raided by French-backed Indians, who killed fifty people and kidnapped the rest. When Henry Adams was an old man, the United States owned Alaska, Hawaii, and the Philippines, and President Roosevelt had won a Nobel Prize for making peace between Russia and Japan. Ideas of republic and empire, and the tensions between them, had been present throughout American history. What was the American system of government? It had a written system of fundamental laws, but what was its essence? Would geographical expansion change the political system? How could America expand on a continent full of rivals?

The Declaration of Independence said that all men were created equal; perhaps that was the essence of republicanism. If so, then John Adams was out of luck, for he quarreled with the Declaration. John Quincy Adams quoted it, notably in his argument in the *Amistad* case, and in defense of the Haverhill petition. Yet John Quincy's birth, his years at foreign courts, and his obvious pride in an intellect that recognized only Calhoun's as its peer made most Americans outside New England doubt that he really believed in equality. Henry Adams never deigned to seek a fellow citizen's vote, and his arrogance was leavened by an irony that was yet more frigid. But the scorn he heaped on leaders, and the praise he offered ordinary men, individually and in the mass, made him, in the *History* at least, the family's one true egalitarian.

Assenting to the doctrine that all men are created equal does not settle all political questions: The details must be worked out in cases. American politics took up several hard cases during the Adamses' lifetimes, on which it is still working.

In 1910, Theodore Roosevelt gave a speech in which he called for "a more substantial equality of opportunity." Roosevelt was thinking of the opportunity to participate in civic life, as well as to make money. "No man can be a good citizen unless he has a wage more than sufficient to cover the bare cost of living, and hours of labor short enough so that after his day's work is done he will have time and energy to bear his share in the management of the community."[2] Calhoun had told John Quincy Adams that slaves spared freemen the degradation of manual labor. Roosevelt wanted laws that would give laborers enough free time to behave like freemen.

The United States backed into the politics of leveling up. For more than a century before Roosevelt, politicians had been content with symbolic expressions of solidarity with common folk (Lincoln's supporters depicting him as a rail-splitter), or with attacks on selected groups of the rich. Jefferson laid the template for the latter form of class warfare, with his railing against the Tories and Anglomen who profited from Hamilton's financial system. Abolitionists turned the tables when they railed against southern slaveowners.

The Adamses followed the slow trajectory of the nation on this issue. They would not, of course, try to ingratiate themselves with common people, or with anyone, but they often scorned rich enemies. John feared the rich and the poor alternately, depending on who seemed most menacing. In the middle of his career, mobs and civil commotion in America and France made him criticize the poor; at the end of it, the scheming of rivals in the Federalist party turned him against the rich. As an old man, he swapped denunciations of banks and bankers with numerous pen pals, including Jefferson, Benjamin Rush, and John Taylor of Caroline, a learned theorist of southern agrarianism. John Quincy and Charles Francis scourged northern manufacturers and the southerners who shipped them cotton picked by slaves. Schooled by his early journalism and his hatred of Jews, Henry brought abusing the rich to an art. Rich men deflated the currency to make themselves still richer; his brother Brooks showed him that the process had been going on since ancient times.

Henry's anger was frivolous; it never moved beyond the level of hermetic rhetoric. He liked to call himself a conservative Christian anarchist, but this was not a program, still less a worldview, only a gesture of irritation. "As a convinced, conservative, Christian anarchist," he wrote his friend Mrs. Cameron in the 1890s, ". . . turning out a set of cheap politicians in order to put in a cheaper, seems to me scavenger's work, necessary but low, at least as compared with the bomb, which has some humor in it, and explodes all round, making an effectual protest against the whole thing."[3] But Henry made neither bombs nor protests, only noise. Brooks did pull him far enough in the direction of practical politics to convert him to free silver—an inflationary movement that sought to benefit credit-starved farmers—and its champion, William Jennings Bryan, who ran for president as a Democrat and a Populist in 1896. But Adams's friendship with Hay tugged him back toward McKinley and the Republicans. Moving pieces on the chessboard of nations was more interesting to him than destroying society.

After the Revolution, the state of New Jersey made an abortive experiment with women's suffrage, giving the vote to property-holding widows. They tended to be Federalist, and the Jeffersonians disenfranchised them as soon as they came to power in the state. The Adamses, with the example of Abigail before them, were well aware of the intelligence and power of women, though they conceived of it in extrapolitical terms.

Abigail's famous 1776 appeal to John to "remember the ladies" was written with a light touch—"If perticuliar care and attention is not paid to the laidies we are determined to foment a rebelion"—though there were serious issues behind it: John's neglect, arising from his absorption in politics; Abigail's sense that her already-formidable talents would have been improved by formal education (she spelled much more wildly than John, to take a minor example, though she wrote as well). John chose to respond to the light tone, in the traditional badinage of the war of the sexes: "We [men] have only the name of masters, and rather than give up this, which would completely subject us to the despotism of the peticoat, I hope General Washington, and all our brave heroes, would fight."[4]

John put more serious thought in a letter from Paris to his eighteen-year-old daughter Abigail, whom he urged to read history, so that her children should profit by it. "When I hear of an extraordinary man, good or bad, I naturally . . . inquire who was his mother?"[5] Decades later, he gave the same advice to his daughter's daughter: To educate her own children, she should know Locke, Descartes, Berkeley, and Hume. Women had to be smart and well-educated if their children were to be virtuous. Their sons might become leaders; their daughters, mothers of still more leaders, though not leaders themselves.

Many of the petitions John Quincy presented to Congress were gath-

ered by women. His enemies typically greeted them with humorous proposals to calm the ladies down by providing them with husbands. John
Quincy silenced one such joker by calling a roll of politically engaged
heroines, from the Old Testament to the volunteer nurses of the American Revolution. Did they "bring discredit" on their sex "by mingling in
politics?" Still, he told early suffragists that he did not support giving
women the vote: "I look to the women of the present age," he wrote a
feminist cousin, "with the feelings of a father." The radical reformers of
the mid–nineteenth century split on the issue themselves, quarreling
over whether the enfranchisement of black men should take precedence
over women's rights. Why should "Sambo," complained Elizabeth Cady
Stanton, make laws for "the daughters of Adams and Jefferson"?[6]

In his medieval period, Henry worshiped women, not just the Queen
of Heaven. Man in the Middle Ages "was always getting himself into
crusades, or feuds, or love, or debt, and depended on the woman to get
him out. The story was always of Charles VII and Jeanne d'Arc." By ele-
vating women above men, Henry tried to be less of an Adams, to break
the chain of presidential parthenogenesis. But despite all his efforts to
pay homage—however carefully he measured the houses of the Virgin in
Normandy, or the breasts of girls in Samoa—he felt alienated from what
he admired. "[M]an is pretty vile," he wrote Mrs. Cameron from the
South Seas; ". . . woman might partly compensate for him, if one knew
where to find her."[7] To which Mrs. Cameron might have responded,
"I'm here, reading your letter," but it would not have made Henry feel
less bereft.

The Adamses never had much luck dealing with white ethnic minori-
ties. During John's administration, the Republicans spread rumors
among the Germans of eastern Pennsylvania that the president would
marry one of his sons to a daughter of George III. A mob of farmers,
alarmed by these reports and by high taxes, chased a federal marshal out
of the town of Bethlehem. After the ringleaders were arrested by the
army and convicted of treason, Adams ultimately pardoned them (he
called them "obscure, miserable Germans, as ignorant of our language as
they were of our laws"), but the ethnic group was lost to Federalism, and
to Adams. John Quincy threw away a tool he might have used to woo
them back: When he was running for re-election as president, he refused

to address German-Americans in their native tongue, even though he had lived in Germany and spoke German fluently, on the grounds that it would be pandering. Charles Francis had a consistent record on ante-bellum nativism, which was directed primarily against Irish Catholics, rejecting repeated invitations to join Nativist political parties in the 1840s and 1850s. Yet he became a whipping boy of Irish-American politicians when, as minister to England, he only helped jailed Irish nationalists if they were American citizens. Perhaps that encouraged him to write in his diary that "the Irish" and "the negro" together had lowered the general level of American intelligence perilously. "We are taking far too many chances against ourselves."[8] Sometimes the Adamses blundered, sometimes they were only being principled, but their errors and their virtues struck ethnics as equally tone-deaf.

But the assimilation of white ethnics is not, after all, a first-order problem in American history; no Civil War was ever fought over it. On African-Americans the family's position was clear, and clearly limited.

John Adams never owned a slave, though he was certainly prosperous enough to do so, and until 1780 the laws of Massachusetts allowed it. Among the many founders who criticized slavery, he was one of the few with absolutely clean hands. Most of his generation hoped, rather against the evidence, that slavery would die a natural death. They did not see that blacks were reproducing as fast in North America as whites, so they could imagine that ending the slave trade would keep the slave population small. They could plainly see that the tobacco economy of the upper south was doomed, but then the same minds who invented the steamboat invented the cotton gin. The Founders did not look harder at the tenacity of slavery because they did not want to be forced to make hard choices. Whatever choices were to be made were left, by a tacit bargain, to the southerners whose particular problem slavery became, after northern states began abolishing it in the late eighteenth century.

But as the founding generation died off, John could see that the bargain had not been kept. He hinted as much in an 1821 letter to Jefferson. "I constantly said in former times to the Southern gentlemen, I cannot comprehend this [subject]; I must leave it to you."[9] His implication—he was writing during the Missouri controversy—was that the southern gentlemen had done nothing about it. Jefferson did not address Adams's silent rebuke. By this time, Calhoun had already told John Quincy that slavery was good for republican government.

After John Quincy lost his presidential hopes, he, his son, and his grandson spent thirty-five years fighting slaveowners and their allies. But once the Civil War was won, the surviving Adamses thought no more about former slaves than Elizabeth Cady Stanton did. At the *fin de siècle*, Henry toyed with the notion that "the dark races are gaining on us," and whites might be "shut up, north of the fortieth parallel" (Quincy and Normandy lie above it, though not Washington, D.C.). But since he claimed to "prefer niggers to whites," he was not bothered.[10] All this was no more serious than his chatter about bombs and the gold standard. To the Adamses, the issue of slavery was distinct from the issue of race. It was a breach in the contract of the founding, which was a contract with their family. When the defaulters had been brought to justice, the issue ended.

Even as Americans argued about what their system entailed, they quarreled over how and whether it should expand. Jefferson and his followers supported expansion that was peaceful and covert: purchase, or private-sector colonizing and invasion. Texas became independent by the latter means; William Walker tried the same methods in Central America, and Aaron Burr may have been hoping to use them in Mexico.

The preferred military arm of the Adams family was the navy—John pushed for an American navy in the Continental Congress—in part because the Adamses were suspicious of army officers in politics. Time and again, great heroes like Washington and Grant, or slightly meretricious ones like Roosevelt, thwarted or bemused them. John Quincy admired Jackson as long as he thought he could use him, but once Jackson went his own way, John Quincy consigned him to darkness. Brooks greatly admired Roosevelt—"Thou hast it now," he wrote the new president after McKinley's assassination, "King, Cawdor, Glamis" (an odd way to congratulate someone, comparing his ascent to that of a doomed villain). Brooks's admiration only made Henry bemused with his younger brother. The Adamses did not naturally understand generals and had little patience for figuring them out. "Grant wrecked my own life," Henry wrote operatically in 1911, "and the last hope . . . of lifting society back to a reasonably higher plane."[11] Fairest of the Adamses was John (who had, it is true, the greatest of generals under his eye). In his last public appearance, addressing a corps of West Point cadets from his porch when he was eighty-five, he told them to model themselves on George Washington.

Was America an ideological empire, the incarnation of an ideal? In his later years, Henry ostentatiously denied that the United States represented principles, any more than an explosion or a chain reaction did. "This country is terribly interesting," he wrote in 1904. "It has no character but prodigious force," which he calculated at twenty million horsepower. John Quincy had the most complex views in the family. He scoffed at Clay for thinking that, just because the republics of North and Latin America used similar phrases in their founding documents, they would be similar societies. He did think, as senator and secretary of state, that the United States was carrying enlightenment from Europe westward, the star of freedom and good government following the star of empire. As his opinion of the slave power soured, he came to see his country as its tool, and in his old age he turned against both. He celebrated the Fourth of July, 1844, a week before his seventy-seventh birthday, by staying home: "the noise and bustle and excitement and ranting of this day having become irksome to me." Even at the beginning, not twenty years after the first Fourth of July, John feared that his country might become a force for oppression in the world: America, he wrote Abigail during his vice presidency, when Americans were quarreling with English creditors about prewar debts, was as "insolent" as Britain, and could "become as great a scourge to mankind." [12] The Adamses were skeptical about their country because they were skeptical about man. Henry might put a limited faith in horsepower, but none of them believed in the automatically cleansing effect of any idea.

America's first field of expansion was North America, but to control it, the country had to dispose of rival claimants. The crucial victory in the United States' Indian wars was the defeat and death of Tecumseh in the War of 1812. He was the last Indian with the talent, and the foreign allies, to have impeded American growth. John Quincy invoked religion and natural law to tie up the loose ends at Ghent. He wanted to tell the British commissioners that their proposal to erect an Indian buffer state was unacceptable, since the Indians did not work the land they occupied and hence had no just claim to it, whereas Americans acknowledged a "moral and religious duty" to "settle, cultivate, and improve their territory." Clay found the argument "canting," and Adams dropped it.[13] He revived it, however, ten years later when it worked to the benefit of Indians. By the 1820s the Cherokees of the old southwest had become Christian farmers, newspaper readers, and slaveowners, as settled and industrious as their white neighbors; nevertheless, when gold was discovered on their land, the state of Georgia drove them off it. As president, John Quincy tried vainly to intervene, and he considered Jackson's support for their dispossession to be one of his many sins.

But it was European powers—France, England, and Spain—that loomed largest on the rising empire's horizon. France was the earliest enemy, threatening the Adamses and other colonists from Louisburg and from beyond the Alleghenies. France's grand strategy—a policy of encirclement, using the rivers and lakes of North America, from the St. Lawrence to the Mississippi, as the noose—was an excellent one, though the French lacked the numbers on the ground to make it work. They did not finally abandon it, however, until the army that Napoleon had sent to occupy Louisiana was destroyed in Haiti by black resistance and yellow fever. Napoleon's failure not only boosted Jefferson's reputation, by allowing him to buy Louisiana, it retrospectively saved John's reputation for selfless prudence, by making his efforts to end the Franco-American war of 1798 seem free of any risks but political ones to himself. If Napoleon had managed to establish himself in New Orleans, the Federalist war hawks would have gone down as prescient patriots.

From John's youth to Henry's maturity, Britain changed from mother country, to enemy, to ally. In the mid-1890s, the United States complained that Britain was bullying Venezuela in a border dispute with British Guiana. Worried by the rise of Germany, London concluded that it must never quarrel with the United States again—a policy it would follow throughout the twentieth century. Henry took satisfaction in Britain's humbler attitude and saw it as the fulfillment of "the chief effort of his family," going back to the 1760s—"bringing the government of England into intelligent cooperation with the objects and interests of America."[14]

The most tenacious imperial rival, surprisingly, turned out to be

Spain. Spain was already the sick man of Europe by the time John Adams was born, and the Spain of the Armada and the Inquisition was nothing more than an ancient bogeyman. Madrid abandoned North American territories at the lightest pressure from the United States; when the upper classes of Latin America turned against the empire in the early 1820s, it fell in a heap. Mexico, the successor state in North America, was even less effectual than Spain had been. Cuba and Puerto Rico remained under Spanish control as late as 1898 only because of northern unwillingness to create Caribbean slave states fifty years earlier.

After centuries of weakness and incompetence, all Spain left behind it in the New World was people: black, Indian, or mestizo, speaking Spanish and practicing Catholicism, if they had been weaned from Indian tongues and pagan religions. Henry did not have to go to Normandy to find the Virgin; the Virgin of Guadaloupe was across the border.

Now she is on both sides of it. At Ghent John Quincy boasted to the British commissioners that the population of the United States was eight million, and growing. "[W]as it in human experience, or in human power, to check its progress by a bond of paper? . . . It was opposing a feather to a torrent."[15] Other times, other torrents. Spain's power is a memory, but she turns out to have been playing a very long game, which is not yet done.

John Quincy's Monroe Doctrine had envisioned the United States and the European powers staying each within their own hemispheres. But in the late nineteenth century America began to expand beyond the New World. The first steps were taken by Seward, who coveted naval bases as far afield as Borneo, and actually managed to claim the uninhabited Midway Island in the northern Pacific, as well as buy Alaska from Russia. In the 1890s, the United States annexed Hawaii and eastern Samoa (which Henry had explored only a few years before), and took Guam and the Philippines in the western Pacific from Spain. Many of these acquisitions were justified by steam power, which required navies to have convenient coaling stations. In the twentieth century, the country took part in European wars. Henry, the only Adams who would witness these developments, was not as expansionist as Lodge or Roosevelt—he thought taking the Philippines was premature, but that was a prudential judgment only. He was caught up with Hay's global politics and thought the United States should develop northern China. Westward and eastward the star of empire took its way.

John's quirky talk of monarchical republics can jar us into realizing that both the republican and the imperial models, in their pure forms, have shortcomings. Critics of empire—as John Quincy became in his old age—appear throughout American history, although they are usually argued down. Republicanism has fewer critics, though it deserves them. In its classical form, as practiced in the ancient world and praised by writers like Machiavelli, it is a ferocious ideal, demanding complete dedication to politics and sacrificing all for liberty, including liberty itself— Calhoun was well within the classical republican consensus when he argued that slavery liberated free men. In its popular demotic form, it can be bullying, as the Adamses saw firsthand, from cousin Samuel's rioters to Theodore Roosevelt's dinner-table monologues. Empires, especially commercial ones, can mollify republics by offering other objects besides politics, while republican institutions can restrain the militarism and energy of empires. John Adams was not supple enough to explain how republic and empire could moderate each other, but he was acute enough to see that moderation is needed.

Legacy and Merit

WHEN CRAZY JOHN RANDOLPH called the Adamses the American House of Stuart, he was not just accusing them of being monarchists—a charge that members of the first Republican party habitually threw at their opponents. He was comparing them to the most villainous dynasty in recent English history, according to the Whig myth. To the American mind, weaned on that myth, the Stuart kings—James I, Charles I, Charles II, and James II—who reigned from 1603 to 1688, represented crypto-Catholicism (which, in the dynasty's last days, became open Catholicism) and absolutism. For these sins, Oliver Cromwell cut off Charles I's head, and Parliament drove James II into exile. The Stuarts remained a live issue for decades: Stuart pretenders schemed to regain the throne until the middle of the eighteenth century, and images of them were among the devil-totems that Samuel Adams's Boston mobs rioted over on Pope Day.

The political sin of the Stuarts was advocating the divine right of kings—the notion that they were entitled to the throne by birth, and that no degree of incompetence or religious waywardness could entitle the nation to rebuke them. By John Randolph's lifetime, the Adamses wished to be, and had plainly become, a political dynasty. How could they maintain themselves over time, without justifying Randolph's accusation? How could they leave a legacy that would also be earned?

One obvious condition for would-be American dynasts was to produce children—and since American public life, during the span of the Adamses' greatness, was conducted mostly by men, they had to produce sons. Most of the earliest presidents failed to accomplish this. The Father of His Country had no children. Washington brooded on his lack, and transferred his paternal feelings to a number of surrogates, notably Lafayette. He did have one step-son, Jack Custis, who was a bad lot: Jack's eldest daughter remembered him teaching her bawdy songs, which she was too young to understand, and making her sing them for his gentlemen friends. Happily, he died young. Jefferson, Madison, and Monroe were called the Virginia Dynasty, but their bond was political only, since Jefferson and Monroe had only daughters, and Madison, who married late, only had a wild step-son. Jackson's marriage, which excited such bitter partisan attack, was, like Washington's, childless. Martin Van Buren was the next president after the Adamses to have an adult son of his own. John Van Buren—"frank . . . generous . . . gifted," according to one contemporary; possessed of "wit" and "unbounded self-assurance," according to another[1]—stumped the nation for his father in the Free Soil campaign of 1848, and his admirers believed that if he had re-mained politically independent instead of returning to the Democratic fold, he might have been the presidential candidate of the second Re-publican party in 1856. Only three of the first eight presidents produced potential successors, but three of those sons were considered presidential timber—John Quincy, Charles Francis, and John Van Buren—and one of the three made it.

If heirs were available, they had to be impressed with a proper con-sciousness—American, not Stuart. Though their family's position might stimulate them, they would have to rise, if not entirely by their own ef-forts, then with considerable exertion. The Adamses were impelled to strive by the Calvinist culture of New England. The dogmas of this cul-ture might flit away: In his late seventies, John Quincy confided to his diary that he could not believe that Christ died for man's sins ("It is not true. It is hateful. But how shall I contradict St. Paul?");[2] Henry, like a late Stuart, even became a Catholic, at least on paper. But the mindset of predestinate believers arduously laboring for signs that they had been saved outlasted the beliefs that had produced it, and was a persistent goad. The Adamses had their own family culture of striving to goad them. It was already in place before they made a mark in the world, when Deacon John made John cut thatch so he would become sick of farming. Success beyond the Deacon's wildest imaginings reinforced it. Given the peppery temper of most of the family, the ritual exhortations to achieve could be screechy, even demented, though the prickliest Adamses were also capable of softness and sympathy, even if they did not offer them at the right time, or in sufficient amounts.

On the threshhold of his own greatness, John Adams saw firsthand an instance of a dynasty maintaining itself in the wrong way. Thomas Hutchinson, the colonial official who had written the damning letter about the need to abridge traditional liberties, sowed the government of Massachusetts with relatives. Adams hated Hutchinson, for his nepotism as well as his politics, and he held him up as a bad example. "If [my] journal should ever be read by my own family," he wrote, "let them know that there was upon the scene of action, with Mr. Hutchinson, one determined enemy" of the system "to which alone he owes his and his family's late advancement."³ John was committing the Adams family to behave differently. Twenty years after Hutchinson and his clan had fled to England as Tories, President John Adams gave a diplomatic assignment to his eldest son, but John Quincy Adams had already earned the good opinion of George Washington. President Adams also tried to make his son-in-law, William Smith, a brigadier general. But Smith was an incompetent, and Congress refused. The exception proved the rule: Smith was undeserving, but after all, he was not an Adams.

The goal of a dynasty's striving, finally, had to be public service. Science, business, or the arts would not do, though Adamses pursued all three. In New England's first century, the public good had been most conspicuously served by clergymen, and the ministry was a vocation that was often passed down in families. Richard Mather, an English Puritan minister, moved to Massachusetts in the 1630s; his son, Increase Mather, was a minister and president of Harvard; his son, Cotton Mather, was a minister now known mostly for believing in witches, though he was also an early advocate of vaccination. A genealogist has calculated that Richard Mather had eighty descendants who were clergymen. Jonathan Edwards of Connecticut, who led the Great Awakening of the 1730s, became president of Princeton, as did his clergyman son-in-law Aaron Burr. Aaron's son, also named Aaron, did not pursue the ministry, but John Adams claimed in his old age that the clerical prestige of the younger Burr's father and grandfather earned him one hundred thousand pious votes in his political career.⁴

Much of New England was initially a religious venture, not of individual souls, but of communities of saints, who came out from the ungodly to found Zion. As religion ceased to be the organizing principle of society, New England's wars against absolutist France, imperial Britain, and the slave-owning south made it (in many minds, at least) a community struggling to uphold liberty. Communities never spontaneously act in unison, except at moments of extraordinary stress: They need institutions and leaders; they need politics. Public service in New England, during the lifetimes of the Adamses, was not just a job but an essential moral and social task.

Yet even when all the pieces were in place, the Adams dynasty was difficult to perpetuate. Their dizzying initial success set the bar very high. Supplying congressmen, as the Frelinghuysens have done for New Jersey off and on for more than 220 years, is a feat of endurance. But it was more impressive to produce a president and a signer of the Declaration of Independence (the two achievements reinforced each other, since there were many obscure signers, and many less than stellar presidents): impressive, and intimidating. The Adamses defined themselves as a dynasty of greatness.

Unlike a royal family, a family of achievers could not move along the automatic track of primogeniture. John, it is true, was the eldest son in his generation, as was John Quincy. But the great Adamses of the third and fourth generation were both third sons. How were the repositories of Adamshood selected? How was the burden of greatness passed on, and taken up?

When sons did not become great, it was not for lack of advantages. John's younger brothers, Peter and Elihu, did not go to Harvard, but all of his sons, and most of his grandsons and great-grandsons, did. After college, many of them had the benefit of special political experiences. When John's third son, Thomas Boylston, was twenty-two, he sailed to Europe to be his older brother's secretary in Holland and Prussia; when he came home four years later, he carried an important message from Talleyrand to his father the president. John Quincy's second son, John II, became his father's private secretary in the White House at age twenty-two (this opportunity, it is true, followed a disgrace, for John II had been expelled from Harvard for joining in a student riot). When Charles Francis's second son, Charles Francis, Jr., was twenty-five, he took a political train trip with William Seward, met the presidential candidate Abraham Lincoln (who had "a mild, dreamy, meditative eye"), then spent a month in Washington as the secession winter turned into the secession spring. Charles Francis's fourth son, Brooks, accompanied his father to Switzerland for the arbitration of the *Alabama* claims and labored in the quixotic effort to win him the presidency by acclamation in 1876 (Brooks complained that Carl Schurz, the noncampaign's manager, "was no more a leader than the man in the moon")[5] Other young men besides Adamses ran errands, served as secretaries, pulled wires, and went on the campaign trail. But an Adams could partake of these experiences as a matter of course. Names, finally, confer symbolic advantage: As soon as a child is self-conscious, it wants to know what its name means, and who else had it. Three Adamses were named after presidents: John Quincy's older boys, George Washington and John II, and Charles Francis's eldest boy, John Quincy II.

Yet most of the Adamses, favored by education, experience of the world, and christening, were either simply talented, or simply normal, or simply failures. They never did a great thing, either because they shunned the effort (John Quincy II wanted "to be left alone"), or because they shunned life (George Washington wanted to be left alone so badly that he drowned himself), or because, for all the abilities of scions like Charles Francis, Jr., and Brooks, they could not find or make their chance for greatness.

Charles Francis offers the strangest clash of will and destiny in the whole family. The spectacle of his father's naked but unacknowledged ambition appalled him. He disliked politics intensely, and by shifting to journalism and history he became, in some measure, a spectator, and a curator. Although the history he edited and wrote was the nation's, it was also family history, and thus a step on the short, dusty road to compiling genealogies, the favored activity of those who do nothing memorable themselves. He had, in addition, a deeply conventional mind, bound to his family's principles as he understood them, and uninterested in stretching them, as John and John Quincy were willing to do, by their wide and miscellaneous reading. And yet, because of his name and his principles, this quiet, self-contained man was thrust into a vice presidential campaign, and almost thrust into a presidential one. Between the two, President Lincoln assigned him to a necessary and difficult task, which he did well. In his old age, John Adams said, foolishly, that he had never been a great man. Charles Francis Adams might have said it, with more truth. But he did a great thing. All his inclinations ran counter to his responsibilities, except for one—his inclination to do his duty, and his duty made him, with respect to the Whig party and Great Britain, at least, a rebel and a troublemaker.

The Adamses, finally, passed on burdens as well as incentives. The heaviest was alcoholism. Charles Francis thought the vice was inherited, and modern science agrees that it has a genetic component. If so, it may have been introduced into the family via Abigail Adams, whose brother was a drunkard. Alcohol laid waste two-thirds of the second and third generations, and John Quincy, learned in Madeiras, clearly had inclinations in that direction, which someone slightly less busy and less rigidly self-controlled might have followed.

Another inherited burden, the family attitude toward politics, ruined only presidencies, not lives. It is not surprising that heirs should feel themselves to be above office-seeking. The only diplomatic post Henry might have wanted was ambassador to England, but he was too proud ever to ask, even his friend Hay. In the early 1880s, Secretary of State Frederick Frelinghuysen told Marian Adams that her husband could go to Guatemala City as ambassador to Central America. Given Henry's later role in Cuba, the offer was almost prophetic, but the Adamses were not going to leave their pleasure dome for such a posting. Mrs. Adams told the secretary it was "an unwise appointment."[6] Yet John himself, the founding politician, was a hapless practitioner of his trade, insisting that he was above parties. All the founding fathers agreed with him, yet all practiced politics, and Washington and Jefferson, his great foils, were the best politicians of their day. Pride and principle impelled the Adamses to serve, and hobbled them in the techniques of service.

As the Adams dynasty reached its fourth generation, the social context of the country changed, and with it the nexus of the pursuit of greatness. New England and America came less and less to see themselves as communities of freedom fighters, much less of saints. *The Education of Henry Adams* attempts to track this development, and if Henry had written it with less irony and bile, he might have tracked it more effectively. When Tocqueville came to America in the 1830s, he found a nation of subcommunities, of people engaged in private institutions and associations. Henry's introduction to his *History* depicted a nation of Americans with yet narrower views, working like beavers at their farms and inventions. Abraham Lincoln's first notable speech, given to a young men's lyceum in Springfield, Illinois, when he was thirty-two, described the changing focus of American aspiration and attributed it to the success of the Founding. What was there for leaders to do once the country was up and running? "This field of glory is harvested, and the crop is already appropriated."[7] Lincoln was premature—the need for great public men had not ended, because history never ends. But the call on the Adamses, or on any other family, to produce a great public man every twenty-five years or so was becoming attenuated, because the public's attention was elsewhere. If the Adamses were not going to revert to farming again, perhaps they could take up some other private pursuit, such as art.

John Adams foresaw such a development. In 1780, he wrote a letter to Abigail about the gardens of Paris. He wanted to describe the statues on the grounds of the Tuileries Palace, but his thoughts were too full of "schemes" and "anxiety" to do them justice. "I could fill volumes with descriptions of temples and palaces, painting, sculptures, tapestry, porcelaine, &c. &c. &c.—if I could have time. But I could not do this without neglecting my duty. . . . I must study politicks and war that my sons may have liberty to study mathematicks and philosophy. My sons ought to study mathematicks and philosophy, geography, natural history, naval architecture, navigation, commerce and agriculture, in order to give their children a right to study painting, poetry, musick, architecture, statuary, tapestry and porcelaine."[8] John simultaneously predicted the future and issued a challenge to it: He presented the sciences and the arts as flowers of freedom and peace, which he would not enjoy, an intellectual promised land that, like Moses, he could see, but never enter. At the same time, he asserted the primacy of his specialties, war and politics. As they are first in time, so they are also, implicitly, first in importance, for they make wisdom and beauty possible.

John's prediction was not immediately fulfilled, for however much his descendants dabbled in weights and measures, poetry, or tending the Brooks inheritance, they chiefly devoted themselves to politics and war, whether as politicians or historians. But toward the end of Henry's life, at the end of the end of the dynasty, he did produce, in *Mont Saint Michel and Chartres,* a work of art about a work of art. In doing so, he answered John's challenge. The most important thing was to name beauty, love, and woe. To give voice to grieving mothers, dead children, and doubting intellectuals was as important as founding a state.

But art was not a dynastic enterprise. Bali has villages of hereditary woodcarvers, and Germany had the Bachs, but for Henry, at the beginning of the twentieth century, art was a personal achievement. In any case, he had no children, and he was tired.

Death

CHAPTER 17

ENRY ADAMS WAS seventy-six years old, riding in an automobile through the French countryside, when he heard the ringing church bells that marked the outbreak of World War I. He closed up his Paris apartment and returned, with his attendant nieces and their friends, to Washington. After decades of vehemently predicting apocalypses and millenniums, he found that the arrival of an actual catastrophe left him little to say. "[F]or the first time in fifty years," he wrote a friend, he was "surrounded by talk of war and weapons," which had "less meaning to me now than they had" during the Civil War. But he continued his Washington dinner parties, at which he continued to whisper aside to his guests, of the politicians he pretended not to notice, "Well, tell me, what are they up to?" In April 1917 America entered the war; Prussian lieutenants would have occasion to learn what the United States were. Almost a year later, in March 1918, he retired to bed after dinner and conversation; his last words, addressed to his secretary, an adoring young woman, were "Good night, my dear."[1] He died in his sleep, age eighty, and was buried in Rock Creek Park.

Henry Adams had escaped one of the fates he most feared—an end like his father's. Charles Francis Adams, whom Henry credited with "the only perfectly balanced mind that ever existed" in the family, "singular" for its "poise," lost his faculties. In the spring of 1880, at the age of seventy-two, he was preparing a lecture for a learned society and found that he could not organize his notes. His reaction to his disability was dictated by his sense of obligation: If he could not perform his duties well, he would not perform them at all. "I cannot be blind to the necessity of marking out a line of life as private as it can be made."[2] He gave up his clubs, his public engagements, and even his diary, which had not missed a day for over half a century. He lived to 1886 and age seventy-nine, but the last years were pitiful. He lost the ability to speak; he was a shell of himself, trapped in a shell of silence. Only one blessing was granted him: he could recognize his wife, and rose whenever she entered the room.

John Quincy Adams's last years had been far different, conducted in the blaze of public life that Charles Francis so disliked. After a stroke in 1846, a month after he had turned seventy-nine, he was unable to write more than brief entries in his diary or occasional shaky notes. But he continued to attend the House regularly. One of his last letters, to Charles Francis, expressed his fortitude: "A stout heart, and a clear conscience, and never despair."[3] He had much to despair of. His victory in the fight over petitions had been poisoned by the annexation of Texas, and then by the war with Mexico that followed it. Adams was one of a small band of northern congressmen who opposed every war measure, however necessary—the decision to fight having once been taken—or slight. On February 21, 1848, he called out "No" to a roll call on one such proposal, rose to speak against it, then collapsed at his desk, from another stroke. He was carried to a couch in the office of the Speaker, where he lingered for two days. One of the last people he recognized in a brief lucid interval was a weeping Henry Clay. One of his pallbearers was his partner in intellect and strife, John Calhoun.

The circumstances of John Quincy Adams's death riveted the nation. But not as much as the simultaneous passing, twenty-two years earlier, of John Adams and Thomas Jefferson. "I wish your health may continue to the last much better than mine," Adams had written Jefferson in February 1825. "The little strength of mind and the considerable strength of body I once possessed appear to be all gone, but while I breathe I shall be your friend." The two patriarchs, aged ninety and eighty-three respectively, pushed their ruined, ailing frames into the spring and summer of 1826. With wonder, the nation learned, as rapidly as news could travel in those pretelegraph days, that both men had died on July 4, the fiftieth anniversary of the Declaration of Independence. When Caesar died,

> *Strange tremors shook the Alps*
> *. . . Cattle (dare I tell it?)*
> *Spoke; rivers ceased to flow and the earth gaped;*
> *In temples ivories wept and bronzes sweated.*

Caesar aspired to be emperor, and after his death was named a god. Adams and Jefferson were men who had founded a republic; the timing of their deaths seemed miracle enough. "The time, the manner, the coincidence," wrote John Quincy Adams in his diary, were "visible and palpable marks of Divine favor, for which I would humble myself . . . before the Ruler of the universe."[4]

John Adams was mindful of the timing of his death, though he could not know of its coincidence with Jefferson's. His last words on the Fourth were: "Thomas Jefferson still survives." Since there was nothing more in this world that he could have gained from the connection with his vanquisher, they stand, purged of self-interest, as an expression of pure friendship. More interesting were the words he had given the Fourth of July committee of Quincy, which had hoped for an appearance and a brief address, but had settled, as his health failed, for a toast to be read for him. John Adams offered them a brief, almost Delphic slogan. It was an odd toast for the founder of a family so bound to itself, and its role in public life. But it honored John's greatest achievement, which was the precondition of all the Adamses' achievements, and failings. Henry's art, Charles Francis's devotion to duty, John Quincy's determination, John's patriotism, all presupposed freedom to act, for good or ill. So John Adams gave the toast, "Independence forever."

NOTES

CHAPTER 1

1. L. H. Butterfield, Marc Friedlander, and Mary-Jo Kline, eds., *The Book of Abigail and John: Selected Letters of the Adams Family 1762–1784* (Cambridge: Harvard University Press, 1975), p. 207.

2. Allan Nevins, ed., *The Diary of John Quincy Adams 1794–1845* (New York: Longmans, Green and Co., 1928), p. 12.

3. Ibid., p. 165.

4. Martin B. Duberman, *Charles Francis Adams* (Boston: Houghton Mifflin Company, 1961), pp. 428, 151.

5. J. C. Levenson, Ernest Samuels, Charles Vandersee, and Viola Hopkins Warner, eds., *The Letters of Henry Adams* (Cambridge: Harvard University Press, 1982), Vol. II, p. 95.

6. Page Smith, *John Adams* (Garden City: Doubleday & Company, 1962), p. 254.

7. George A. Peek, Jr., ed., *The Political Writings of John Adams* (Indianapolis: The Bobbs-Merrill Company, 1954), p. 135.

8. Paul C. Nagel, *Descent from Glory* (New York: Oxford University Press, 1983), p. 53; Duberman, p. 21.

9. Butterfield et al., pp. 9–10.

10. Carl Van Doren, *Benjamin Franklin* (New York: The Viking Press, 1938), p. 694; Ernest Samuels, *Henry Adams* (Cambridge: Harvard University Press, 1989), p. 337.

11. Butterfield et al., pp. 142, 145; Newton Arvin, ed., *The Selected Letters of Henry Adams* (New York: Farrar, Strauss and Young, 1951), p. 242.

12. Nevins, p. 201.

13. Peter Shaw, *The Character of John Adams* (Chapel Hill: University of North Carolina Press, 1976), p. 29.

CHAPTER 2

1. Perry Miller and Thomas H. Johnson, eds., *The Puritans* (New York: Harper and Row, 1963), pp. 108, 110.

2. Peek, pp. 13, 7, 9.

3. John Ferling, *John Adams: A Life* (New York: Henry Holt, 1996), p. 12.

4. Shaw, p. 4.

5. Ferling, pp. 232, 21; Joseph J. Ellis, *The Passionate Sage* (New York: W. W. Norton & Company, 1993), p. 49.

6. Shaw, p. 54; Miller and Johnson, p. 227.

7. L. H. Butterfield, ed., *The Diary of John Adams* (Cambridge: Harvard University Press, 1961), p. 20; L. H. Butterfield, ed., *The Earliest Diary of John Adams* (Cambridge: Harvard University Press, 1966), p. 73.

8. Francis Russell, *Adams: An American Dynasty* (New York: American Heritage Publishing Co., 1976), p. 28.

9. Van Doren, p. 445.

10. John C. Miller, *Sam Adams: Pioneer in Propaganda* (Stanford, Calif.: Stanford University Press, 1960), p. 16.

11. Ibid., p. 70.

12. Joseph Galloway, *Historical and Political Reflections on the Rise and Progress of the American Revolution* (New York: Johnson Reprint Corporation, 1972), p. 67; John R. Galvin, *Three Men of Boston* (New York: Thomas Crowell, 1976), p. 117.

13. Ferling, p. 73.

14. Shaw, pp. 79, 97.

15. Smith, p. 175; Butterfield et al., p. 79.

16. Benson Bobrick, *Angel in the Whirlwind* (New York: Simon & Schuster, 1997), pp. 95–96; Smith, p. 170; Butterfield et al., pp. 55, 60, 71.

17. Ibid., p. 78.

18. Peek, p. 60.

19. Butterfield et al., pp. 80, 89.

20. Ibid., pp. 82–83; Bobrick, p. 143.

21. Butterfield et al., pp. 90–91.

22. Ibid., p. 96.

23. Ibid., p. 114.

24. Thomas Paine, *Collected Writings* (New York: Library of America, 1995), p. 46.

25. Adrienne Koch and William Peden, eds., *The Life and Selected Writings of Thomas Jefferson* (New York: The Modern Library, 1944), pp. 13–14.

26. Butterfield et al., p. 106; Ferling, p. 123.

27. Butterfield et al., p. 136.

28. Ferling, p. 169.

29. Ibid., pp. 149–50; Smith, p. 269.

30. Butterfield et al., p. 168.

CHAPTER 3

1. Van Doren, p. 559.

2. Ibid.

3. George Washington, *Writings* (New York: The Library of America, 1997), pp. 155–56.

4. Smith, p. 201.

5. Butterfield et al., pp. 91–92, 87; Smith, p. 202.

6. Ibid., p. 201; Zoltan Haraszti, *John Adams and the Prophets of Progress* (Cambridge: Harvard University Press, 1952), p. 3.

7. Butterfield et al., pp. 120–21.

8. Shaw, p. 101; Ferling, p. 164.

9. John J. Gallagher, *The Battle of Brooklyn, 1776* (New York: Sarpedon, 1995), p. 119.

10. Ferling, p. 181.

11. James Thomas Flexner, *George Washington in the American Revolution* (Boston: Little, Brown and Company, 1967), p. 275; Preston Russell, "The Conway Cabal," *American Heritage Magazine,* February–March 1995, p. 91; Ferling, p. 181.

12. Butterfield et al., p. 317.

13. Ferling, p. 269.

14. Butterfield et al., pp. 104–5.

15. Conor Cruise O'Brien, *The Long Affair* (Chicago: University of Chicago Press, 1996), p. 3.

16. H. W. Brands, *The First American* (New York: Doubleday, 2000), p. 610; Ferling, p. 203.

17. Dumas Malone, *Jefferson and the Rights of Man* (Boston: Little, Brown and Company, 1951), p. 36.

18. Ferling, p. 225; Shaw, p. 144.

19. Butterfield et al., p. 318.

20. Ibid., p. 305.

21. Ferling, p. 247.

22. Butterfield et al., pp. 327, 338.

23. Ferling, p. 256; Van Doren, p. 694; Shaw, p. 196.

24. O'Brien, pp. 13–15.

25. Lester J. Cappon, ed., *The Adams–Jefferson Letters* (Chapel Hill: University of North Carolina Press, 1959), pp. 175–76, 84.

26. Shaw, p. 297.

27. Ferling, p. 297.

28. Fawn Brodie, *Thomas Jefferson: An Intimate History* (New York: W. W. Norton and Company, 1974), p. 337.

29. Kenneth R. Bowling and Helen E. Veit, eds., *The Diary of William Maclay* (Baltimore: The Johns Hopkins University Press, 1988), pp. 31, 17.

30. Paine, p. 370.

31. Peek, pp. 191–92; Shaw, p. 237.

32. Forrest McDonald, *Novus Ordo Seclorum* (Lawrence, Kan.: University Press of Kansas, 1985), p. 181.

33. Ferling, p. 309; O'Brien, p. 103.

34. Smith, p. 1084.

35. Shaw, p. 97.

36. Ferling, p. 335.

37. Washington, p. 1046.

38. Joseph J. Ellis, *Founding Brothers: The Revolutionary Generation* (New York: Alfred A. Knopf, 2000), p. 191; Stanley Elkins and Eric McKitrick, *The Age of Federalism* (New York: Oxford University Press, 1993), p. 556; Ferling, p. 345.

39. Elkins and McKitrick, p. 601.

40. Ellis, *Founding Brothers,* p. 191.

41. Ferling, p. 378.

42. Ibid., p. 395.

CHAPTER 4

1. Ferling, pp. 406, 388.

2. Shaw, pp. 275, 280; Ellis, *The Passionate Sage,* pp. 70, 73.

3. Shaw, p. 245; Cappon, pp. 586, 411; Ellis, *The Passionate Sage,* p. 175.

4. Ferling, p. 446.

5. Joseph J. Ellis, *American Sphinx* (New York: Alfred A. Knopf, 1997), p. 77; Cappon, pp. xxxvi, 13; Ellis, *Passionate Sage,* p. 115.

6. Cappon, p. 274.

7. Ibid., pp. 291, 594.

8. Ibid., pp. 338, 610.

9. Bobrick, p. 196; Ellis, *American Sphinx,* p. 50.

10. Helen A. Cooper, ed., *John Trumbull* (New Haven: Yale University Art Gallery, 1982), p. 78.

11. Ellis, *The Passionate Sage,* p. 64; Cappon, p. 393; Haraszti, p. 174.

12. Koch and Peden, eds., p. 719; Peek, p. 96. The Massachusetts constitutional convention, which ratified Adams's draft in 1780, changed "equally" to "equal."

13. Cappon, pp. 371, 388–89.

14. Ibid., pp. 401, 408–9.

15. Peek, p. 134.

16. Ibid., p. 180; Cappon, p. 609.

CHAPTER 5

1. Nevins, p. 11.
2. Butterfield et al., pp. 68–70, 94.
3. Ibid., p. 253.
4. Nevins, p. 397.
5. Lynn Hudson Parsons, *John Quincy Adams* (Madison, Wis.: Madison House Publishers, 1998), p. 27; Butterfield et al., p. 359.
6. Paul C. Nagel, *John Quincy Adams* (Cambridge: Harvard University Press, 1997), p. 45.
7. Nagel, *Descent from Glory,* p. 553.
8. Parsons, p. 55.
9. Ibid., pp. 56–57.
10. Nevins, pp. 91, 92, 425.
11. Parsons, p. 62; Nagel, *John Quincy Adams,* p. 125.
12. Ellis, *The Passionate Sage,* p. 31; John C. Miller, *Alexander Hamilton: Portrait in Paradox* (New York: Harper & Bros., 1959), p. 481.
13. Nagel, *John Quincy Adams,* p. 102.
14. Ibid., p. 132.
15. W. B. Allen, ed., *Works of Fisher Ames* (Indianapolis: Liberty Classics, 1983), p. 1455.
16. Samuel Eliot Morison, *By Land and By Sea* (New York: Alfred A. Knopf, 1953), p. 197.
17. Nevins, p. 229; Henry Adams, *John Randolph,* Robert McColley, ed. (Armonk, N.Y.: M. E. Sharpe, 1996), p. 2.
18. Nevins, pp. 28–29, 409.
19. Miller, *Alexander Hamilton,* p. 563.
20. Nagel, *John Quincy Adams,* p. 153.
21. Parsons, p. 111.
22. Henry Adams, *History of the United States of America During the Administration of Thomas Jefferson* (New York: Library of America, 1986), p. 1042.
23. Nevins, p. 56.
24. Ibid., p. 57.
25. Nagel, *John Quincy Adams,* p. 185.
26. Nevins, pp. 88, 79, 72.
27. Henry Adams, *History of the United States of America During the Administration of James Madison* (New York: Library of America, 1986), p. 528.
28. Nevins, p. 103.

CHAPTER 6

1. Nevins, p. 129; Robert V. Remini, *Henry Clay: Statesman of the Union* (New York: W. W. Norton & Company, 1991), p. 131.

2. Remini, pp. 514, 252, 23; Nevins, pp. 148–49.

3. George Dangerfield, *The Era of Good Feelings* (New York: Harcourt, Brace and Co., 1952), p. 72; Nevins, p. 129.

4. Parsons, p. 119.

5. Nevins, p. 151.

6. Henry Adams, *Madison,* p. 1117.

7. Nevins, pp. 170, 179.

8. Nevins, p. 317; Nagel, p. 261.

9. Nevins, pp. 259, 354.

10. Ibid., pp. 265, 248.

11. Arthur M. Schlesinger, Jr., *The Age of Jackson* (Boston: Little, Brown and Company, 1946), p. 40; Robert V. Remini, ed., *Age of Jackson* (New York: Harper & Row, 1972), p. 22.

12. Nevins, p. 195.

13. Ibid., p. 199; Parsons, p. 142.

14. Remini, *Henry Clay,* p. 253.

15. Nevins, p. 274.

16. Ibid., pp. 292, 277.

17. Ibid., pp. 193–94, 257.

18. Cappon, pp. 570–71.

19. Nevins, p. 231.

20. Ibid.

21. Ibid., p. 232.

22. Ibid., p. 226; Parsons, p. 157.

23. "Ferdinand VI," article in *Encyclopedia Britannica,* 11th edition (New York, 1910–11), Vol. X, p. 267.

24. Nevins, p. 192.

25. James F. Hopkins, ed., *The Papers of Henry Clay* (University of Kentucky Press, 1961), Vol. II, p. 517; Nevins, pp. 262–63; Parsons, p. 147.

26. Cappon, p. 524.

27. Parsons, p. 149.

28. Koch and Peden, eds., pp. 708–9.

29. Nevins, pp. 170, 302–3.

30. "Ali, known as Ali Pasha," article in *Encyclopedia Britannica,* 11th edition (New York, 1910–11), Vol. I, p. 660; Hopkins, ed., op. cit., Vol. III, p. 598.

31. Parsons, p. 153.

32. Winston S. Churchill, *The Great Democracies* (New York: Dodd, Mead and Company, 1957), p. 22.

33. Nevins, p. 304. For May's argument, see Ernest R. May, *The Making of the Monroe Doctrine.*

34. Washington, p. 329.

35. Ellis, *The Passionate Sage,* p. 191.

36. Nevins, p. 342.

37. Ibid., p. 362.

38. Michael Lind, *Hamilton's Republic* (New York: The Free Press, 1997), pp. 226–27.

39. Nevins, p. 115; Lind, p. 226; Nagel, *John Quincy Adams,* p. 302.

40. Elkins and McKitrick, p. 43.

41. Henry Adams, *John Randolph,* p. 1.

42. Nevins, p. 349.

43. Ibid., pp. 382–83.

44. Ibid., p. 387.

CHAPTER 7

1. Nevins, pp. 463, 483.

2. Ibid., p. 439.

3. Nagel, *John Quincy Adams,* p. 346.

4. William Preston Vaughn, *The Antimasonic Party* (Lexington, Ky.: University Press of Kentucky, 1983), p. 9.

5. Schlesinger, p. 43.

6. Vaughn, pp. 20, 58.

7. Parsons, p. 243.

8. Nevins, p. 508.

9. Ibid., p. 518; Parsons, p. 240.

10. Parsons, p. 239.

11. Nevins, p. 475.

12. Nevins, pp. 574, 571; Ulysses S. Grant, *Personal Memoirs* (New York: Penguin Books, 1999), p. 25.

13. Nevins, p. 430.

14. William Lee Miller, *Arguing About Slavery* (New York: Alfred A. Knopf, 1996), p. 149.

15. Ibid., p. 127.

16. Ibid., pp. 210, 231.

17. Nevins, p. 430.

18. Ibid., pp. 493, 551–52.

19. Koch and Peden, pp. 729–30; Miller, *Arguing About Slavery,* p. 257.

20. Nevins, p. 479.

21. Miller, *Arguing About Slavery,* p. 430.

22. Ibid., pp. 440, 442.

23. Cappon, p. 610.

24. Nevins, pp. 557, 555.

25. Ibid., p. 575. Among the things the "just and steady-purposed man" does not fear, according to Horace, are the south wind (*"Auster"*) and "a mob of citizens clamoring for injustice" (*"civium ardor prava iubentium"*).

CHAPTER 8

1. Duberman, p. 8.

2. Nagel, *John Quincy Adams,* p. 204; Duberman, pp. 12, 18.

3. Ibid., p. 21.

4. Ibid., pp. 38, 27, 357, 153, 142; Ernest Samuels, *Henry Adams* (Cambridge: Harvard University Press, 1989), p. 307; Duberman, p. 41.

5. Levenson et al., eds., Vol. I, p. 478.

6. Parsons, p. 197; Nagel, *John Quincy Adams,* p. 342; Parsons, p. 207.

7. Nagel, *John Quincy Adams,* p. 335.

8. Duberman, p. 70.

9. David Hackett Fischer, *Albion's Seed* (New York: Oxford University Press, 1989), pp. 850–52.

10. Duberman, p. 85.

11. Ibid., p. 101.

12. Ibid., pp. 95–96.

13. Ibid., pp. 443, 103, 118.

14. Ibid., p. 90.

15. Duberman, p. 104; Kevin Phillips, *The Cousins' Wars* (New York: Basic Books, 1999), p. 357.

16. Nagel, *John Quincy Adams,* p. 367; Duberman, p. 68; Henry Adams, *The Education of Henry Adams* (Boston: Houghton Mifflin Company, 1961), pp. 62–63.

17. Duberman, pp. 105, 195.

18. Ibid., p. 69.

19. Robert C. Winthrop, Jr., *A Memoir of Robert C. Winthrop* (Boston: Little, Brown, 1897), p. 71; Duberman, pp. 131, 447.

20. Schlesinger, p. 439; Philip Van Doren Stern, ed., *The Life and Writings of Abraham Lincoln* (New York: Random House, 1940), p. 285; Wendell Glick, ed., *Great Short Works of Henry David Thoreau* (New York: Harper & Row, 1982), p. 138.

21. Edward L. Pierce, *Memoir and Letters of Charles Sumner* (Boston: Roberts Brothers, 1877), Vol. III, p. 148; Hoar, George F., *Autobiography of Seventy Years* (New York: Charles Scribner's Sons, 1903), p. 155.

22. Duberman, p. 151.

23. Ibid., pp. 78, 151.

CHAPTER 9

1. Duberman, pp. 163, 178.

2. Levenson et al., eds., Vol. I, p. 205; Henry Adams, *The Education*, p. 104; Charles Francis Adams, Jr., *An Autobiography* (Boston: Houghton Mifflin Company, 1916), p. 59; Glyndon G. Van Deusen, *William Henry Seward* (New York: Oxford University Press, 1967), p. 123.

3. Van Deusen, p. 138.

4. Arvin, p. 198.

5. Glick, ed., p. 282.

6. David Donald, *Sumner and the Coming of the Civil War* (New York: Alfred A. Knopf, 1967), p. 296.

7. Duberman, p. 219.

8. Ibid., p. 220; Philip Lopate, ed., *Writing New York* (New York: Library of America, 1998), p. 211.

9. Duberman, p. 248; Levenson et al., eds., Vol. I, p. 217.

10. Charles Francis Adams, Jr., p. 104; Levenson et al., eds., Vol. I, pp. 205, 212; Charles Francis Adams, Jr., p. 83.

11. Duberman, p. 249.

12. Ibid., p. 253; Charles Francis Adams, Jr., pp. 96–98.

13. Duberman, p. 257.

14. Henry Adams, *The Education*, p. 135.

15. Ibid., p. 123.

16. Duberman, p. 289.

17. Ibid., pp. 295, 481. Bertrand Russell's anecdote may be found in *Unpopular Essays* (New York: Simon and Schuster, 1950), pp. 168–69.

18. Duberman, p. 311.

19. Ibid.

20. Ibid., pp. 481–488.

CHAPTER 10

1. Charles Francis Adams, *Diary* (unpublished), May 1, 1865.

2. Duberman, p. 339; Levenson et al., Vol. I, p. 498.

3. Charles Francis Adams, *Diary*, January 4, 1864.

4. Ulysses Grant, p. xxiii.

5. Duberman, p. 359.

6. Ibid.

7. Ibid., p. 390; Robert C. Winthrop, Jr., pp. 295–96.

8. Robert C. Winthrop, Jr., pp. 295–96.

9. Parsons, p. 207.

10. Francis Russell, *Adams,* p. 281.

CHAPTER 11

1. Paul C. Nagel, *Descent from Glory* (New York: Oxford University Press, 1983), p. 242.

2. Charles Francis Adams, Jr., pp. 124, 170, 190.

3. Henry Adams, *The Education,* p. 37.

4. Levenson et al., eds., Vol. II, p. 196.

5. Henry Adams, *The Education,* pp. 12–13. Adams thought he was "not much more than six years old at the time—seven at the utmost"; his biographer Ernest Samuels makes him five (see Samuels, pp. 2, 466).

6. Henry Adams, *The Education,* p. 16.

7. Ibid., p. 46.

8. Levenson et al., Vol. I, pp. 22, 66, 167.

9. Edward Gibbon, *Memoirs of My Life* (New York: Funk & Wagnalls, 1966), p. 136; Levenson et al., Vol. I, p. 149.

10. Levenson et al., Vol. I, p. 204.

11. Ibid., pp. 208, 223, 231.

12. Ibid., pp. 208–9, 221, 224.

13. Samuels, pp. 45–46, 53.

14. Levenson et al., eds., Vol. I, p. 239; Henry Adams, *The Education,* p. 115.

15. Levenson et al., eds., Vol. I, p. 298.

16. Ibid., pp. 426–27.

17. Ibid., p. 458.

18. Ibid., p. 494.

CHAPTER 12

1. Samuels, p. 79.

2. Henry Cabot Lodge, *Early Memories* (New York: Charles Scribner's Sons, 1913), p. 297.

3. Samuels, p. 83; Levenson et al., eds., Vol. II, p. 326.

4. Henry Adams, *The Education,* p. 268.

5. Levenson et al., eds., Vol. II, p. 56; Samuels, p. 43.

6. John Steele Gordon, *The Great Game* (New York: Scribner, 1999), p. 144.

7. Ibid., p. 112; Edwin G. Burrows and Mike Wallace, *Gotham* (New York: Oxford University Press, 1999), p. 914.

8. Elizabeth Stevenson, ed., *A Henry Adams Reader* (Garden City, N.Y.: Doubleday and Company, 1958), p. 72.

9. Ibid., pp. 55–56.

10. Ibid., p. 86.

11. Levenson et al., eds., Vol. II, p. 68.

12. Ari Hoogenboom, "Henry Adams and Politics," *Transactions of the American Philosophical Society* (Philadelphia, 1993), Vol. 83, Part 4, p. 31; Levenson et al., eds., Vol. II, pp. 69, 217.

13. Henry Adams, *The Education*, p. 294.

14. Samuels, p. 105.

15. Ibid., p. 95; Lodge, p. 187.

16. Levenson et al., eds., Vol. II, pp. 217, 247.

17. Ibid., p. 68; Forrest McDonald, *The American Presidency* (Lawrence, Kans.: University Press of Kansas, 1994), p. 432.

18. Leon Edel, *Henry James: The Conquest of London* (New York: J. B. Lippincott Company, 1972), p. 377; Levenson et al., eds., Vol. II, p. 133.

19. Henry Adams, *John Randolph*, p. 194.

20. Ibid., p. 80.

21. Levenson et al., eds., Vol. II, p. 371.

22. Ibid., p. 303; Henry Adams, *The Education*, p. 106; Levenson et al., eds., Vol. II, p. 477.

23. Leon Edel, *Henry James: The Middle Years* (New York: J. B. Lippincott Company, 1962), p. 30; Samuels, p. 175.

24. Henry Adams, *Democracy* (New York: Penguin Books, 1961), pp. 54, 82.

25. Samuels, p. 195.

26. Ibid., p. 95; Edel, p. 166.

27. Levenson et al., eds., Vol. II, p. 643.

CHAPTER 13

1. Arvin, pp. 193, 197; Samuels, p. 378.

2. In 1955, one of Marian's nieces, Louisa Hooper Thoron, told biographer Edward Chalfant that her aunt had practiced contraception. Chalfant assumed that Thoron's source for this information was her father, Marian's brother, and concluded that Henry and Marian had no children so that he could be undistracted in his work. Edward Chalfant, *Better in Darkness* (Hamden, Conn.: Anchor Books, 1994), pp. 310, 764–65.

3. Arvin, p. 142; Henry Adams, *The Education*, p. 409; Arvin, p. 188; Samuels, p. 255.

4. Henry Adams, *The Education*, pp. 3, 238.

5. Henry Adams, *History . . . Jefferson*, p. 550.

6. Henry Adams, *History of the United States During the Administrations of James Madison* (New York: Library of America, 1986), p. 1334.

7. Samuels, p. 276; Levenson et al., eds., Vol. II, p. 491; Henry Adams, *History . . . Jefferson,* p. 1135.

8. Henry Adams, *History . . . Jefferson,* pp. 119, 121.

9. Henry Adams, *History . . . Madison,* p. 1300.

10. Levenson et al., eds., Vol. II, p. 403.

11. H. L. Mencken, *Prejudices: A Selection* (New York: Vintage Books, 1958), p. 59; Edmund Morris, *The Rise of Theodore Roosevelt* (New York: Ballantine Books, 1979), p. 162; Edith Wharton, *The Age of Innocence* (New York: Collier Books, 1993), p. 345.

12. Morris, p. 569.

13. Samuels, p. 329.

14. Morris, p. 656; Samuels, p. 347.

15. Arvin, pp. 235–36, 241–42.

16. Ibid., p. 242.

17. Samuels, pp. 306–7.

18. Henry Adams, *Mont Saint Michel and Chartres* (New York: Penguin Books, 1986), p. 7.

19. Ibid., pp. 8–9.

20. Ibid., pp. 201, 82.

21. Ibid., p. 347.

22. Ibid., pp. 185–86.

23. Samuels, p. 381.

24. Henry Adams, *The Education,* pp. 380, 100, 143.

25. Ibid., pp. 266, 33.

26. Ibid., pp. 496, 501, 505.

27. Ibid., pp. 47–48.

28. Arvin, p. 267.

29. Samuels, p. 444.

CHAPTER 14

1. *Horace in English* (New York: Penguin Books, 1996), 213; Fawn Brodie, *Thomas Jefferson: An Intimate History* (New York: W. W. Norton & Company, 1974), p. 745.

2. Shaw, p. 278.

3. Zoltan Haraszti compares these and other passages of Adams and Smith, pp. 169–70. The Adams may be found in Peek, p. 183; the Smith in Adam Smith, *The Theory of Moral Sentiments* (Amherst, N.Y.: Prometheus Books, 2000), p. 71.

4. Maclay, p. 56.

5. Butterfield et al., p. 349; Ellis, *The Passionate Sage,* p. 190; Nevins, pp. 368, 568; Charles Francis Adams, Jr., pp. 10, 14.

6. Haraszti, pp. 59–60.

7. Cappon, pp. 200, 203.

8. Ibid., p. 595; Haraszti, p. 257.

9. Henry Adams, *The Education*, p. 230.

10. Stevenson, ed., p. 360.

11. Ibid., p. 390.

12. Levenson et al., eds., p. 350.

13. Alexis de Tocqueville, *Democracy in America* (New York: Vintage Books, 1945), Vol. II, pp. 90–93.

14. Henry Adams, *History . . . Madison*, pp. 1333–34.

CHAPTER 15

1. Peek, pp. 166–67.

2. Lind, pp. 277–78, 280.

3. Arvin, pp. 212–13.

4. Butterfield et al., eds., p. 123.

5. Ibid., p. 360.

6. Parsons, p. 229; Nagel, *John Quincy Adams*, p. 368; Barbara Goldsmith, *Other Powers* (New York: Alfred A. Knopf, 1998), p. 181.

7. Henry Adams, *Mont Saint Michel and Chartres*, p. 232; Levenson et al., eds., Vol. III, p. 280.

8. Charles Francis Adams, *Diary* (unpublished), January 4, 1864.

9. Cappon, p. 571.

10. Arvin, p. 183.

11. Samuels, p. 348; Arvin, p. 266.

12. Ibid., p. 245; Nevins, p. 571; Shaw, p. 243.

13. Nevins, pp. 132, 137.

14. Henry Adams, *The Education*, p. 114.

15. Nevins, p. 132.

CHAPTER 16

1. Schlesinger, p. 399. John Van Buren also had many vices; after losing five thousand dollars at cards, he bet his mistress, Maria Vespucci, and lost her too.

2. Nagel, *John Quincy Adams*, p. 407.

3. Shaw, p. 67.

4. Cappon, p. 399. Adams's assertion makes no sense literally: The Jefferson/Burr ticket did poorly in the Congregationalist parts of the northeast. But Burr's background did help make him seem trustworthy to certain New England Federalist leaders.

5. Charles Francis Adams, Jr., p. 65; Duberman, p. 508.

6. Samuels, p. 171.

7. Stern, ed., p. 238.

8. Butterfield et al., eds., pp. 259–60.

CHAPTER 17

1. Samuels, pp. 459, 456, 461.

2. Henry Adams, *The Education,* p. 27; Charles Francis Adams, *Diary* (unpublished), May 25, 1880.

3. Nagel, *John Quincy Adams,* reproduces this letter in his illustrations.

4. Cappon, p. 610; the grandiose portents are described in the first of Virgil's *Georgics;* Nevins, p. 360. John's last words and toast are in every biography of him.

INDEX

ABOUT THE AUTHOR

Richard Brookhiser is the author of *Alexander Hamilton, American* (1999), *Founding Father: Rediscovering George Washington* (1995), and *The Way of the WASP* (1991), all published by The Free Press. He is a Senior Editor at *The National Review* and a *New York Observer* columnist. He contributes to such publications as *American Heritage* and *The New York Times*. He lives in New York City.

Don't miss the other biographies of American founders by Richard Brookhiser.

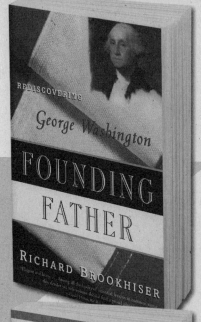

FOUNDING FATHER
Rediscovering George Washington

Brookhiser peels back the folk legend to reveal George Washington the man, tracing his amazing accomplishments as a statesman, soldier, and founder of a great nation in a quarter century of activity that remains unmatched by any leader.

"**Elegant and lively.** . . . Among all the books of remedial lessons in common virtue, this slender yet rich volume should find a proud place."
—DANIEL J. SILVER,
The Wall Street Journal

ALEXANDER HAMILTON, AMERICAN

Brookhiser traces the arc of Alexander Hamilton's fascinating (and tragically brief) life, demonstrating how one of the least understood of the founding fathers was also one of the most important and inspiring.

"**A dramatic, compact biography that fairly gallops through Hamilton's picaresque life.** *Alexander Hamilton, American* brilliantly succeeds in arguing that Hamilton deserves greater credit than he usually gets for his brainpower, idealism, and vision."
—MICHAEL BESCHLOSS,
The New York Times Book Review

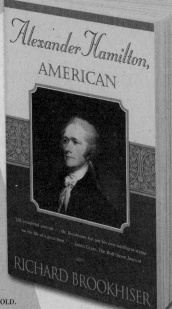